# FROM THE CLOSET
# TO THE COURTROOM

OTHER BOOKS BY CARLOS A. BALL

*The Morality of Gay Rights:*
*An Exploration in Political Philosophy*

*Cases and Materials on Sexual Orientation and the Law*
(with William Rubenstein and Jane S. Schacter)


OTHER BOOKS IN
THE QUEER ACTION SERIES

*Come Out and Win: Organizing Yourself,*
*Your Community, and Your World,* by Sue Hyde

*Out Law: What LGBT Youth Should Know*
*about Their Legal Rights,* by Lisa Keen


OTHER BOOKS IN
THE QUEER IDEAS SERIES

*Beyond (Straight and Gay) Marriage:*
*Valuing All Families under the Law,* by Nancy D. Polikoff

# FROM THE CLOSET
# TO THE COURTROOM

## Five LGBT Rights Lawsuits
## That Have Changed Our Nation

CARLOS A. BALL

QUEER ACTION/QUEER IDEAS
*A Series Edited by Michael Bronski*

BEACON PRESS, BOSTON

Beacon Press
25 Beacon Street
Boston, Massachusetts 02108-2892
www.beacon.org

Beacon Press books
are published under the auspices of
the Unitarian Universalist Association of Congregations.

13  12  11  10      8  7  6  5  4  3  2  1

This book is printed on acid-free paper that meets the uncoated paper
ANSI/NISO specifications for permanence as revised in 1992.

Composition by Wilsted & Taylor Publishing Services

Library of Congress Cataloging-in-Publication Data

Ball, Carlos A.
From the closet to the courtroom : five LGBT rights lawsuits
that have changed our nation / Carlos A. Ball.
p. cm.
Includes bibliographical references and index.
ISBN 978-0-8070-0078-6 (hardcover : alk. paper)
1. Gay rights—United States—Digests. 2. Homosexuality—Law and
legislation—United States—Digests. 3. Discrimination—Law and legislation—
United States—Digests. 4. Gay couples—Legal status, laws, etc.—United
States—Digests. 5. Actions and defenses—United States. I. Title.
KF4754.5.A53B35 2009
342.7308′7—dc22      2009027667

To Miguel Braschi, Jamie Nabozny, Angela Romero,
Genora Dancel, Ninia Baehr, John Lawrence,
and Tyron Garner for their courage.

And to Richard Storrow, Emmanuel Ball-Storrow,
and Sebastian Ball-Storrow for their love.

# CONTENTS

# A Note from the Series Editor

SOCIAL-JUSTICE MOVEMENTS are tapestries woven from many threads: justice, anger, compassion, courage, pain, and a firm sense of legal right and wrong. But we frequently forget that these valiant, admirable qualities are always embodied by people—often everyday, average people—whose lives, emotions, and fears are integral not only to the movements but to how change happens. These lives are some of the most brilliant, striking—and emotionally moving—threads in the tapestry, and they are the most overlooked.

The lesbian, gay, bisexual, and transgender movement in the United States is relatively young. Although it began just over five decades ago it has, along with feminism, radically changed how we think about sexuality and gender, families and relationships, love and even death. Much of this change has been driven by the long and difficult legal battles that LGBT activists have fought. Carlos Ball's *From the Closet to the Courtroom: Five LGBT Rights Lawsuits That Have Changed Our Nation* reminds us in vivid prose and wonderful detail that these legal battles are, in the end, about people and their stories. Ball has taken five landmark decisions from the dry, academic pages of law journals and the livelier pages of newspapers and placed them in the larger, engaging, far broader context of human experience and everyday life. Ball isn't just recounting great stories here—although they are as complex and gripping as any invented fiction—but is telling us a profound truth about politics. No matter what lofty ideals are at play, no matter what high moral stands are taken, when you cut right to the heart of the matter progressive politics is about the importance of people's lives. These are the lives that make up *From the Closet to the Courtroom*, and they are the lives that have changed our world.

MICHAEL BRONSKI
*Series Editor, Queer Action/Queer Ideas*

# Introduction

THE LGBT RIGHTS MOVEMENT has had many heroes, some who have received a great deal of national attention, and others whose names we will never know. Indeed, the advancement of LGBT rights has come about through struggles large and small—on the streets, around kitchen tables, in newspapers and on the Internet, and in courtrooms across the country. The list of individuals who have participated is long, and it includes the drag queens who congregated at the Stonewall Inn and who decided in 1969 to push back against police harassment and intimidation; the gay rights activists who in 1978 defeated a California ballot measure that would have led to the firing of gay public school teachers throughout the state; the thousands of volunteers who in the 1980s helped to care for, and fought on behalf of, people with AIDS; and the many who came together to mourn and celebrate the life of Matthew Shepard, who in 1998 was brutally beaten to death in Laramie, Wyoming, for being gay.

One important piece of the struggle for LGBT rights has involved lawsuits. This book tells the story of five lawsuits that have worked in conjunction with political mobilization and social protests to remake our nation's political, social, and moral landscape.

In many ways, overcoming invisibility is the first step in successfully demanding basic civil rights. In fact, it is perhaps no coincidence that *Invisible Man*, Ralph Ellison's novel about the pain and misery associated with the invisibility of black people in America, was published only two years before the Supreme Court issued its opinion in *Brown v. Board of Education*. *Brown* compelled our country to recognize the capabilities and hopes of African Americans. Black people after *Brown* may still have been hated by some and feared by others, but they were no longer invisible. After *Brown*, it was no longer tenable to reject out of hand the claims of African Americans to basic equality.

Similarly, the five lawsuits explored in this book have required our nation to take seriously the claims of LGBT people to equal citizenship. The primary goal of laws and policies that discriminate on the basis of sexual orientation is to discourage LGBT individuals from being open about who they are and whom they love. In contrast, the five lawsuits chronicled here have helped to make LGBT people visible by forcing society to grapple with both their existence and their aspirations.

In *Braschi v. Stahl Associates* (1989), an American appellate court for the first time concluded that it is possible for two men in an intimate relationship to constitute a family. Prior to *Braschi*, same-sex relationships, no matter how close or long-lasting, had no greater legal significance than those of friends or roommates. As we will see, the LGBT rights movement used the *Braschi* litigation to encourage the courts—and, through them, the public—to take a hard look at a particular loving relationship between two men in order to make its case that LGBT people are as capable of forming close and lasting familial ties as are straight people.

As a result of *Nabozny v. Podlesny* (1996), a jury in rural Wisconsin concluded that school officials violated the constitutional rights of a gay teenager when they permitted other students to harass him in violent and demeaning ways because of his sexual orientation. Prior to this case, the intense physical and emotional suffering of countless LGBT students in American schools at the hands of homophobic students went largely unacknowledged by school officials and the public at large. It took a federal constitutional lawsuit to render visible the plight of the many LGBT students who have to cope with repeated instances of violence and harassment in the hallways and bathrooms of the country's public schools.

Because of *Romer v. Evans* (1996), the U.S. Supreme Court held that it is unconstitutional to deny LGBT people the opportunity to seek antidiscrimination protection under the law. At issue in *Romer* was a Colorado state constitutional amendment that would have made it illegal to protect sexual minorities against discrimination based on their sexual orientation. Supporters of the amendment hoped to push LGBT people back into the closet, but the Court rejected this effort, making it clear that LGBT people are equals under the law and that the government has an obligation to treat them accordingly.

When the Hawaii Supreme Court ruled in *Baehr v. Lewin* (1993), it became the first American court to question the constitutionality of denying same-sex couples the opportunity to marry, and, in the process, it ignited the marriage equality movement. The same-sex marriage cases, of which *Baehr* was the first important one, have done more to increase the visibility of LGBT people than any other strategy pursued by the LGBT rights movement in the last twenty years. The lawsuits have forced the country as a whole to grapple with the question of whether it is legally and morally defensible to deny an entire group of individuals access to the hundreds of rights and benefits that our society allocates through the institution of marriage. As a result of *Baehr*, and of the same-sex marriage cases that followed, it has become much more difficult for Americans to continue to pretend that LGBT people either do not exist or that their needs and aspirations are not worth considering.

In *Lawrence v. Texas* (2003), the U.S. Supreme Court held that the government cannot criminalize private and consensual gay sex. For decades prior to *Lawrence*, those who supported discrimination against LGBT people contended that society was entitled to use the criminal law to express disapproval of same-sex sexuality and relationships. The Court in *Lawrence* ruled that such a position is inconsistent with our nation's most cherished principles aimed at protecting individual dignity and autonomy. Rather than relegating same-sex sexuality to the realm of the hidden, shameful, and degrading, the Court made it clear that the choices LGBT people make about sexual intimacy are as closely linked to their dignity as human beings as are those of heterosexuals.

As we will see, the five lawsuits explored in this book have changed the country's treatment and understanding of LGBT people in fundamental ways. Before turning to those suits, it is worth pausing to tell the story of a little-known legal case from Austin, Texas, that was brought in the late 1970s. It was around the time of the Austin case that the LGBT community began a concerted effort to pursue a judicial strategy as a way of advancing and protecting the interests of its members. The strategy, largely modeled on the one pursued earlier by the civil rights movement, sought to challenge discriminatory laws and policies in court with the objective of creating the necessary legal, economic, and social conditions that would permit LGBT people to lead lives that were both open and dignified.

▲

The Driskill Hotel, in downtown Austin, is one of the most famous buildings in the state of Texas. Built by a wealthy cattleman in 1886, the cream-colored brick and limestone Victorian structure is where most Texas governors in the last century have held their inaugural balls. President Lyndon Johnson and his wife Lady Bird had their first date at the Driskill, and it was there that they watched the results of the 1964 presidential election. In 2000, George W. Bush and his advisors set up camp at the hotel as they waited for courts to determine the outcome of that year's contested presidential election.

The Driskill has been commercially successful for most of its history, except during a brief period in the late 1970s. In 1977, the hotel owners, looking to increase revenues, opened a dance bar called the Cabaret. The disco attracted young people from throughout Austin, some of whom were gay; although the gay clientele at the dance club was not large, the hotel's managers grew concerned that the Cabaret might become a gay dance club. Their solution to this perceived problem was to institute a house rule prohibiting same-sex couples from dancing together. A few days later, a hotel staff member approached two men dancing on the disco floor and asked them to leave the premises.

If the hotel had instituted its new dance policy two years earlier, it could have done so with legal impunity. In 1976, however, the Austin City Council enacted an ordinance making it a misdemeanor, punishable by a fine of up to $200, for places of public accommodation to discriminate on the basis of sexual orientation.

Word of the hotel's dance policy quickly spread throughout Austin's LGBT community. A group of local activists approached the couple that had been asked to leave by the hotel's staff to inquire whether they would be interested in taking legal action under the new ordinance. The two men demurred, wanting to avoid the publicity that would inevitably accompany the filing of a legal complaint against the hotel. A few days later, four students at the University of Texas, who were also members of a local gay community group, stepped forward and volunteered to help.

On February 11, 1978, the four students—two men and two women —went to the Cabaret, accompanied by a city attorney and by a member of the Austin Human Rights Commission, the agency charged with enforcing the city's antidiscrimination laws. Shortly after the party of six arrived at the disco, the four students started dancing together, dividing themselves into two different-sex couples. At a predetermined moment during a particular song, the dancers switched partners, transforming themselves into two same-sex couples. A hotel manager quickly approached the students, informing them of the house rule against same-sex dancing. When the students protested that such a rule violated the local ordinance, the manager responded by saying that he did not care. He then ordered the students to stop dancing as same-sex couples or leave the premises.

The following week, the students filed a complaint with the Human Rights Commission, which began an investigation. The hotel refused to cooperate with the investigation, and the Commission— not surprisingly, given that one of its members had observed what occurred on the Cabaret's dance floor—concluded that there was enough evidence to turn the case over to the city attorney's office for prosecution.

When the hotel owners learned that they would likely be prosecuted under the local ordinance, they responded not by changing their policy but by suing the city instead. The lawsuit claimed that the city lacked the authority, under state law, to enact an ordinance prohibiting sexual orientation discrimination. The city attorney assigned the case to a young lawyer named Clayton Strange. Strange, a self-described cowboy who grew up on a cattle ranch in West Texas, knew nothing about gay issues. The first thing he did after being assigned the case was to ask around for the name of a lawyer who might know something about gay rights laws. The name that he kept hearing was that of Matthew Coles, a San Francisco attorney.

Coles had graduated from law school only the year before. As a law student at the University of California's Hastings Law School in the mid-1970s, he had helped to found the San Francisco Gay Democratic Club (later renamed the Harvey Milk Democratic Club). One of the club's first political objectives was to convince the San Francisco Board of Supervisors to enact a gay rights law. There was, however, one slight problem: none of the members knew what a gay rights law should say. It became Coles's responsibility, as the only member of the group with legal training, to figure that out.

Coles contacted city attorneys' offices in most of the roughly two dozen municipalities that then had gay rights laws on their books to request copies of their ordinances. As the material arrived, Coles read through the laws, noting the wording that he thought made the most sense, and typed up a draft law that would prohibit employers, landlords, and owners of public accommodations from discriminating on the basis of sexual orientation. A year later, thanks largely to the lobbying efforts of the San Francisco Gay Democratic Club, the City's Board of Supervisors enacted into law a gay rights ordinance, the origins of which could be traced back to Coles's typewriter.

When Strange reached Coles on the telephone in May 1978, the latter was practicing as a lawyer in San Francisco's predominantly gay Castro district. Strange told Coles about the Driskill Hotel case and asked whether he, as a national expert on municipal gay law, would be willing to help. Although amused at the notion that he, twelve months out of law school, could be an expert at anything, Coles nonetheless agreed.

Coles's first responsibility was to write a brief defending Austin's authority, under Texas law, to enact a gay rights ordinance. While working on the San Francisco gay rights law the year before, Coles had done extensive research on the authority of municipalities, under home rule principles, to enact antidiscrimination ordinances. It was clear to Coles that Austin had acted well within its power under state law when it enacted the gay rights measure and he argued so in his brief. Several months later, the state court agreed with Coles, dismissing the hotel's challenge to the ordinance. The discrimination case was now ready to be tried before a jury.

The day before the trial was scheduled to begin in the summer of 1979, Coles flew to Austin to meet with Strange at the city attorney's office and discuss their trial strategy. Coles knew that the hotel's main defense during the trial would be that its staff had not asked the four college students to stop dancing *because* of their sexual orientation. The hotel's legal position was that it had not violated the city ordinance prohibiting discrimination on the basis of sexual orientation because its house rule applied equally to both gays and straights; patrons, the hotel would argue at the trial, were not allowed to dance with others of the same sex *regardless* of their sexual orientation.

To counter this argument, Coles had lined up four local psychiatrists and psychologists who agreed to testify to the seemingly obvious proposition that club patrons usually dance with members of the sex to whom they are attracted. This testimony would allow Coles to establish that a policy which prohibited individuals of the same sex from dancing together had, in legal terminology, a "disparate impact" on lesbians and gay men, and was therefore illegal under the Austin ordinance.

When Coles, the day before the trial, called the four witnesses whom he had lined up to testify, they all told him that they were no longer willing to help with the case. This turn of events left Coles sus-

pecting that someone had contacted his potential witnesses and convinced them—perhaps even threatened them—not to testify against
the hotel. Coles was annoyed, but it was too late—the trial started the
next day—to line up new medical experts.

As Coles thought about his predicament, it occurred to him that he
might not need medical experts after all. Perhaps the point he wanted
to make in court the following day—essentially that people who dance
with others of the same sex are usually gay—could be made through
the testimony of a dance bar owner. He got on the phone and called a
handful of local gay activists, seeking their help. At eleven o'clock that
evening, he found himself in the modest home of Bunch King Britten,
who had owned two discos in Austin, one gay and one straight. Britten at first was understandably incredulous that a lawyer was in his
home late at night asking him to testify the following day about how
most people who danced with others of the opposite sex at his straight
disco were straight and how most people who danced with others
of the same sex at his gay disco were gay. But when Coles explained
that the prosecution of the Driskill was an important discrimination
case that would test Austin's new antidiscrimination ordinance, Britten agreed to do his part and testify.

The trial began the next morning in the courtroom of municipal
court judge Steve Russell. Russell, a Native American of Cherokee de-
scent, was born and raised in Oklahoma. He quit school in the ninth
grade, later joined the air force, and eventually acquired his education
(including a law degree from the University of Texas) through the GI
Bill. Upon completing his legal education, Russell worked as a civil
rights lawyer in Austin for several years, after which the city council
appointed him to the bench.

In the late 1970s, municipal courts in Texas dealt with minor of-
fenses, such as drinking in public and traffic violations, which carried
fines of no more than $200. So when Russell first learned that he
would be presiding over the case against the Driskill, he realized immediately that he had an unusual municipal court case in his hands.
Suspecting that many potential jurors might be uncomfortable with
the topic of homosexuality, the judge asked his assistant to fill the

courtroom with as many potential jurors as could be accommodated. A few minutes after 9:00 a.m. on June 10, 1979, Russell walked into his courtroom and addressed a crowd of over sixty potential jurors. He thanked them for their service and informed them that they might be chosen to serve on a case that involved possible discrimination on the basis of sexual orientation. When Russell asked the potential jurors how many might find it difficult to be impartial in a case that involved homosexuality, most of them raised their hands. He proceeded to explain to the jurors that he was not there to pass moral judgments on their personal views of homosexuality. Instead, his job, and that of the lawyers, was to find jurors who were willing to listen to the evidence carefully and to apply the law as written.

From the beginning of the proceedings, Russell created an atmosphere in the courtroom that encouraged the potential jurors to express themselves freely. In fact, at one point, the following colloquy took place between Russell and a potential juror:

> POTENTIAL JUROR: Judge, I believe that every individual person has the right to decide who he wants to serve [in his establishment].
>
> JUDGE RUSSELL: I understand that sentiment, sir, but I'm just trying to determine if you can follow the law the way it's written. What about the law that requires everyone to serve blacks?
>
> POTENTIAL JUROR: That's different. Blacks are human beings.[1]

Although Russell was startled by the man's comment, he politely thanked the potential juror and told him that he was free to leave.

After three hours of careful questioning by Russell and the lawyers, a group of six individuals—three men and three women—was chosen to hear the case. It took only two additional hours to try the case. Two of the college students who had visited the Driskill the year before testified that they had been asked to stop dancing with their same-sex partners. One of the students noted how the hotel's actions "made me feel like a second class citizen. And that made me angry because here they were telling me I could not dance with my life partner of four years." That same student also testified about how difficult it was to be openly gay in a society that was so intolerant and fearful of homosexuality. When asked why he had decided to challenge publicly the Driskill Hotel's policy, the young man replied that his parents had raised him to confront injustice whenever possible.[2]

The hotel's lawyer, while cross-examining Bunch King Britten (Coles's "expert" witness), tried to establish that even if most people who dance with someone of the same sex at a club are gay, that did not mean that a policy that was meant to prevent same-sex dancing was necessarily antigay. The lawyer returned to this point during his closing argument, telling the jurors that they should find the hotel not guilty because its dance policy applied to everyone regardless of their sexual orientation.

In the end, the jurors were not persuaded that an ostensibly neutral policy that prohibited all patrons from dancing with someone of the same sex was not ultimately aimed at gay people. After deliberating for about thirty minutes, they returned to the courtroom to announce a finding of guilt. Judge Russell thanked them and closed the proceedings after fining the hotel $200.

As they walked out of the courthouse, Strange thanked Coles for his help, noting that Coles's obvious trial experience had made a big difference in the case. As a bemused Coles was telling Strange that, in fact, this had been his first trial, he noticed that one of the jurors, a librarian at a local Bible college, was walking a few feet ahead of them. Coles quickened his pace and politely asked the middle-aged woman if he could talk to her about the trial. She agreed. When Coles inquired why the jury had voted to convict the hotel, the woman replied as follows:

> You know, Mr. Coles, there was a lot of discussion during the trial about who dances with whom and the lawyers and the judge went on and on talking about "disparate impact," but

none of us really understood any of that. We just figured that if they can stop gay folks from dancing at a disco, then they can deny them jobs, and if they can deny them jobs, then they can deny them housing, and if they can do it to gays, well, the next thing you know, they can do it to Jews. But honestly, Mr. Coles, I am not sure I understood the case at all.

Coles looked at the woman in amazement for a moment, and then replied: "No, ma'am. You understood the case perfectly. Thank you."[3]

▲

At its most basic level, the case against the Driskill Hotel was successful because the jury concluded that the defendant had discriminated against LGBT people. Just as importantly, the trial provided a mechanism for the LGBT community, with the help of lawyers, to make a *public* demand for equal treatment. Behind the seemingly trivial question of who should be allowed to dance with whom at a disco stood an important principle—that LGBT people are equal citizens who are entitled to the opportunities enjoyed by everyone else.

A few weeks after the trial, the hotel filed a motion with Russell requesting a new trial. In the months that followed, he received phone calls from several leaders of Austin's business community warning him that they would pressure the city council not to reappoint him to a new term on the bench if he ruled against the hotel. Despite these threats, Russell denied the defendant's motion. In his written decision, he noted that the issue in the case was ultimately "one of human dignity, of the right to go about one's daily life without being publicly marked as inferior, less than human. The Austin City Council faced this issue [when it enacted the law], as did the jury in this case. This Court can do no less."

The lawsuit did not just encourage those who were present in the courtroom to grapple with the place of LGBT people in society. The Driskill case, as gay rights cases usually do, received considerable media coverage, including several articles in the local newspaper. It is unlikely, of course, that everyone who heard about the case was convinced that the hotel should have been penalized for instituting its "no dancing by gay people" policy. It is likely, though, that many who learned about the case gave some thought—perhaps for the first time —to the fact that some of their neighbors were gay and that others in their community felt entitled to discriminate against them based on that fact.

It is also likely that the case encouraged at least some members of the public to view LGBT people in ways that undermined preju- dices and stereotypes. As Coles told a reporter a month after the trial, LGBT people "accomplished more at this trial simply by exposure and personal contact than they did by winning the case." He added that "having straights see what gays look like, what they are and how they act . . . [and] that they are just plain folks like anyone else, will go a long way to changing the stereotypes."[4]

When the four college students at the Driskill disco that winter night in 1978 swapped partners, they made a public statement that they were, as LGBT people, entitled to equal treatment. The students could have made that statement regardless of whether the hotel's danc- ing policy was proscribed by law. But it was the legal prohibition that forced the local community, as a result of the litigation, to take notice of the hotel's policy and its impact on Austin's gay residents. Ironically, then, a policy such as the Driskill's, which was meant to keep LGBT people closeted, had the opposite effect. Gay activists, with the as- sistance of lawyers, brought public attention to the policy, and in the process educated the community about the fact that LGBT people exist and that they too have rights.

▲

One day in the summer of 1982, as Michael Hardwick was leaving the gay bar in Atlanta where he worked, he threw a beer bottle into a trash can in front of the building. Moments later, police officer Keith Torick drove up beside him, ordering him to get into the cruiser. After Torick asked Hardwick what he was doing in the area, he answered that he worked at the bar, a statement that suggested to the officer that Hardwick was gay. Torick then proceeded to ticket Hardwick for drinking in public, despite his protestations that he had not.

Torick inadvertently wrote down the wrong court date on the summons. As a result of the officer's mistake, Hardwick did not appear in court on the correct day and a warrant was issued for his arrest. A few hours later, Torick took the unusual step—unusual because the charge was so minor—of going to Hardwick's apartment to arrest him. Hardwick was not home, but when he learned from his roommate that a police officer was looking for him, he went down to the county clerk's office, paid a $50 fine to settle the matter, and hoped that he would never see Torick again. But three weeks later, a determined Torick went back to Hardwick's place to arrest him.

When Torick arrived at the apartment, the door was unlocked. The officer made himself at home, walking through the premises to a back bedroom. The door to the bedroom was slightly ajar; Torick opened it further, went in, and saw Hardwick engaging in oral sex with another man. Torick then announced to the startled men that they were under arrest. After Hardwick and his friend dressed, Torick handcuffed them and drove them downtown where he had them booked for violating Georgia's sodomy law.

Hardwick spent twelve hours in jail before being released. Prosecutors, recognizing the questionable legality of the arrest based on an invalid warrant, eventually dropped the sodomy charge. By that point, the ACLU had already contacted Hardwick offering to represent him, and Hardwick readily agreed. On Valentine's Day, 1983, the ACLU filed a complaint on his behalf in federal court in Atlanta challenging the constitutionality of the law under which he was arrested.

A few months later, a meeting took place in New York City in the office of Abby Rubenfeld, a civil rights lawyer from Nashville, who had recently been named legal director of the Lambda Legal Defense and Education Fund. (The group later changed its name to Lambda Legal. In this book, I will refer to the organization simply as "Lambda.") Lambda—the oldest gay rights legal organization in the United States—was founded by a handful of young gay lawyers in

New York City in the early 1970s. When the lawyers first attempted to register their new organization as a public interest law firm, a court denied the petition, concluding that there was no evidence that lesbians and gay men were unable to obtain adequate legal representation.[5] Even though that ruling was eventually overturned, Lambda, during its first years of existence, had little money and was unable to take on many cases. Funding improved in the early 1980s—at around the time Rubenfeld became legal director—allowing the group to litigate a greater number of cases.

Rubenfeld called the meeting in 1983 because, despite the consensus among activists that sodomy laws were the biggest obstacle to attaining full equality for LGBT people, there was little coordination among the handful of lawyers who were working on the issue. In fact, the 1983 meeting turned out to be of historic importance because it constituted the first time that LGBT rights lawyers from across the country gathered to discuss ongoing cases and plan for future ones. In addition to Lambda, several other organizations were represented that day, including the Texas Human Rights Foundation, Boston's Gay and Lesbian Advocates and Defenders, and two San Francisco groups: the Lesbian Rights Project (which later became the National Center for Lesbian Rights) and the National Gay Rights Advocates. Also present that day were lawyers from the ACLU, the organization that was representing Hardwick in his constitutional challenge to Georgia's sodomy law.

Although the ACLU was widely recognized as one of the nation's leading liberal organizations, it took the group a long time to add gay rights to its legal repertoire. During the 1950s, the organization had refused to represent government employees who were fired because of their sexual orientation, going so far as to issue a policy paper stating that homosexuality was "a valid consideration in evaluating the security risk factor in sensitive positions." Around the same time, the civil liberties group also took the position that sodomy statutes were constitutional and that "[i]t is not within [the organization's] province to evaluate the social validity of the laws aimed at the suppression or elimination of homosexuals."[6]

After much agitation from some of its more liberal affiliates, the ACLU began changing its position on gay issues in the mid-1960s, first by calling on the government to refrain from penalizing individuals for engaging in private and consensual gay sex and then by agreeing to start representing former military and civilian employees whom the federal government had dismissed upon the belief that they were gay. Also in the 1960s, the ACLU helped to represent a Canadian immigrant who unsuccessfully challenged the government's authority to deport him solely because he was gay.[7] And, in the 1970s, the ACLU was involved in some of the earliest constitutional challenges to sodomy laws. All of this activism culminated—three years after the meeting held in Rubenfeld's office—with the ACLU's formation of the Lesbian and Gay Rights Project. That unit, which was headed initially by Nan Hunter, an experienced ACLU lawyer, was the first of its kind created by a national legal organization.

From the initial Rubenfeld meeting in 1983, a group called the Ad-Hoc Task Force to Challenge Sodomy Laws was formed, with its members meeting periodically to discuss how best to challenge sodomy laws in court. In 1986, the group was renamed the Gay Rights Litigators' Roundtable, a change that reflected the fact that the movement's lawyers were involved in a broad range of legal actions beyond sodomy challenges, including cases involving custody and adoption, relationship recognition, and employment discrimination.

That same year, the Supreme Court issued a ruling rejecting Hardwick's argument that his constitutional right to privacy was violated.[8] In doing so, the Court dismissed as "facetious" the claim that the Constitution recognized the right of LGBT people to choose their sexual partners. The devastating loss in Hardwick's case turned out to be the low watermark in the LGBT rights movement's pursuit of civil rights though the courts. In the two decades that followed, the movement went on to attain many impressive legal victories, including the five that are chronicled in this book.

Although this book focuses on the main LGBT rights lawyers who litigated the five cases, it is important to emphasize that many other attorneys have contributed in crucial ways to the LGBT rights movement's legal successes.[9] These lawyers include not only Lambda's Abby Rubenfeld and the ACLU's Nan Hunter, but also the Gay and Lesbian Advocates and Defenders' Mary Bonauto and Shannon Minter of the National Center for Lesbian Rights. A complete list of the lawyers who have made important contributions to the LGBT rights cause would include many additional names.

▲

LGBT rights attorneys have not received the attention they deserve given that their work over the last two decades is comparable to that carried out by the NAACP Legal Defense Fund lawyers in the 1940s and 1950s. In both instances, a group of attorneys, carefully and methodically, used the courts to advance the interests of a marginalized group in ways that fundamentally changed society. LGBT rights lawyers, like their earlier civil rights counterparts, have successfully used litigation as a means to promote greater equality and freedom for the members of the communities they serve.

It is in many ways not surprising that the legal advocacy that was part of the civil rights movement has received much greater attention than that of the LGBT rights movement. To begin with, several decades have elapsed since the civil rights movement achieved its most important judicial victories, giving legal historians and other commentators considerable time to explore and evaluate the lawyers' accomplishments. In addition, the LGBT rights movement, quite simply, has not had a towering figure like Thurgood Marshall, the man who played such a crucial role in almost all of the important civil rights cases of the 1940s and 1950s. It is not possible, when assessing the legal work done on behalf of the LGBT rights movement, to focus to the same extent on the work of any one person. Thus, this book examines the accomplishments of seven different LGBT rights attorneys.

Part of the story that I tell about these lawyers relates to their sexual orientation. In the same way that most of the attorneys who worked for the NAACP Legal Defense Fund in the 1940s and 1950s were black, and most of the lawyers who worked for the ACLU's Women's Rights Project and the NOW Legal Defense Fund in the

1970s and 1980s were women, most of the lawyers profiled in this book are either gay or lesbian.

Interestingly, the LGBT attorneys profiled here began their legal education while still largely in the closet. The story is fairly consistent: at the same time that they were acquiring—at some of the nation's leading law schools—the legal skills necessary to advocate successfully on behalf of a social movement, they were also coming to terms with their sexual orientation. It is remarkable that these lawyers, only a few years later, found themselves handling some of the most important LGBT rights cases in the country's history. The handful of years that elapsed between their coming out of the closet and their legal advocacy on behalf of the LGBT community constituted a period of exceptional personal and professional growth that not only benefited them as individuals but also contributed significantly to improving the lives of LGBT people across the country.

▲

The LGBT rights movement's legal strategy has its critics, including those who agree with many of the movement's ends but not with its means. One common criticism is that the movement has spent too much time and resources working through the courts rather than through the political process. This view is bolstered by political science and legal scholars who contend that even iconic cases such as *Brown v. Board of Education* play a relatively minor role in changing social attitudes.[10]

There are, to be sure, limits to what any social movement can accomplish through the courts. The judiciary, after all, is dependent on the other two branches of government for the application and enforcement of its rulings. In addition, although judicial decisions can change people's behavior—as long as the rulings are enforced—it is probably true that courts can do little to change deeply held prejudices about certain groups, be they African Americans, women, or LGBT people. As a result, court-mandated change can sometimes proceed at a frustratingly slow pace, even when the nation's highest court orders that it be carried out with "all deliberate speed."

Despite these limitations, courts offer groups that have historically been shut out of the political process a vehicle through which their claims can be heard and assessed. The issue of same-sex marriage provides an illustrative example of this point. In the early 1990s, before the gay plaintiffs' initial legal success in the Hawaii same-sex marriage litigation, no state legislature had been willing to address the implications for LGBT people of being denied access to the institution of marriage. The socially entrenched idea that marriage is by definition a heterosexual institution, coupled with the relatively small number of voters who are LGBT, meant that political and legislative processes offered little hope of progress. It was not until courts began grappling with the constitutionality of denying LGBT people access to the institution of marriage that the nation as a whole started paying attention to the issue of whether same-sex relationships merit legal recognition.

Courts, unlike legislatures, are required to address the substance of claims properly brought before them by citizens. And, under our system of government, courts have the authority to strike down laws and regulations that are inconsistent with constitutional provisions. It is for both of these reasons that minority groups in the United States frequently rely on the courts when seeking the rights and opportunities that accompany equal citizenship.

None of this means that a social movement will be able to achieve all of its goals through the courts. It bears remembering, for example, that it was a legislative act—the enactment by Congress of the Civil Rights Act of 1964—that dealt the mortal blow, a full decade after the Supreme Court decided *Brown*, to segregationist policies in America. Judicial civil rights victories, then, are frequently the beginning of the process rather than the end. The move toward greater equality, however, has to begin somewhere, and under our system of government, that somewhere is frequently the courts.

It is unclear, at the beginning of the twenty-first century, whether the LGBT rights movement will ultimately prevail in achieving its most important goals. It is clear, however, that the nation, at the very least, is grappling with the place of LGBT people in society. This is a monumental shift from thirty years ago, when the country hardly took notice of their existence, much less struggled in meaningful ways with their claims to equal citizenship. LGBT rights cases, and the lawyers who litigate them, have played a crucial role in making this happen.

# CHAPTER I

# Family

## The Facts

When Leslie Blanchard, a fifty-two-year-old gay man, died of AIDS at a Newark, New Jersey, hospital on September 14, 1986, he did so in the arms of his partner, Miguel Braschi. For the previous ten years, the two men had lived together in a rent-controlled apartment on East 54th Street in Manhattan, with only Blanchard's name on the lease. Three months after Blanchard died, the landlord threatened Braschi with eviction. As Braschi waited for the new year—his first without Blanchard in more than a decade—he had to cope with not only the loss of the man whom he loved but also with the possibility of being thrown out of his home.

▲

As a young boy growing up in Vermont, Blanchard was particularly close to his grandmother, who lived with his parents and him. "Gram," as he called her, seemed to pay special attention to Blanchard, her eldest grandchild. She taught him how to cook and garden, two activities that would remain lifelong passions.

One night, when Blanchard was ten, the two were at home listening to the radio, when the boy absentmindedly picked up a hairbrush and started combing Gram's hair. Surprised by how much he enjoyed stroking her hair with the brush, Blanchard soon found himself brushing it every night as the two sat listening to the radio. A few weeks later, he shampooed his grandmother's hair over the kitchen sink, and she taught him how to set it. Blanchard loved all of it—the feel of the hair, the smell of the shampoo, and, in particular, the way in which Gram smiled when she looked at herself in the mirror after the grooming was over.

When Blanchard was eighteen, he moved to Boston to attend a beauty school. After graduating, Blanchard held several jobs in different salons in Boston and New York, specializing in hair coloring. Dissatisfied with the commercial products available at the time, he developed his own color formulas that worked surprisingly well in showing off the richness and texture of his clients' hair. Word that there was a new and talented kid on the hair-coloring block soon spread throughout the beauty industry, leading Clairol, the country's largest manufacturer of hair-coloring products, to hire him as a consultant.

In the 1960s, Saks Fifth Avenue set up a special salon for Blanchard, which became the first in New York to specialize in hair coloring. The salon's clientele soon grew to include many Hollywood stars, including Gloria Swanson and Joan Fontaine. In 1970, he left Saks to open his own salon on the second floor of a building on East 62nd Street. Business thrived, with the list of clients now including Barbara Walters, Mary Tyler Moore, Meryl Streep, Robert De Niro, and Donald Sutherland. In 1975, overwhelmed with bookings, Blanchard expanded the salon to two other floors.

In December of that year, Blanchard took a few days off from work and traveled to Puerto Rico on vacation. It was during that trip that he met, and fell in love with, the twenty-year-old Braschi. Blanchard had known that he was gay since a young age. There were many gay men working in the beauty industry, and Blanchard dated a handful of them through the years. Yet his intimate relationships seemed to lack permanence—that is, until he met Braschi.

Braschi was born and raised in San Juan. He was an athletic child who at a young age developed a love for tennis. As a teenager, he became one of the best tennis players on the island, eventually receiving a full tennis scholarship at Ohio State University.

The two men met at a gay bar on December 27, 1975. They spent the next ten days traveling around the island together. Blanchard felt an immediate attraction to Braschi, who was tall, dark, muscular, and extremely handsome. The attraction went beyond the physical, however. Blanchard was also drawn by Braschi's apparent boundless energy; he loved the fact that Braschi seemed determined to find joy in every activity, no matter how prosaic or mundane. Despite the twenty-year difference in their ages, and despite their different cultural backgrounds, the two men quickly grew quite fond of each other.

After a handful of heady days together in Puerto Rico, Braschi returned to Ohio to finish his junior year of college and Blanchard went back to New York to resume his demanding work schedule. On every weekend of that spring, however, Braschi got on a plane and headed to New York. The couple spent most of their time in Manhattan, with Blanchard making the younger man feel at home in his one-bedroom apartment on East 54th Street, the one that would eventually be the subject of the LGBT rights lawsuit. As winter turned to spring, they also started taking frequent weekend trips to Yellow Iris Farm, Blanchard's one-hundred-acre property in northern New Jersey.

As summer approached, Blanchard invited Braschi to spend it with him in New York. Braschi immediately agreed. The two flew down to Puerto Rico in late May, and Braschi introduced Blanchard to his parents. At first, the family had reservations about the relationship, not because Blanchard was a man—they were accepting of their son's sexual orientation—but because he was twenty years older than their son. Braschi's parents, however, quickly realized that the two men loved one another deeply, and that their son was happy, which in the end was all that mattered.

After returning to the mainland, Blanchard and Braschi had a wonderful summer together, enjoying each other's company and spending time with friends, both in the Manhattan apartment and at the New Jersey farm. In August, Braschi made the life-altering decision not to return to Ohio to finish college and instead moved in with Blanchard. A month later, he began working at the salon as an assistant manager, helping with the day-to-day operation of the business.

Both men soon settled into a busy and happy routine. They worked hard during the day, running what had arguably become the most famous hair salon in New York. And they played hard at night, usually in their own apartment, surrounded by friends. The apartment, in fact, became the center of their social lives. Both men were tireless hosts who offered some of the more sought-after invitations in town. Dinner parties at their apartment were almost nightly events, with extravagant and delicious meals prepared by Blanchard's Chinese cook. Several of Blanchard's famous Hollywood clients would drop by periodically, adding to the allure of the parties. For his part, Braschi made sure that there was always salsa music playing on the stereo so that their guests could dance late into the night.

The two men seemed happy and at peace with themselves, primarily because they had each other. Blanchard's friends in particular were thrilled that he had found a companion with whom he could share his home. As one of those friends would later state in an affidavit, "the home that they created in their apartment [seemed] like the home of any happily married couple."

Blanchard and Braschi, of course, did not have the option of marrying, but as 1976 drew to a close, they wanted to commemorate their first anniversary in some way. They purchased Cartier love bracelets as symbols of their commitment to each other, and one night in their apartment, the two men exchanged the bracelets, along with kisses and statements of love. A decade later, as Blanchard lay dying in the hospital, Braschi removed Blanchard's bracelet and placed it on his wrist, next to his own, where it would remain for years to come.

As the years went by, the relationship between Blanchard and Braschi remained a strong and vibrant one. They both had peripatetic tendencies, traveling to Rome every year for a decade and to Brazil every Christmas between 1977 and 1981. They also routinely traveled to San Juan, spending time with Braschi's parents, and to Vermont to visit with Blanchard's family.

In short, for several years after they met, Blanchard and Braschi were a happy couple, leading active and fulfilled lives. But by the early 1980s, there was a public health crisis looming in the horizon that would soon have a devastating impact on countless people across the country, including Blanchard and Braschi.

▲

The first indication that something was amiss came in early 1980 when gay men in San Francisco started complaining to doctors about swollen glands. It was clear that these men's immune systems had shifted into overdrive, but no one knew exactly why. A few months later, gay men in New York and California started developing unusual diseases such as Kaposi's sarcoma, a skin cancer that until then had mainly afflicted older men of Mediterranean extraction, and Pneumocystis carinii pneumonia, a rare disorder. The Centers for Disease Control (CDC) issued its first bulletin on the AIDS epidemic in June of 1981, reporting on a small cluster of Pneumocystis cases in Los Angeles. A month later, the *New York Times* published a brief but ominous article titled "Rare Cancer Seen in 41 Homosexuals."[1]

At first, public health officials were unsure what was causing so many young gay men to become sick. The transmission of some kind of organism, perhaps through sex, was only one of several theories in the early days of the epidemic. Other possible causes included the use of certain recreational drugs or the frequenting of specific locations such as bars. It was not until June of 1982 that the CDC uncovered evidence linking together forty gay men with AIDS in a network of sexual relationships in ten different cities, strongly suggesting that the disease was caused by a single infectious agent transmitted sexually and perhaps in other ways as well.

The gay community quickly mobilized to share the little that was known about the disease and how it was transmitted, as well as to begin to care for the hundreds of gay men who were becoming sick every month. The community also began mobilizing politically to try to address the rampant discrimination—especially in employment, housing, insurance, and health care—that was already becoming pervasive in a society that, even before the epidemic, was deeply suspicions of gay men and their sexuality.

The vilification of gay men intensified in 1983 when it was discovered that the disease could also be transmitted through blood, meaning that anyone who needed a blood transfusion was potentially at risk of developing AIDS. Even though heterosexuals—including, but not limited to, hemophiliacs and intravenous drug users—also started coming down with the disease, the media kept the spotlight almost exclusively on gay men and their sexual practices.

In April 1984, when the government first announced the scientific finding that AIDS was caused by a specific virus, later to be named HIV, there were over four thousand reported AIDS cases in the United States. A year later, when a test was finally developed to detect the presence of the virus in the blood, the number of reported cases nationwide had doubled, with three thousand of them in New York City alone.

For Blanchard and Braschi, as for many gay men across the country, particularly those living in San Francisco and New York, there was no escape from the sheer relentlessness of the disease. First, there was the constant fear of becoming sick, with every cough and fever, no matter how innocuous, a possible indication of imminent death. Second, there were frantic visits to hospitals to comfort stricken friends, frequently followed by sad trips to funeral homes to memorialize the lives of those same friends. And third, there was the anxiety caused by hearing about so many gay men with AIDS who were, in their greatest time of need, losing not only their jobs, housing, and health insurance, but also, in some instances, even the support of their own families.

Blanchard and Braschi tried, as best they could, to remain sane amidst such chaos. One way of doing this was to continue working hard; another was to leave the city as frequently as possible to spend time surrounded by the bucolic serenity of the Yellow Iris Farm. In the spring of 1986, *Architectural Digest* sent a reporter and photographer to do a feature on Blanchard and his farm. The article described how Blanchard had lovingly restored the old farmhouse to its original grandeur, filling it with beautiful objects, while using the farm to raise and train prize-winning horses. The glossy photographs accompanying the piece showed handsomely decorated rooms and beautifully manicured gardens. The reporter ended the article with a description of Blanchard's plans to use the property as a summer retreat for underprivileged urban children unaccustomed to living among lush greenery and beautiful animals. By the time the article appeared in June of 1986, however, it was unclear whether Blanchard would be able to implement those plans anytime soon.[2]

▲

It began in May, with what at first seemed like a bad case of the flu. When Blanchard's high fever and debilitating fatigue failed to go away, he visited his physician in New York and then an immunology specialist in New Jersey. Both doctors conducted tests and came to the same conclusion: Blanchard had AIDS.

There was, at the time, no treatment for the disease. The discovery that an old cancer drug called AZT could, for some people, slow down the spread of the virus in the body was still a year away. By now, there were some individuals who had been living with AIDS for several years, suggesting that the disease might spare the lives of some who had it. But such a possibility offered only a thin reed of hope, given that the mortality rate of people with AIDS in 1986 was extraordinarily high.

Blanchard, who was not feeling well enough to continue going in to the salon every day, told Braschi that he wanted to go to the farm to recover. Friends offered to visit him there, but Blanchard balked, telling everyone that he would soon be better and able to return to the city. The truth was that Blanchard was in no position to play social host, as he had done so many times, both at the apartment on East 54th Street and at the farm. He felt like he needed to conserve all of his energies to fight the virus. And the only person whom he wanted with him was Braschi.

Both men left for the farm in late May, uncertain when they would return to New York. Blanchard continued to feel ill, suffering from a lack of appetite, high fevers, and night sweats. In June, his condition deteriorated significantly, requiring that he be hospitalized. While at the hospital, Blanchard had to confront the reality that he might soon be unable to manage his own affairs. He therefore asked his lawyers back in New York to draft a power-of-attorney document in favor of Braschi, giving him full authority to make decisions on Blanchard's behalf, including those related to medical care and finances. Blanchard signed the document in late June while lying in his hospital bed, with Braschi by his side.

A few days later, Blanchard started feeling better, and the doctors told him he could go home. The two men drove back to the farm, where they spent the rest of the summer. July and August were relatively good months; as Blanchard health's stabilized, the couple was able to enjoy many quiet and tender moments together.

In early August, Blanchard traveled to the offices of his Manhattan lawyers to execute a will. Years later, in the course of the litigation involving the apartment on East 54th Street, the landlord's lawyer would contend that the relationship between Blanchard and Braschi was not as close as the latter claimed because the will repeatedly referred to Braschi simply as "my friend." The problem, of course, was that in the mid-1980s, there was still no word in common usage that accurately described someone in a committed same-sex relationship. The term that was most prevalent at the time was "lover," but it seemed to emphasize the sexual component of committed relationships at the expense of emotional attachment. So Blanchard's lawyers settled for the word "friend," even though it failed to capture the depth of the men's devotion to each other.

The will designated Braschi as the co-executor of Blanchard's estate. Braschi was also to receive the bulk of the estate, including the farm and the many works of art that Blanchard had purchased through the years. In addition, Blanchard knew that the salon was too closely associated with his talents, reputation, and public persona to survive his death. He therefore ordered in his will that the company through which Blanchard owned the salon (and the building where it was located) be liquidated with all of the proceeds going to Braschi. In the end, Blanchard's estate would be valued at more than $5 million, all of which, except for $150,000, would go to Braschi.

With his financial affairs in order, Blanchard returned to Yellow Iris Farm, knowing there was a good chance that he would be dead before the end of the year. The only person, other than Braschi, whom Blanchard allowed to visit him that summer was his mother, who came down from Vermont in August to spend a few weeks caring for her son.

Shortly after Blanchard's mother went back home, his condition took a turn for the worse. In early September, he was once again rushed to the hospital, this time to St. Michael's, a Catholic hospital in Newark. Blanchard had not eaten solid food for several days, and his body seemed unable to retain the intravenous nutrients ordered by the doctors. There was, in the end, little that anyone could do for him except try to make him as comfortable as possible as his body surrendered to the virus.

Blanchard would live for another ten days. During the last forty-eight hours of Blanchard's life, Braschi did not leave his bedside, repeatedly caressing his partner and telling him that he loved him. In the few minutes before his death, when it became clear that Blanchard was taking his last, difficult breaths, Braschi lay down next to him for one last time and embraced him.

A few days after Blanchard died, about a dozen of his friends congregated at the farm for a simple memorial service. Braschi spoke to the group about how much Blanchard had accomplished in his life, how he had surrounded himself with friends who adored him, and how much Blanchard had meant to him. He had met Blanchard when he was a young man who, like many twenty-year-olds, was unsure of what the future might bring. Blanchard had been the first and only man whom he had truly loved. He had given up his college degree, and even a potential career as a tennis pro, because he wanted to spend as much time as possible with Blanchard. Blanchard had welcomed him into his world with open arms, making it clear that he wanted to share every part of his life with Braschi. And they had had ten wonderful years together, something that not even HIV, with its cruel determination to cut short vibrant and brilliant lives, had been able to take away.

Blanchard had requested that he be cremated and that his ashes be strewn among his flowers at the farm. After he spoke, Braschi gave each guest a handful of the ashes. The group then dispersed among the flowers beds, scattering the remains in silence.

▲

The weeks and months after Blanchard's death were difficult ones for Braschi. He missed his partner immensely; the pain of the loss was almost physical. Dealing with the complexities of settling the estate provided a distraction of sorts, but even that entailed the sad prospect of selling the salon and the farm, two places that were intimately associated with Blanchard's life and passions. Soon, the most important and tangible thing that would remain of their lives together would be the apartment on East 54th Street.

Braschi knew that Blanchard had moved into the rent-controlled apartment many years earlier and that under applicable regulations, the landlord had been prohibited from evicting Blanchard as long as he paid his rent. Braschi assumed that it would be relatively straightforward to have the lease put under his name—he had, after all, been living in the apartment with Blanchard for more than ten years, sharing in all matters related to it, including the paying of the rent. Stanley Stahl, the owner of the building, however, had other ideas.

Stahl, the son of a Brooklyn butcher, became a real estate broker in 1947, at the age of twenty-three. Two years later, he turned an initial investment of $12,000 in a Manhattan building into a modest but growing real estate development business. In the late 1950s, Stahl staked everything he owned to build what at the time was a pioneering fifty-story Park Avenue office tower. That building became the centerpiece of a New York City real estate empire that eventually included ownership of over four million square feet of office space, residential buildings with more than three thousand apartments, and several Broadway theaters and restaurants. One of Stahl's properties was the building on East 54th Street where Braschi had lived with Blanchard for more than a decade.

Stahl was known in the real estate world as a ferociously tough competitor and negotiator. This engendered considerable resentment among others in the high-stakes world of New York real estate. When a reporter once asked a developer who had had extensive dealings with Stahl whether anyone in the business liked him, the person replied that "even Hitler must have had a couple of friends."[3]

Stahl, like most New York City landlords, grew to despise the Rent Control Law that limited the profitability of many of his properties. Under New York law, the death of the tenant whose name is on the lease offers landlords the best opportunity to free the property from the clutches of rent control. Once the apartment is no longer subject to rent control regulations, the landlord is permitted a one-time increase in rent as determined by market conditions. After that, most apartments are subject to the Rent Stabilization Law, which also places caps on how much rent can be charged. Those caps, however, are significantly higher than they are under the Rent Control Law.

When Blanchard died, therefore, Stahl and his lawyers were prepared to do whatever was necessary to free the apartment from the rent control regime. The only obstacle that stood in their way was Miguel Braschi. Stahl was a businessman who was used to getting his way. What he perhaps did not count on was that Braschi was an equally determined person, albeit one with significantly less power and money than Stahl. As Braschi would tell a friend several times as the litigation over the apartment dragged on in the years to come, the landlord and his people "do not know who they are messing with."[4]

In November 1986, a little more than two months after Blanchard died, Stahl and his lawyers began sending Braschi letters threatening him with eviction if he did not move out of the apartment. Braschi decided to consult with a lawyer, setting the legal wheels in motion that would eventually lead a court to rule, for the first time in the nation's history, that a sexually intimate relationship between two individuals of the same sex can constitute a family.

## The Lawyer

Bill Rubenstein graduated from law school during the same month that Leslie Blanchard learned that he had AIDS. A year later, Rubenstein joined the ACLU, quickly becoming, while still in his twenties, one of the nation's leading lawyers working on gay rights and AIDS issues.

Rubenstein, the son of an accountant and a former schoolteacher, was born in 1960 and grew up in Squirrel Hill, a predominantly Jewish neighborhood in Pittsburgh. Although he knew that he was gay from a young age, Rubenstein remained in the closet throughout his four years of college at Yale. In fact, it was not until the summer of 1982, a few months after he graduated from college, that Rubenstein first came out to a friend. That friend proceeded to warn him about a mysterious disease that seemed to be afflicting gay men in New York and San Francisco. Rubenstein had not heard about the illness and did not give the matter much thought. Shortly after arriving at Harvard in 1983 to pursue a law degree, Rubenstein joined the gay law student organization and came out to members of his study group, most of whom were straight men. Much to his relief, none of them seemed to care.

While Rubenstein was taking small yet determined steps to come out of the closet, AIDS was transforming itself from a relatively rare illness into a national epidemic of frightening proportions. The stigma that accompanied the spread of AIDS pushed some gay men back (or further) into the closet. But for Rubenstein, as for many LGBT people of his generation, AIDS had the opposite effect. As it became clear that the epidemic would soon have a devastating impact on thousands of gay men across the country, Rubenstein started feeling a growing sense of solidarity both with those who were becoming ill and with the partners and friends who were caring for them.

Rubenstein's education as a gay man took place primarily in the bars and cafés of Boston and Cambridge. There was not much to learn on the subject, however, from his law school classes, where the topic of homosexuality never arose. Perplexed by this silence, Rubenstein spent an evening at the Harvard law library looking for what legal books had to say about homosexuality. Despite searching for several hours, he found no discussion of homosexuality as a legal topic, much less any reference to actual lives led by lesbians and gay men. It was as if LGBT people, as far as the law was concerned, were invisible.

After receiving his law degree in 1986, Rubenstein moved to Washington, D.C., to clerk for a federal district judge. In his spare time, he volunteered for the Whitman-Walker Clinic—the largest AIDS service organization in the nation's capital—by drafting wills for its clients. On many early evenings after leaving the judge's chambers, Rubenstein stopped by the Clinic to pick up files containing interviews of gay men about their dying wishes. Most of these men had few assets, their bequests consisting of leaving small bank accounts, furniture, and pets to partners and friends. In his apartment at night, Rubenstein drafted wills based on these modest requests, dropping them off at the Clinic the following morning on his way back to work. He did not meet any of the men whose final wishes he transcribed into legal documents, though he frequently saw their names in the local gay newspaper's obituary pages. He also sometimes recognized their names stitched into the colorful patches of the AIDS quilt that was spread out like an ocean of grief on the Washington Mall.

By the middle of the 1980s, the AIDS epidemic had become the leading cause of death among twenty-five- to forty-four-year-olds in the United States. In doing so, it reversed, as one writer put it, "the natural order of life as the old buried the young and the young buried one another."[5] Surrounded by so much death and dying, Rubenstein came to assume that the disease would kill him before he reached the age of thirty. With a perceived life expectancy of less than five years, he decided in 1987 to dedicate his professional life as a lawyer to doing whatever he could to help people with AIDS. As a result, he got a job with the ACLU's Lesbian and Gay Rights Project (as well as its recently created AIDS Project).

In his first year at the ACLU, Rubenstein represented a woman with AIDS quarantined by public health officials in South Carolina. The young lawyer filed a habeas corpus petition in federal court in

Charleston, demanding that the government justify the continued detention of his client. The case was assigned to district court (now U.S. Court of Appeals) judge Karen Henderson, a Reagan appointee. When Rubenstein showed up in Judge Henderson's courtroom to argue the petition, he noticed that the furniture had been rearranged so that the quarantined woman and her lawyer would have to sit in the back of the courtroom. It seemed that the judge, apparently fearing that she might contract HIV from the mere presence of Rubenstein's client in the courtroom, wanted her as far away from the bench as possible. Rubenstein was forced to make his legal arguments from the back of the room, practically shouting in order to be heard. Perhaps not surprisingly, Judge Henderson denied the habeas corpus petition. Rubenstein then went across the street to the state courthouse and, with the assistance of a local lawyer, convinced a judge there to issue an order releasing his client from confinement.

Another one of Rubenstein's early cases involved Parkland Memorial, the Dallas hospital where President John F. Kennedy was taken in 1963 after he was shot. In the mid-1980s, Parkland administrators adopted several measures aimed at discouraging individuals with AIDS from seeking medical treatment at their facility. One policy prohibited hospital staff from dispensing the medicine AZT, even though it had been approved by the Food and Drug Administration for the treatment of HIV. The hospital also placed a cap on the number of beds that were allocated to AIDS patients. This meant that if a person with AIDS showed up at the hospital when all of the "AIDS beds" were taken, that individual, no matter how ill, would not be admitted until a patient with AIDS either died or was discharged. Although it is inconceivable that a hospital would ever treat cancer or heart patients in the same way, these types of policies, sadly enough, were not that unusual in the early days of the AIDS epidemic. Rubenstein helped a group of local attorneys bring a lawsuit charging the hospital with discriminating against people with AIDS. The lawsuit, and the attention it received, eventually embarrassed the hospital sufficiently that it rescinded its discriminatory policies.[6]

In another instance, Rubenstein threatened to sue the state of

Alabama when it refused to use Medicaid money to pay for AZT prescribed to individuals with AIDS. When confronted with the possibility of a lawsuit brought by the ACLU, the state relented and agreed to pay for the medication. The evening after state officials announced their change in policy, a group of Alabamians with AIDS gathered at a Birmingham apartment to celebrate the good news. From there, one of them called Rubenstein at his New York office to thank him for his help with the case. As Rubenstein spoke to the caller, and as he heard the celebratory din in the background, he felt pleased that he had been able to help his clients in a tangible way; as a direct result of his advocacy, after all, the state government had agreed to pay for their AIDS treatment. But he also suspected, as in fact would turn out to be the case, that every person with AIDS present in that Birmingham apartment that evening would be dead in a few years.

Death was an inescapable part of Rubenstein's early professional life as an attorney, and the young lawyer tried to deal with this awful reality as best he could. Rubenstein found some solace in the fact that the legal work he was doing was challenging and fascinating. There had never before in the United States been an epidemic quite like this one; the disease tested not only political and medical institutions but also legal ones. Although Rubenstein was aware that there were limits to what the law could accomplish, he also knew that it could be deployed in certain instances to benefit people with AIDS in tangible ways. There was also a creativeness to the AIDS activism of the late 1980s that motivated Rubenstein to keep fighting for his clients. AIDS activists during that time did everything from chaining themselves to drug companies' trucks to demonstrating with cardboard tombstones in front of government buildings to draping antigay U.S. senator Jesse Helms's house with a gigantic condom. There was a theatricality and an inventiveness to the political activism that Rubenstein found mesmerizing and captivating. In the end, Rubenstein felt proud to be manning the barricades, so to speak, with individuals, most of whom were quite young, who were committed to fighting until their last breaths to pressure, cajole, and embarrass those in power to treat the epidemic with the seriousness that it demanded. There was a dignity and pride in this perseverance that, despite the relentlessness of the disease, was inspiring.

In the spring of 1988, less than a year after Rubenstein joined the ACLU, he learned about a series of housing cases percolating in the New York courts in which the owners of rent-controlled apartments were trying to evict survivors of deceased tenants. Several of those cases involved the same-sex partners of tenants who had died of AIDS. One of them was Miguel Braschi.

## The Law

If Braschi was going to have the right to remain in the home that he had shared with Blanchard for a decade, it would be because of a law passed forty years earlier. After World War II, many American cities found themselves confronting a severe housing shortage caused by the return of thousands of service members. This sudden jump in the demand for housing led many landlords to start charging exorbitant rents. Nowhere in the country were the rents higher than in New York City. The New York legislature attempted to address this housing emergency by enacting the Rent Control Law, which placed strict caps on how much landlords could charge for rental properties built before 1947. The Rent Control Law not only limited the discretion of landlords to increase rents but also constrained their ability to evict both named tenants and their survivors. In fact, the state agency responsible for enforcing the Rent Control Law eventually issued a regulation prohibiting landlords from evicting "either the surviving spouse of the deceased tenant or some other member of the deceased tenant's family who has been living with the tenant."

As far as the landlord Stahl was concerned, Braschi was neither Blanchard's spouse nor a member of his family. He was, therefore, not legally entitled to remain in the apartment after Blanchard died. Braschi's ability to do so would depend on whether Stahl and his lawyers were correct in their view that two men in an intimate relationship could not, as a legal matter, constitute a family.

▲

The lawyer who first represented Braschi was Owen Wincig, a young attorney working in a small Manhattan law firm headed by his father. When Wincig began researching the law on behalf of Braschi, he ran across several cases—all decided in the previous six months—in which the gay partners of deceased tenants in rent-regulated apartments had successfully thwarted their landlords' efforts to evict them. The cases were promising because they were factually nearly identical to Braschi's case. Although none of them had been reviewed by appellate courts, the cases nonetheless showed a willingness by at least some trial judges to accept the notion that those who had been in committed same-sex relationships with now deceased tenants in rent-regulated apartments were entitled to anti-eviction protection under the law.[7]

Relying on these precedents, Wincig sought a preliminary injunction prohibiting Stahl from evicting Braschi. In February 1987, the case went before Justice Harold Baer Jr., a former assistant U.S. attorney who, in the 1960s, had supervised the work of the young prosecutor Rudolph Giuliani. Baer eventually issued an order prohibiting Stahl from evicting Braschi until he had an opportunity to review the merits of the latter's legal arguments. Braschi was elated when Wincig called to tell him that the judge had issued the temporary order. For now, at least, he would be able to stay in the apartment. Wincig cautioned Braschi, however, that the landlord would likely appeal.

The line of trial court cases, of which Braschi's was now only the latest, broadly interpreting the meaning of family in eviction law constituted a new roadblock for landlords who hoped to free their apartments from the clutches of rent control regulations. From the landlords' perspective, it was one thing for the law to require, as it had for many decades, that upon the death of a tenant in a rent-controlled apartment, those who were related to the tenant by marriage, blood, or adoption be allowed to remain in the unit. It was another thing altogether for the law to require landlords to provide that same opportunity to *any person* whom the courts concluded had a sufficiently close relationship with the deceased tenant to be deemed a family member.

The landlords in the other cases involving the partners of deceased gay tenants had not appealed. Stahl decided that he would be the first to do so. Sooner or later, an appellate court would have to rule on this issue. Stahl figured that it might as well be in his case.

▲

If landlords viewed cases like Braschi's as threatening their financial bottom line, LGBT rights litigators saw them as having great potential to advance the interests of the LGBT community. Although there were some in that community who, in the mid-1980s, were already pushing for the recognition of same-sex marriage, the movement's lawyers were not (yet) focusing on marriage. There had been a handful of same-sex marriage cases brought in the early 1970s but those had all failed miserably. There was little appetite among the movement's lawyers in the 1980s to bring same-sex marriage claims, largely because they perceived those cases as certain losers. Rather than focus on marriage, the movement's lawyers in the 1980s, when it came to relationship recognition and family law issues, concentrated instead on domestic partnership benefits and on the custody and visitation rights of LGBT parents.

The ACLU's Bill Rubenstein first heard of Braschi's case at a meeting of the Gay Rights Litigators' Roundtable held in early 1988. As Rubenstein and the other lawyers present began discussing the lawsuit, a consensus emerged that it could potentially be one of great importance to the movement. The benefits of a legal victory in this case would not be limited to one housing issue; if an appellate court ruled that Braschi and Blanchard had been a family, such a ruling would make it more likely that same-sex couples would have equal access to a whole series of benefits granted to family members, including health insurance benefits, bereavement leave, and hospital and jail visitation privileges.

▲

After consulting with others at the ACLU, Rubenstein filed an amicus (or "friend of the court") brief with the New York Appellate Division on behalf of Braschi arguing that landlord Stahl's interpretation of the anti-eviction regulation—one that would limit its applicability to cases where there were ties of marriage, blood, or adoption —rendered it unconstitutional. There was no rational justification, Rubenstein noted, for treating two individuals who were not related in one of the traditional ways differently than those who were so related. As the facts of the case showed, the former could lead lives that were as emotionally and financially interdependent as the latter. The differential treatment of these similarly situated individuals, Rubenstein contended, violated constitutional principles of equality.

A few months later, however, the Appellate Division rejected Braschi's claim that a same-sex couple could constitute a family.[8] Relying on *Matter of Adoption of Robert Paul P.*—a 1984 New York Court of Appeals case in which a gay man had unsuccessfully attempted to adopt his partner of many years in an effort to gain legal recognition of their relationship—the appellate court ruled that only the legislature could recognize same-sex relationships.[9]

▲

If there were likely considerable benefits for the LGBT rights movement from an appellate opinion concluding that a gay couple could be legally deemed a family, then the opposite was also true: a ruling that rejected that argument would be a significant setback. If there was a clear judicial precedent holding that a gay couple could *not* constitute a family for purposes of the Rent Control Law, then opponents of LGBT rights would be able to argue, both inside and outside of courtrooms, that same-sex relationships should not be deemed families for other legal purposes. From the gay rights movement's perspective, it was now imperative that the New York Court of Appeals review the lower court's ruling.

After the Appellate Division's ruling, Rubenstein persuaded Wincig, and through him Braschi, that the ACLU should take over the lawsuit. The mere fact that Braschi was now represented by the ACLU sent a signal to the state's highest court that this was an important case that merited careful attention. And indeed, a few months later, the New York Court of Appeals agreed to hear the case.

As Rubenstein reflected more deeply on the lawsuit in preparation for the appeal, he realized that it was an unusual LGBT rights dispute. The case, of course, had an LGBT rights component to it since Braschi and Blanchard had been in a same-sex relationship for ten years; however, if the Court of Appeals reinstated Justice Baer's preliminary injunction, it would likely not base its ruling on the fact that the two men were gay. In other words, if the right to the anti-eviction protection afforded by the Rent Control Law was applicable in this case, the sexual orientation of the parties should not matter. What seemed more important was the extent to which the men's relationship was sufficiently close and permanent enough to qualify as a family. It was important, therefore, that the court view the case as one that asked what constitutes a family as opposed to whether the landlord's interpretation of the regulation impermissibly discriminated on the basis of sexual orientation.

Rubenstein's principal objective, then, became to persuade the court that it was both appropriate and necessary to define the meaning of family functionally by focusing on the extent of the emotional and financial interdependence of the parties rather than formalistically by focusing on whether the parties were linked through ties of marriage, blood, or adoption. These links were simply proxies: their existence allowed courts to *assume* that the relationship between the survivor and the deceased tenant had been a close and durable one. The proxies, however, were imprecise. For example, a niece who was related to an uncle by blood would automatically be eligible for anti-eviction protection under the landlord's interpretation of the regulation regardless of whether the two had a close and interdependent relationship. Rubenstein wanted the court to focus on the characteristics of the relationship in question, rather than on the presence or absence of proxies.

It was possible to frame the case in such a way as to make it a more explicitly LGBT rights lawsuit. The rent control regulation, after all, provided eviction protection to a *spouse* or a family member of the deceased tenant. Rubenstein, therefore, had the option of arguing that Braschi was Blanchard's de facto spouse. Some LGBT rights activists, in fact, advised Rubenstein to do precisely that; as they saw it, it would be more consistent with the facts of the case to argue that Braschi was Blanchard's spouse than to contend that the former was simply a member of the latter's family. To suggest anything less was demeaning and disrespectful to their relationship. These activists also reasoned that to argue that Braschi was a member of Blanchard's family, as opposed to his spouse, constituted an implicit acknowledgment that two men (or two women) could not have a relationship that was marital in nature regardless of its closeness and permanency.

Rubenstein rejected this approach for both legal and political reasons. As to the former, the term "spouse" had a very specific meaning in the law that was inevitably linked to the existence of a legally valid marriage. Rubenstein feared that if he followed the activists' advice, he would make it too easy for the court to dismiss Braschi's claim on the ground that he was not Blanchard's spouse. While the meaning of "spouse" was clear, that of "family" was considerably more ambiguous and contestable, especially given that the anti-eviction regulation at issue in the case did not define the term. Rubenstein believed that it was the ambiguousness (and potential open-endedness) of the word "family" that provided Braschi with the best opportunity of prevailing in his appeal.

Rubenstein also disagreed that it would, as a political matter, be more progressive to argue that Braschi was Blanchard's spouse rather than a family member. In the unlikely event that the Court of Appeals ever held that Braschi, for purposes of the Rent Control Law, was Blanchard's "spouse," such a ruling would only help those who could establish that their relationship with a deceased tenant was analogous to a *marital* one. It would exclude many other potential familial arrangements that, while evincing economic and emotional interdependency, lacked the sexual or romantic component that characterized the relationship between Braschi and Blanchard. The potential impact of a positive ruling by the Court of Appeals, then, was considerably greater if Braschi argued that he was Blanchard's surviving family member rather than his surviving spouse. This strategic way of framing the case did not mean that the intimate nature of Braschi and Blanchard's relationship had to be hidden from the court. It did mean, however, that the court should be discouraged from seeing the case only through the lens of the men's sexual orientation.

While some activists believed that Rubenstein should argue that Braschi and Blanchard were effectively spouses, others were concerned that the relationship between the two men was *too* analogous to a traditional marital relationship. This was potentially problematic because it might set the bar too high for future claimants. The fear was that there might be some couples who deserved legal protection but who would be denied such protection because they could not match Braschi and Blanchard's extensive degree of emotional and economic interdependency.

But Rubenstein saw matters differently. The starting point of any successful impact litigation case is the presence of good facts. "Good" in this context means facts that are likely to lead the court to rule in a way that advances the cause of legal reform. Courts are intrinsically conservative institutions that seek to ground today's decision in yesterday's rulings. It is essential, when lawyers ask a court to depart somewhat from those rulings, therefore, that they do so in a case with compelling facts. It was precisely the fact that the relationship between Braschi and Blanchard was in many ways indistinguishable from that of a married heterosexual couple that might convince a majority of the judges that the anti-eviction regulation was also meant to protect same-sex partners in committed relationships. If the court was going to be persuaded to apply an expansive definition of the word "family," it was likely to first do so in a case where the relationship in question, putting aside the gender of the parties, seemed familiar to it. Once the definition of family was, as a legal matter, loosened from its formalistic moorings, the opportunity would then present itself for advocates to go back to the courts to seek further protections. The key point was that the quasi-marital relationship between the two men increased the chances that the court would apply an expansive definition of family, one that could later be used by advocates to seek to extend legal protections to other types of families that also did not fit the traditional mold.

▲

Another strategic question that Rubenstein confronted when he took over the *Braschi* litigation was what role AIDS should play in the case. (Although everyone involved in the lawsuit knew that Blanchard had died of AIDS, it was Braschi's wish that the disease not be mentioned in any of the legal papers that Wincig filed with the trial court.) Rubenstein knew that, as a matter of legal doctrine, it was irrelevant that Blanchard had died of AIDS; but Rubenstein also understood that the case's social significance was inexorably intertwined with AIDS.

By the late 1980s, the issue of AIDS-related homelessness in New York had reached emergency proportions. At the time, there were between two thousand and five thousand New Yorkers—some gay, some poor, some members of racial minorities, and some a combination of all three—who were homeless (or were confronting the likelihood of homelessness) because of AIDS. Many of these homeless individuals had AIDS themselves; others were the relatives of people who had died of AIDS or who were in the process of dying. This deplorable state of affairs was caused by an unfortunate confluence of factors that created a perfect storm of deprivation and need around the intersection of AIDS and housing.

The first factor that contributed to this problem was a marked increase in poverty. Twenty-four percent of New York City residents lived below the poverty rate in 1984, compared to fifteen percent in 1975. A second factor was that the federal and state governments—under pressure from the antigovernment ideology that prevailed in the United States in the 1980s—were drastically cutting back spending on programs intended to protect public health and assist the poor. Furthermore, the administration of Mayor Edward Koch, either because of negligence or indifference or both, failed to respond with any discernable urgency to the growing numbers of New Yorkers who were dying of AIDS. By 1985, for example, Koch's administration had spent only about $75,000 in AIDS-related public education and community services, while San Francisco, which had far fewer reported AIDS cases, had spent over $16 million. Even more inexplicably, the Koch administration, as late as 1987, was committed to reducing the number of public hospital beds despite the fact that the total number of days that individuals with AIDS were spending in hospitals was growing at an annual rate of 20 percent. In addition, the city in 1987 was operating only one small facility with a few dozen beds to shelter the thousands of homeless individuals with AIDS.

By the end of the 1980s, there was a growing consensus that the government, at all levels, had failed to adequately respond to the AIDS crisis. The *Braschi* case provided the Court of Appeals with an opportunity to issue a ruling that would have a positive impact on the AIDS crisis by helping to reduce the human suffering that surrounded the intersection of AIDS and housing. For at least some New Yorkers who were survivors of people with AIDS (some of whom were themselves HIV positive), the ability to remain in rent-controlled apartments was the difference between having a shelter over their heads and living in the streets. Although an opinion that sided with Braschi would obviously not solve the entire problem of AIDS-related homelessness, it would help some AIDS survivors avoid the terrible fate of losing their homes.

Given the fact that the legal issue related to the scope of the anti-eviction protection afforded by the Rent Control Law did not turn on the existence or impact of the AIDS epidemic, Rubenstein decided not to address the AIDS-related policy issues arising from the case in his main brief. Instead, he chose to coordinate with other organizations in the writing of amicus briefs that would inform the court about the AIDS crisis and the potential ameliorative effect of its ruling on that crisis. Thus, Lambda, in a brief written by its then legal director Paula Ettelbrick, provided the court with data on the thousands of same-sex couples living in New York City, none of which would qualify for anti-eviction protection if the court adopted the landlord's interpretation of the law. The Lambda brief also gave the court a sense of the magnitude of the AIDS epidemic in New York City, including the fact that a City Council report had recently concluded that the number of homeless people with AIDS in the five boroughs could soon reach the tens of thousands.

A brief submitted by the city's AIDS organizations provided the court with summaries of about twenty cases in which landlords had succeeded in evicting, or were attempting to evict, the survivors of tenants who had died of AIDS. Given the lack of services and support for such survivors, the brief argued, it was likely that many of them would end up living in the streets. A third brief submitted by the Legal Aid Society emphasized the vulnerability of poor and disabled people to eviction and homelessness. The brief also noted that the poor and disabled were more likely to live in familial arrangements that were not defined through either marriage, blood, or adoption. A refusal by the court to interpret the legal meaning of family in a way that went beyond the traditional definition would have a disproportionate impact on these vulnerable groups. In short, the goal of the amicus strategy pursued under Rubenstein's direction was to give the court a sense of the lawsuit's real-world implications.

▲

In writing the main plaintiff's brief in the case, Rubenstein raised two principal arguments. The first was that the anti-eviction provision of the Rent Control Law should, as a matter of statutory interpretation, be read to define family in a functional manner. The second was that it would be unconstitutional to interpret the provision in a way that denied protection to Braschi because there was no rational justification for treating him differently than survivors who were related to deceased tenants by marriage, blood, or adoption.

Rubenstein knew that courts generally prefer to avoid broad constitutional rulings when they can decide cases on narrower statutory grounds. A holding that the state was required, as a matter of constitutional law, to recognize that a same-sex couple could constitute a family would have greater repercussions than one that limited itself to determining the scope of the Rent Control Law. The former holding, for example, might call into question the constitutionality of the denial of health insurance benefits to the same-sex partners of government employees. A ruling on constitutional grounds in *Braschi* might even undermine the validity of bans against same-sex marriage. Rubenstein suspected that the court would want to avoid these types of thorny constitutional issues in a case that was already quite controversial. Most of the legal arguments in his brief, therefore, addressed the issue of whether the regulation in question, *as a matter of statutory interpretation*, required that Braschi be afforded the same anti-eviction protection provided to those related to deceased tenants by marriage, blood, or adoption.

The greatest obstacle Rubenstein faced in crafting his statutory argument was the fact that when New York legislators enacted the Rent Control Law in 1946, they did not specifically intend to provide same-sex couples with anti-eviction protection. Although little is known about who precisely the legislature intended to protect when it enacted the anti-eviction provision—that provision was not mentioned in any of the legislative reports or statements that accompanied the legislation—it was reasonable to assume that legislators in the 1940s did not have the interests of LGBT people in mind. Rubenstein dealt with this considerable obstacle by arguing in his brief that the court should focus not on the narrow question of whether the legislature specifically intended to protect same-sex couples as such but instead on the broader question of what policy goals the legislature was trying to achieve. The purpose of the legislation, Rubenstein told the court, was to provide a buffer for grieving family members, insulating them from the problems of dislocation and eviction during their bereavement after the death of the named tenant. In addition, the legislature wanted to secure for survivors the family home that they had shared with the deceased. It would be consistent with both of those purposes, Rubenstein argued, to provide anti-eviction protection to survivors like Braschi who had had such a close and committed relationship with the rent control tenant.

In focusing on the purpose of the anti-eviction regulation, Rubenstein relied on a series of cases decided by the New York Court of Appeals in which it had held that municipalities were under a constitutional obligation to define the meaning of family in zoning cases in a *functional* manner.[10] Most municipalities have zoning ordinances that restrict land uses in certain areas to single-family households. The cases relied on by Rubenstein in his brief had struck down ordinances which required that individuals be related via marriage or biology in order to qualify as a family for zoning purposes. What should matter, the court had held, was whether individuals cared for each other as a family rather than whether ties of marriage or blood were present. The same functional approach to the meaning of family, Rubenstein argued, was appropriate in interpreting the anti-eviction provision of the Rent Control Law at issue in *Braschi*.

▲

For his part, Dean Yuzek, Stahl's lawyer and a partner at the corporate law firm of Shea & Gould, relied on several arguments in his brief. First, he contended that since the case was ultimately about who would succeed to a rent-controlled apartment, the court should look to the state's intestacy statute—the law that distributes the property of individuals who die without a valid will—to determine the meaning of family. The intestacy statute limited the right to inherit property to individuals who were related to the deceased by marriage, blood, or adoption. The court, Yuzek argued, should look to those same factors in determining who could succeed to a rent-controlled apartment.

Second, Yuzek reminded the court of its earlier opinion in *Matter of Adoption of Robert Paul P.*, in which it ruled, in the context of interpreting the adoption statute, that if the law was going to recognize same-sex relationships, it had to be through a legislative mandate rather than through judicial action. Third, Yuzek told the judges that one of the purposes of the Rent Control Law was to encourage an orderly and gradual transition of the regulated properties to a free-market system and that an expansive interpretation of the anti-eviction provision, which would keep many properties under rent control for years to come, was inconsistent with that purpose. And lastly, Yuzek warned the court that if it adopted Rubenstein's proposed functional definition of family, it would only encourage more litigation while creating an administrative headache for lower courts as they would have to determine whether any given relationship between any two or more individuals was sufficiently close to merit the label of "family."

▲

After the briefs were submitted, Rubenstein turned his attention to preparing for the oral argument. One of the court's seven members —Chief Judge Sol Wachtler—had recused himself, leaving six to hear the case. In counting heads, Rubenstein was relatively certain that the two judges who were widely considered the most liberal on the court—Judith Kaye, the first woman named to the court, and Fritz Alexander, the first African American appointed to a full term on the court—would be sympathetic to Braschi's claim.

At the same time, Rubenstein suspected that Judges Richard Simons and Stewart Hancock Jr., who hailed from upstate New York and were the two most conservative members of the court, would be reluctant to interpret any law, regardless of its context, in a way that provided legal recognition to an intimate relationship between two individuals of the same sex.

The outcome of the case, therefore, likely depended on the votes of the last two remaining judges, Joseph Bellacosa and Vito Titone. These two jurists constituted the court's ideological center. It helped Rubenstein that the two men were lifelong Democrats. Both were also devout Catholics, which Rubenstein surmised could cut both ways. On the one hand, the Catholic Church's official condemnation of same-sex relationships and its unequivocal opposition to their legal recognition could make the two judges less open to the possibility that two men in a sexually intimate relationship could constitute a family. On the other hand, the fact that the Catholic Church in the 1980s was the largest provider of services to people with AIDS in New York

City might make the two judges more sensitive to the ways in which a narrow definition of family under the Rent Control Law would exacerbate the problem of AIDS-related homelessness.

Rubenstein needed both Bellacosa and Titone to vote his way—if only one of them did so, it would likely leave the court equally divided, which would mean that the lower court's ruling would be upheld. Although there was no way of knowing for sure, Rubenstein suspected that if the case had not had ramifications for people living with AIDS, his chances of winning the votes of both would have been significantly reduced.

About two minutes into the oral argument, held in April 1989, Rubenstein was asked the one question that he knew was coming. How exactly, Judge Hancock wanted to know, was the court supposed to define family? In particular, the judge was interested in whether Rubenstein was suggesting that the court adopt in this case the same interpretation of family that it had applied in the zoning cases cited in his brief. Rubenstein provided a careful and nuanced answer. He explained that it would be appropriate for the court to look to whether the person claiming anti-eviction protection had a relationship with the deceased tenant that was "the functional and factual equivalent" of a family, which was the standard that the court had applied in the zoning cases. That standard, however, might protect someone under the zoning law but not under the Rent Control Law because the two laws had different purposes. Only the month before, for example, the court had concluded that five elderly women sufficiently shared household responsibilities so as to constitute a family for purposes of determining who could live in a single-family residential neighborhood.[11] While wanting the court to adopt the zoning cases' functional approach, Rubenstein acknowledged that those women "might be protected in a zoning context but not necessarily if they did not make this their family home in a rent control context."

Judge Titone then wanted to know why two roommates who shared expenses would not, under Rubenstein's proposed interpretation of the statute, also function as a family. Rubenstein responded by noting that sharing expenses might not be enough and that the court should look to other criteria as well, including whether the individuals held themselves out as a family. Since roommates do not usually consider themselves a family, nor are they usually considered as such by others, Judge Titone's scenario was distinguishable.

Judge Kaye asked about the administrative burden that would accompany the court's adoption of a functional definition of a family. After all, every time a rent control tenant died leaving behind a survivor to whom he or she was not related in one of the traditional ways, a determination would have to be made whether the relationship in question was sufficiently close to qualify as a family. In his response, Rubenstein reminded the court that a hearing already had to be held before anyone could be evicted from a rent-controlled apartment. Even when the parties were biologically related, those hearings could involve complicated factual scenarios. As an example, Rubenstein referred to a recent case where a trial court had to determine whether a granddaughter had been living with the deceased grandmother for a sufficiently long period of time to qualify for anti-eviction protection. All that his client was asking the court, Rubenstein explained, was that individuals in functional families "be given the benefit of that hearing."

During his oral argument, Yuzek told the court that it was for the legislature and not for the courts to determine whether same-sex relationships should be recognized by law. He added that Braschi's real grievance was against the statute that prohibited him from marrying Blanchard rather than against the Rent Control Law. Sensing that some of the judges might be concerned with the difficulty of determining what constitutes a functional family, Yuzek urged the court to define family by relying on "objective criteria, such as documentary evidence of birth, or participation in a marriage ceremony, instead of requiring individualized proof on a case by case basis."

After thirty minutes of oral arguments, the judges thanked the lawyers and the court adjourned. The legal work in the case was over. The only thing to do now was to wait for the court's decision.

▲

The wait was not long; the court issued its opinion six weeks after it heard oral arguments. In the end, the court, in a plurality opinion written by Judge Titone and joined by Judges Kaye and Alexander, did what Rubenstein asked it to do by rejecting a definition of family that only looked to whether individuals "have formalized their relationship by obtaining, for instance, a marriage certificate or an adoption order." The opinion added, in surprisingly strong language, that "the intended protection against sudden eviction should not rest on fictitious legal distinctions or genetic history, but instead should find its foundation in the reality of family life." The court went on to state that "in the context of eviction, a more realistic, and certainly equally valid, view of a family includes two adult lifetime partners whose relationship is long term and characterized by an emotional and financial commitment and interdependence. This view comports both with our society's traditional concept of 'family' and with the expectations of individuals who live in such nuclear units."[12]

The fact that the court dismissed traditional means of establishing familial relationships (such as through marriage) as constituting little more than "fictitious legal distinctions" was nothing less than extraordinary. The court could not have been clearer that what ultimately mattered in determining what constitutes a family, at least in the eviction context, was not the form that familial relationships took but instead the ways in which the relationships actually functioned.

In explaining the court's decision, Judge Titone noted that a less rigid and more expansive definition of family was consistent with the changes that had taken place in the composition of American families over the previous decades. The court, in other words, adopted a dynamic rather than a static definition of family, acknowledging that that definition was subject to modification as the nature of familial relationships changed over time.

Regarding how to determine whether a familial relationship existed between the deceased tenant and the person seeking protection

from the anti-eviction regulation, the court followed Rubenstein's suggestion by relying on the factors that lower courts had considered in
similar cases. Those factors included "the exclusivity and longevity of
the relationship, the level of emotional and financial commitment,
the manner in which the parties have conducted their everyday lives
and held themselves out to society, and the reliance placed upon one
another for daily family services." The court emphasized that none of
those points was dispositive, and that lower courts, in determining
what constitutes a family, must look to "the totality of the relationship as evidenced by the dedication, caring and self-sacrifice of the
parties."

Judge Bellacosa wrote a separate opinion, also voting to reverse the
Appellate Division's decision, but doing so on much narrower grounds.
Bellacosa reasoned that the Appellate Division's ruling should be reversed because it would be irrational to interpret the anti-eviction
regulation in such a way that would deny Braschi protection given his
close relationship with Blanchard. Bellacosa, however, did not want to
go beyond such a case-specific ruling, believing that it was improper
for the court to set forth general criteria for future cases as to what
constitutes a family. Only the legislature, Bellacosa concluded, had the
authority to define the meaning of family.

Judge Simons wrote a dissenting opinion, joined by Judge Hancock, in which he concluded that a definition of family which looked
to "objectively verifiable relationships based on blood, marriage and
adoption" was the best way of balancing, on the one hand, the interests of survivors in remaining in rent-controlled properties and, on
the other, the interests of landlords in regaining possession of their
properties. Simons worried that expanding the definition of family
beyond its traditional meaning would cover many new types of relationships, making it considerably more difficult for landlords to relet
their properties at market rates after the death of named tenants. He
then added that the traditional definition of family promoted certainty
and consistency while avoiding the need for protracted litigation aimed
at determining "the strength and duration of the relationship and the
extent of the emotional and financial interdependency."

It took little time before news of the court's ruling was disseminated by every major news outlet in the country. Within hours of the opinion's release, Rubenstein was interviewed by the *New York Times* and the *Washington Post*, and the next day he appeared on CNN and ABC's *Nightline*. In an ACLU press release, the lawyer was quoted as saying that "this decision marks the most important single step forward in American law toward legal recognition of lesbian and gay relationships." He then added that, given the broad criteria adopted by the court in defining the legal meaning of family, "the ruling will benefit not only gay couples, but all people who live in committed family relationships throughout society."

It had been a long legal struggle, lasting more than two and a half years, but in the end, Braschi prevailed. The principle that he and his lawyers had fought so hard to establish—that family is ultimately about love, caring, and commitment rather than about legal formalities—had been recognized by the highest court of the state.

Sadly, Braschi was unable to enjoy his legal victory for very long. A few months before the Court of Appeals issued its opinion, he became ill and was diagnosed with AIDS. By the end of 1989, he left New York and returned to Puerto Rico, where he died the following year at the age of thirty-four.

We do not know what Braschi was thinking when he closed the door of the Manhattan apartment behind him for the last time. It is likely, however, that he was thinking of Blanchard and of their life together in the apartment. It is also likely that he felt a certain amount of pride and satisfaction in being able, despite his illness, to leave the apartment under his own terms rather than as a result of being evicted. The landlord had contended in court that whatever kind of relationship Braschi had had with Blanchard, it was not worthy of legal recognition as a family. Braschi had proven him wrong.

## The Impact

In many ways, the *Braschi* litigation represented the culmination of an important shift in the LGBT rights movement's views and expectations of the government. Prior to the 1980s, LGBT people for the most part viewed the government largely as a source of discrimination and harassment. For example, agencies of the federal government, especially those involving national defense and intelligence, had for decades dismissed gay employees for no reason other than their sexual orientation. For their part, police departments across the country routinely arrested LGBT people for doing nothing more than congregating in gay bars or showing affection in public. In its early days, therefore, the LGBT rights movement largely focused on protecting sexual minorities *from* the government. The best thing that the government could do, most LGBT people believed through the 1970s, was to simply leave them alone.

This attitude began changing in the 1980s, primarily for three reasons. The first was that LGBT people in certain parts of the country, particularly in large cities, were increasingly able to have some effect on the decisions made by elected officials. Although this newfound political influence was limited, it did permit the movement to successfully seek the enactment of laws—first in several municipalities, and then in a handful of states—that prohibited discrimination on the basis of sexual orientation.

The second factor that led the LGBT community to turn to the government for help was the advent of the AIDS epidemic. LGBT people now expected the government not only to provide the necessary funds for AIDS-related research and care but also to protect those who were HIV positive from being discriminated against in everything from jobs to housing to health insurance. The government could provide such protection through the enactment of laws, such as the Americans with Disabilities Act of 1990, which prohibited discrimination against people with AIDS. The government could also help many people with AIDS by legally recognizing same-sex relationships. The AIDS epidemic was a painful reminder to LGBT people that they did not have the right to be covered by their partners' health insurance policies or to visit their sick partners in hospitals. The legal recognition by the state of same-sex relationships could change all of that.

A third reason for the shift in the LGBT rights movement's view of government in the 1980s resulted from the growing number of lesbians and gay men (in particular the former) who were raising children together. The fact that these families had no legal status created a great deal of uncertainty and apprehension for their members. This led the movement, primarily working through the courts, to seek governmental recognition and protection of families headed by lesbians and gay men. The goal was to formalize the parental rights of the adults in order to add stability and certainty to the lives of the children.

The skepticism and mistrust that many in the LGBT community felt toward the government prior to the 1980s, then, was replaced with a more complicated view of the state. LGBT people were still not completely trusting of the government (especially given its lethargic response to the AIDS epidemic). Nonetheless, many LGBT individuals came to see the state as potentially useful in protecting them from discrimination both directly through the enactment of antidiscrimination laws and indirectly through the legal recognition of LGBT families and relationships.

The movement's lawyers and activists, in pushing for the legal recognition of the relationships and families of LGBT people, began arguing during the 1980s that what ultimately mattered in determining whether relationships and families merited such recognition was not the existence of a marital license or of a biological connection. Instead, what mattered was whether the individuals in question loved and cared for each other in ways that were similar to those found in so-called traditional families.

The importance of *Braschi* lies not so much in the way in which future courts relied on its holding and reasoning—though the opinion contributed to further changes in the law that positively impacted sexual minorities—but rather in the fact that the highest court of New York adopted the movement's position on what constitutes a family. In doing so, it provided considerable legitimacy to the movement's claim that LGBT people were as capable of forming loving and lasting familial ties as were straight people.

Prior to *Braschi*, relationships such as that of Braschi and Blanchard would have had no greater legal significance than those of friends or roommates. Prior to the opinion, in other words, the true nature of relationships like Braschi and Blanchard's remained invisible to the law. The *Braschi* litigation allowed the movement to bring before the court (and therefore before the public, given the extensive media attention that the case received) one example (out of tens of thousands) of a long-term and committed same-sex relationship.

There were several factors that likely contributed to the New York court's willingness to take what at the time was clearly the bold step of holding that two men in an intimate relationship could constitute a family. One of them was the AIDS epidemic. As already noted, a ruling that would have made it easier for landlords to evict the survivors of LGBT tenants in rent-controlled apartments would have worsened AIDS-related homelessness in New York. Such a socially problematic outcome likely weighed on the minds of the judges who sided with Braschi. A second consideration may have been the fact that one of the two men had already died. The fact that the relationship had ended due to death meant that its legal recognition was retrospective in nature. It was unlikely, in other words, that Braschi would return to the courts seeking the *further* recognition of his relationship with Blanchard.

It was this seemingly limited application of the ruling that in many ways made the case a good vehicle through which to try to convince an important court to adopt the LGBT rights movement's definition of family. Rubenstein was careful not to suggest to the court in either his brief or in his oral argument that the case had wide implications for the status of same-sex relationships. This was one of the reasons why he chose to emphasize the narrower statutory arguments in the case over the broader constitutional ones. The objective was to make the court comfortable with the notion of providing legal recognition to a same-sex relationship in a relatively narrow and safe context. The context was relatively narrow because the case arose from the interpretation of a somewhat obscure provision of New York's Rent Control Law. It was relatively safe because the case involved a relationship that had already ended due to death. If the gay rights movement, in the late 1980s, had tried to achieve something more ambitious through the courts than what it attempted in *Braschi*, the effort would have likely ended in failure.

Despite the relatively narrow and safe context in which the case arose, the court's reasoning in *Braschi* was nonetheless revolutionary. The groundbreaking nature of the ruling becomes especially clear when it is juxtaposed with the almost complete absence of legal recognition of same-sex relationships anywhere in the country at the time the opinion was issued.

The first such recognition had taken place only five years earlier, when the city of Berkeley, California, enacted an ordinance providing benefits to the domestic partners of municipal employees. During the remainder of the 1980s, four other municipalities (Madison, Los Angeles, Seattle, and West Hollywood) enacted domestic partnership ordinances, most of them limited to extending sick and bereavement leaves to city employees with domestic partners. The limited steps taken by these five municipalities constituted the sum total of the legal recognition of same-sex relationships anywhere in the United States at the time of the *Braschi* ruling.

In the particular context of New York law, neither the state nor local governments (including New York City) had taken any steps toward recognizing same-sex relationships. The complete absence of legal recognition of those relationships in New York prior to 1989 is perhaps best exemplified by the case that the landlord in *Braschi* relied on so extensively during the lawsuit. A gay couple in *Matter of Adoption of Robert Paul P.*, as noted earlier, had unsuccessfully attempted to use the adoption statute to formalize their committed relationship. The mere fact that gay couples in New York had to resort to the adoption statute to provide a legal structure to their relationships shows the legal black hole that those relationships found themselves in prior to *Braschi*.

In contrast, a few weeks after *Braschi*, New York City mayor Edward Koch signed an executive order extending bereavement leave benefits to city employees with domestic partners and establishing a mechanism for registering the domestic partnerships of those employees. In addition, a few months later, the state government issued a new anti-eviction regulation that applied to rent-stabilized properties. The court in *Braschi* had made it clear that rent control and rent stabilization were two different regulatory schemes. If a functional definition of "family" was going to apply to the anti-eviction protection provided by the latter, therefore, the change would have to be made by either the legislative or executive branch. The question of whether *Braschi* would be codified into the Rent Stabilization Law was extremely important because it covered about one million apartments, while the Rent Control Law applied to only about 100,000 units.

Although Governor Mario Cuomo's administration at first resisted efforts to extend the anti-eviction protection available under the Rent Stabilization Law, a coalition of LGBT, AIDS, and housing groups successfully used the publicity surrounding *Braschi* to pressure the state government into issuing a new regulation. The regulation codified *Braschi* by making it clear that those "who can prove emotional and financial commitment and interdependence" with the deceased tenant were entitled to succeed to leases in rent-stabilized apartments. The regulation also added that whether a sexual relationship between the parties existed was irrelevant in establishing succession rights, showing how the impact of *Braschi* was not limited to couples in intimate relationships.

In short, when the year of 1989 began, neither New York State nor New York City law explicitly recognized same-sex relationships. But by the end of that year, in addition to the court's issuance of *Braschi*, the city recognized the same-sex domestic partnerships of its employees for some purposes while the state expanded anti-eviction protection to committed same-sex couples (and others in nontraditional relationships) living in thousands of rent-stabilized apartments.

Momentum for recognition continued to build. In the fall of 1989, David Dinkins, while conducting his successful run for mayor of New York City, promised the LGBT community that he would work to expand the city's recognition of domestic partnerships. Dinkins followed through on his promise in 1993 by issuing an executive order creating a city registry through which unmarried city residents (as well as nonresident municipal employees) could register their relationships as domestic partnerships. The order also granted domestic partners visitation rights at city hospitals and jails, as well as the same standing as married couples in qualifying for apartments and in inheriting leases in buildings owned or overseen by the city's housing agencies. A second executive order issued by Dinkins granted registered domestic partners who worked for the city the same leave privileges that married couples enjoyed to care for a new child. Five years later, the city council enacted ordinances codifying both executive orders, and then went beyond them by providing municipal employees with registered domestic partners with the same rights and benefits (including health insurance) afforded to married couples.

It seems clear in hindsight that *Braschi* served as a catalyst for the series of incremental steps taken by both the state and city governments that expanded the forms of recognition of same-sex relationships. LGBT rights activists relied on the Court of Appeals' opinion to pressure state and city officials to grant same-sex couples the type of legal recognition and protection granted by the state's highest court. Although the opinion, strictly speaking, was limited to the issue of rent control, its reasoning, which focused on emotional and economic interdependency rather than on the existence of legal formalities, made it more difficult for government officials to reject out of hand the notion that same-sex couples could constitute families and that they were entitled to at least some of the protections afforded by law. To put it simply, same-sex couples in New York after *Braschi* were no longer legally invisible.

▲

One of the questions that remained after *Braschi* was how courts would interpret and apply the criteria that the Court of Appeals adopted to determine whether particular individuals had a sufficiently close and permanent relationship to be deemed a family. As already noted, some LGBT rights activists, during the course of the litigation, were concerned that it might be difficult for future litigants to match the high degree of interdependence, especially regarding financial matters, that existed between Braschi and Blanchard. Couples with more limited incomes, for example, might not be able to have joint credit cards, or afford life insurance policies, or draft wills naming each other as beneficiaries.

It would have been inconsistent with *Braschi*'s reasoning for courts, in effect, to have applied the functional definition of family in a formalistic fashion by, for example, requiring the existence of certain documents or shared financial accounts before a given relationship could be deemed a "family" under the law. The Court of Appeals in *Braschi* had been clear that none of the factors that it set forth—exclusivity and longevity of the relationship, the degree of emotional and financial commitment, how the parties held themselves out to others, and so on—should be considered dispositive. Instead, what ultimately mattered was, as the court put it, "the totality of the relationship as evidenced by the dedication, caring and self-sacrifice of the parties."

Lower courts have for the most part abided by this principle. In one case, for example, a court rejected the landlord's argument that the survivor of an eight-year same-sex relationship should not succeed to a rent-controlled apartment because there was no documentary evidence that the two men were financially interdependent. The fact that the named tenant provided the household with financial support while the survivor provided domestic support, when coupled with the fact that the latter cared for the former during his four-year illness, was enough to show the existence of a familial relationship. In another case, a court permitted the survivor of a twenty-four-year same-sex relationship to remain in a rent-stabilized apartment despite the fact that the couple had separate banking and credit cards accounts, evincing a lack of financial interdependence. The fact that the two individuals had held themselves out as a couple for more than two decades, when combined with the fact that the named tenant provided the household with financial support while the survivor provided domestic support, established that they had a sufficiently close and interdependent relationship to qualify for legal protection.[13]

There was also a concern among some activists, prior to *Braschi*, that couples who fell short of the apparent sexual fidelity between

Braschi and Blanchard might have difficulty establishing the necessary closeness of their relationships. For the most part, however, courts have taken a lack of complete sexual exclusivity in stride, not allowing it to trump other factors that might establish a relationship's closeness. In one case, for example, a court concluded that the fact that a surviving gay partner may have had an affair during his partner's illness was not enough to preclude a finding that the relationship constituted a family, especially "since peccadillos of this nature seem not to be uncommon, even in the marital life of normally married couples." In another case, a court concluded that the fact that a man in a long-term same-sex relationship might have had an affair with a woman that resulted in the birth of a child did not, by itself, preclude the finding that the relationship between the two men was committed and interdependent.[14]

It has also been possible, after *Braschi*, to provide legal recognition and protection to nonsexual relationships, as Rubenstein and others in the LGBT rights movement hoped. Although the majority of New Yorkers who have benefited from *Braschi* have been survivors of nonmarital intimate relationships (both gay and straight), there have been cases where the relationships in question have not been sexually intimate. In one instance, two women lived together for thirty-four years in a rent-controlled apartment. They were not biologically related, though they considered themselves sisters. When the named tenant died, the landlord sought to evict the other woman, arguing that she was not entitled to legal protection because she had not had an *intimate* relationship with the deceased. As the landlord saw it, this meant that the two women were nothing more than close friends who happened also to be roommates. The court rejected the landlord's position, noting that a sexual relationship was not a prerequisite for legal protection under *Braschi*. The court added that the relationship between the two women had been a familial one because they had shared expenses, traveled together, gone to family functions together, and had been considered by their friends and families to be sisters.[15]

▲

Some courts, both in New York and elsewhere, have adopted a functional definition of family outside of the rent regulation context. The most important of these cases involved a Minnesota appellate court's recognition of what it called a "family of affinity" in ordering, after many years of litigation, that the lesbian partner of a woman who suffered severe injuries in an automobile accident be named as her guardian over the strong objections of her biological family. A trial court in New York, meanwhile, relied on the close and committed relationship between two gay men to grant standing to the survivor who wished to decide how his partner's body should be disposed.[16]

Other courts, however, have refused to adopt a functional approach in deciding whether the law provides some recognition to same-sex couples. A New York appellate court, for example, denied a man the ability to seek a statutory share of his male partner's estate while another denied standing to the survivor of a same-sex relationship who sought to bring a wrongful death lawsuit. Both of these courts distinguished *Braschi* by noting that the statutory term that was at issue in that case (i.e., "family") was more amenable to an expansive interpretation than the term "spouse," which was at issue in the cases before them.[17]

And yet that reasoning does not explain the New York Court of Appeals' unwillingness, only two years after *Braschi*, to interpret the term "parent"—which, like "family," is more open-ended than "spouse" —in a functional manner in a case involving the question of whether a lesbian woman had the right to seek visitation of her former partner's biological child whom she had helped to raise.[18] Many of the considerations that the *Braschi* court relied on to make its decision were also relevant in the visitation case, including the need to account for the changing characteristics of contemporary families, as well as the need to focus on the degree of closeness of relationships as opposed to on formalistic understandings of what constitutes a family. The court, however, chose form over substance when it denied the request for visitation because the petitioner was, as the court put it, "a biological stranger to [the] child."

Three years later, the court returned to the general approach that it had followed in *Braschi* in a case called *Matter of Jacob*.[19] A question in that case was whether a lesbian could adopt her partner's biological child through what is known as a "second-parent" adoption. As it had done in *Braschi*, the court in *Matter of Jacob* focused on the purpose of the statute before it, which in the case of the adoption law, was to advance the best interests of children. The court then noted the many ways in which having a second legal parent benefits children: it increases their economic and emotional security; it renders them eligible to receive governmental benefits in case of either parent's death; and it provides them with the right to sue for wrongful death, to inherit under the intestacy laws, and to be eligible for coverage under both parents' health insurance policies.

The court in *Matter of Jacob* noted that when the legislature in 1937 enacted the particular provision of the adoption statute at issue in the case, it did not consider the possibility that unmarried partners (whether gay or straight) would be adopting together. The court, however, following *Braschi*'s reasoning, found that the lack of explicit legislative intent was an insufficient ground upon which to reject, as a matter of law, an adoption petition that seemed to so clearly promote the best interests of the child in question, and that was therefore entirely consistent with the statute's purpose.

If *Braschi* recognized, for purposes of the Rent Control Law, that the intimate relationship between two adults of the same sex can constitute a family, *Matter of Jacob* recognized that it is often in the best interests of children to have two parents, regardless of their gender or marital status. Although, strictly speaking, the recognition of the relationship between the two adults was not at issue in *Matter of Jacob*, it is clear that the court understood the two women and their child to constitute a functional family unit.

As in *Braschi*, the court in *Matter of Jacob* took account of the realities of modern American families, many of which do not fall under the traditional category of married heterosexual couples with biological children. The court, in both cases, gave considerable weight to the changes in family makeup that have taken place in the last few decades to reject a narrow interpretation of statutes that would have resulted in providing protection only to a limited category of families.

The same court, however, would eventually draw the line at recognizing same-sex relationships as *marital* ones. The court in *Hernandez v. Robles*, a case decided in 2006 (seventeen years after *Braschi*), rejected the view that the ban against same-sex marriage was irrational and arbitrary and therefore unconstitutional.[20] The court reasoned that the legislature could have rationally concluded that the ban against same-sex marriage was necessary in order to provide stability to different-sex relationships. The court noted that same-sex couples can only have children—whether through adoption or alternative insemination—through careful planning. In contrast, different-sex couples can "become parents as a result of accident or impulse." The relationships of heterosexual couples who have children, therefore, are more likely to be unstable than those of same-sex couples who have children. Deploying a rather strained form of reasoning, the court concluded that it was rational for the legislature to provide protection to the more unstable different-sex relationships while denying protection to the more stable same-sex relationships. It was rational for the legislature to conclude, in other words, that children raised by adults in the former category of relationships need greater protection than those raised by adults in the latter category.

The court's position holds water only if we are persuaded that some different-sex relationships will turn out to be less (as the court put it) "casual or temporary" *because of the fact that same-sex couples are prohibited from marrying.* Such a contention, however, makes no sense. Indeed, as one of the dissenting judges stated, "no one rationally decides to have children because gays and lesbians are excluded from marriage." Similarly, no one rationally decides to stay with one's different-sex partner (even after having children with that person) because same-sex couples are excluded from marriage.

At one level, *Braschi* and *Hernandez* are not necessarily inconsistent given that the former was a statutory interpretation case involving a rent control statute while the latter was a constitutional case involving the due process and equal protection provisions of the New York constitution. At another level, however, the court in *Hernandez* was unwilling to do what the court did in *Braschi* (and in *Matter of Jacob*), namely, to look behind form in order to focus on function. For the *Hernandez* court, it did not matter that same-sex relationships can be as close and committed as different-sex relationships (as the court found in *Braschi*) or that children often benefit from having two parents, regardless of the gender or marital status of the parents (as the court found in *Matter of Jacob*). Unfortunately, in upholding the prohibition against same-sex marriage, the *Hernandez* court chose to rely on a rather strained form of reasoning rather than to focus on the reality of contemporary same-sex relationships and families.

▲

The fact that the New York court ultimately drew the line at marriage should not be viewed as diminishing either the impact or importance of *Braschi*. At the time that *Braschi* was decided, the LGBT rights movement was not yet focused on marriage as a civil rights goal to the same extent that it would be four years later after the Hawaii Supreme Court raised constitutional objections to that state's ban against same-sex marriage. In many ways, the Hawaii case replaced *Braschi* as the most important LGBT relationship-recognition lawsuit litigated up until that point. By the mid-1990s, the type of partial equality offered by a legal victory such as *Braschi* was no longer enough to satisfy the LGBT rights movement. There have been so many relationship-recognition lawsuits since then, most of them involving the question of marriage, that it is perhaps easy to forget that it was all preceded by a housing case from New York in which an American appellate court, for the first time in the nation's history, concluded that same-sex relationships are entitled to legal protection and recognition.

# CHAPTER 2

# Harassment

## The Facts

For Jamie Nabozny, it all started in the seventh grade when some of his school peers began taunting him with words like "faggot" and "queer." The harassment grew progressively worse, culminating four years later with Jamie finding himself lying on the floor of his school's library as a boy repeatedly kicked him in the stomach while other kids cheered. On countless occasions during those intervening years, Jamie and his parents pleaded with school administrators to stop the relentless antigay harassment of Jamie; the officials, however, refused to get involved. In fact, no student was ever disciplined for verbally or physically harassing Jamie. This pattern of omission and neglect on the part of school administrators eventually led to a federal lawsuit, one that concluded with a jury finding that the officials' failure to protect Jamie from harm violated his constitutional rights and with a monetary settlement of almost one million dollars.

▲

Jamie was born in Ashland, Wisconsin, in October 1975, the first child of Bob and Carol Nabozny. Both of Jamie's parents grew up in Ashland, a town of about eight thousand people nestled on the shore of

Lake Superior. In the late 1800s, Ashland was one of Wisconsin's largest cities and its port one of the most important on the lake, supporting a bustling paper-mill industry. But the end of the logging era took its toll, and the town became economically depressed in the second half of the twentieth century.

Neither Bob nor Carol graduated from high school. Bob worked when he could, primarily in construction, while Carol worked periodically, usually for about the minimum wage. The family moved from one place to another in rural Wisconsin before Jamie reached middle school—once they even went to Wyoming for several months—in search of better and more reliable jobs. The family's financial prospects never improved much, in part because Bob and Carol were heavy drinkers. And when they drank, they sometimes fought, occasionally in front of Jamie and his younger brothers (Corey, born in 1977, and T.J., born a year after that).

Bob and Carol first married in 1974. They divorced in 1985 and then remarried each other a year after that. (They would do the same a few years later, first divorcing and then remarrying shortly thereafter.) It is fair to say, then, that when Jamie began the seventh grade in the Ashland middle school in the fall of 1988, he had had a difficult life, but he remained a good student, earning straight As and never getting into trouble in school.

Jamie had always been a quiet and soft-spoken child who largely kept to himself. This seems to have contributed to his being victimized by his fellow students; as one of the harassers testified at the trial, they picked on Jamie because "he was silent [and] withdrawn." In addition, the bullies perceived Jamie to be effeminate and immature. As the same harasser put it, Jamie's tormentors were angered by the fact that Jamie, in their opinion, was "girlish" and did not act like "a guy or a . . . grown boy."

When Jamie began coming home complaining that some of his fellow students were harassing him, Bob and Carol decided to send him to live with—and be homeschooled by—an uncle and aunt for a few weeks. The aunt seemed particularly sympathetic to Jamie's ordeal at school, leading him to confide in her that he was gay. The aunt, however, immediately made it clear that she did not approve of his sexual orientation, insisting that he pray with her every night for God to make him straight. All of this made the thirteen-year-old so uncomfortable that he ran away and returned to his parents' house.

When his aunt realized that Jamie had run away, she called the police. A juvenile officer was assigned to the case. In conducting his investigation, the officer asked Jamie's best friend why Jamie had run away and the friend told the policeman that it was related to Jamie being gay. A few days later, the officer and a social worker met with Jamie and his parents in the Naboznys' home to discuss Jamie's running away. At that meeting, the officer asked Jamie directly whether he was gay. Jamie answered that he was.

Bob and Carol, upon hearing this news, started crying. Carol had suspected for some time that Jamie might be gay—a "mother's intuition," she would later call it during a deposition. After she stopped crying, Carol told her son that she loved him and that she was committed to learning more about what it meant to be gay. Bob, however, reacted angrily to Jamie's announcement, storming out of the room after telling the boy that he was going through a stage, one that he would soon outgrow. It is an indication of how far Bob eventually came on this issue that several years later he accompanied Jamie to Washington to lobby Congress to enact a law protecting LGBT students like his son from harassment in schools.

When Jamie returned to the Ashland middle school, he once again found himself subjected to verbal harassment. An increasingly exasperated Jamie went to speak to the school counselor to tell her that a group of boys were constantly calling him names like "faggot," "queer," and "fudge packer." The counselor asked Jamie whether he was gay, and Jamie said that he was. He had not gone around the school telling people he was gay, but he believed—despite his young age—that he should not deny who he was when asked.

The counselor spoke to the boys who had harassed Jamie and the abuse stopped, but after a few weeks it started again. The fact that Jamie had reported the harassment to the school counselor angered the bullies further—they now, in addition to calling Jamie derogatory names, began accosting him in the hallways and bathrooms, frequently pushing and tripping him.

A few months later, the counselor who had intervened on Jamie's behalf left the school, and a new one was hired. The new counselor was also sympathetic to the seventh-grader's ordeal, leading him to set up a meeting between the school principal—Mary Podlesny—and Jamie. At that meeting, Podlesny asked Jamie whether he was gay, and again, Jamie answered that he was.

Podlesny spoke to the harassers, and the abuse stopped temporarily, only to restart after a few weeks. The harassers, furious that Jamie had reported them to the school principal, became more violent, now regularly hitting, kicking, and elbowing him.

Bob and Carol—both of whom had joined Alcoholics Anonymous and stopped drinking—called Podlesny several times in the winter and spring of Jamie's seventh-grade year, asking her to intervene to stop the harassment and discipline the perpetrators. After Podlesny failed to take any action, they took Jamie out of the public school and sent him to a nearby Catholic school, where he finished seventh grade. A few weeks into Jamie's eighth-grade year, the Naboznys removed him because they could no longer afford the tuition. Unfortunately, they had no choice but to return their son to the Ashland middle school.

▲

There is another aspect of Jamie's early life that is vital to understand. When Jamie was eleven years old, he was sexually abused by Nick Rising, an eighteen-year-old who led a youth group at the church that the Naboznys attended. Jamie was confused and angered by Rising's actions, but as often happens in these cases, he kept this awful secret to himself. Rising warned him on several occasions that if he told others what was happening, no one would believe him. One day in the summer between seventh and eighth grades, however, Jamie walked into his bedroom and saw Rising attempting to molest his youngest brother.

Jamie confronted Rising and told him to leave the house. When Rising refused, Jamie stormed out, went to a youth shelter, and called the police to tell them that Rising had molested him several times and had attempted to sexually abuse his brother. Officials at the county department of social services placed Jamie in a foster home for several days while they and the police investigated his allegations. A few days later, Jamie returned home and told his parents what Rising had done to him for over a year and what the man had tried to do to his brother.

Rising was arrested, pled guilty, and served several months in jail. Although Jamie had acted courageously, the sexual abuse scandal, which was reported in the local newspaper, made his life back at the middle school even more miserable than before. The harassers—several of whom were friendly with Rising—now blamed Jamie for the fact that Rising was in jail.

One day that fall, Jamie, now an eighth-grader, and his brother Corey went into one of their school's bathrooms. A pack of angry boys followed them there and started calling Jamie a "faggot" and a "queer." They then pushed his books out of his hands and shoved him violently against a wall.

The Naboznys, after hearing from their two children what had happened in the school bathroom, called the school and demanded to meet with Podlesny. The next day, a meeting was held in Podlesny's office. In addition to the principal, the meeting included Jamie and his parents, a boy named Don Grande—who, along with his brother Roy, was one of Jamie's worst tormentors—and his mother, as well as two other students who had attacked Jamie in the bathroom. At that meeting, Podlesny asked the other kids whether what Jamie said happened in the restroom actually occurred. Not surprisingly, all three boys denied it. More surprisingly, Podlesny seemed willing to take them at their word. After the other boys left her office, the principal ended the meeting by saying that if Jamie insisted on being openly gay in school, then he had to expect that these kinds of incidents would take place. Apparently, from Podlesny's perspective, what was happening to Jamie was his fault.

The fact that Podlesny failed to take any disciplinary action against the harassers seemed only to embolden them. One day, toward the end of eighth grade, Jamie was in his science class when the teacher walked out of the room for a few minutes. Trouble soon started for Jamie. Three boys surrounded him and started touching him in improper ways, calling him "faggot" and "queer," and cursing at him. They then threw him to the ground, and one of the boys jumped on top of him. With the rest of the class standing around watching—many of them laughing and cheering—the harasser straddled Jamie's back while pretending to rape him, all the time saying that Jamie liked that sort of thing.

After a few minutes, Jamie was able to pry himself loose from his tormentor's hold. He ran out of the classroom and went straight to Podlesny's office. He barged past the secretary and told Podlesny, in between sobs, what had happened. The principal then proceeded to berate Jamie for walking into her office without an appointment while brushing off his complaint by saying that "boys will be boys." She told him again that what was happening to him was to be expected if he insisted on being openly gay in school.

A few weeks later, at the end of a day in which he had been mercilessly taunted and harassed in school, Jamie went home, shut his bedroom door, and threw himself on his bed crying. He was distraught and felt total despair. How would he make it through the end of middle school—much less the four years of high school that awaited him after that—given the level of harassment and abuse that he was experiencing almost every day? Believing that there was no way of stopping the pain and humiliation, he went into the bathroom and swallowed every pill he could find. A little later, his parents found him almost unconscious on the bathroom floor. They called an ambulance, and Jamie was rushed to the hospital, where doctors pumped his stomach.

Although Jamie refused to return to the Ashland middle school to complete the last remaining weeks of eighth grade, by the end of that summer he had no choice but to begin high school. Jamie was under no illusion that his ordeal would end simply because he would be attending a new school. After all, most of the boys who had tormented him during the previous two years were also moving on to the same high school. And indeed, soon after Jamie began the ninth grade, the verbal abuse and the physical harassment—the tripping, the kicking, the elbowing, the spitting—began all over again.

One day, before the new academic year was even a month old, Jamie was in a school bathroom standing at a urinal when two boys attacked him from behind. One of the attackers put his knee into the back of Jamie's knee, causing him to fall into the urinal. The other boy then proceeded to urinate on him.

A few minutes later, Jamie ran down the school's main hallway, crying and covered in urine, heading for the office of principal William Davis. The principal was not in his office, but the secretary reached him by phone and told him what had happened. Davis's sole advice, relayed through the secretary, was that Jamie should go home and change his clothes.

The school took no action against the boys who attacked Jamie in the bathroom. Jamie felt humiliated and depressed, not only because of what the harassers were doing to him but also because school officials seemed not to care. He refused to go back to school, and a few days later, he again attempted to commit suicide. His exasperated parents then decided that Jamie should go live with an aunt and uncle who had a home in the town of Drummond, thirty miles away (not the same couple with whom he had briefly lived two years earlier).

Jamie was not happy living in Drummond and missed his parents and brothers terribly. In addition, he was troubled by the deep conservatism of his aunt and uncle. The latter, in particular, seemed to have a problem with his being gay. The last straw for Jamie came when the couple refused to celebrate his fifteenth birthday. A few days after that, Jamie left their house and hitchhiked the almost two hundred miles to Minneapolis.

Jamie often spoke of wanting to live in Minneapolis. When Bob and Carol learned that he had run away, they immediately suspected he had gone to that city. They followed Jamie there, putting up posters and handing out flyers in areas where they were told Jamie was likely spending time. A few days later, Jamie saw one of the missing-child posters that his parents had stapled to a utility pole and started crying. He called the number of the social services agency listed on the poster and was reunited with his parents a few hours later. Jamie told them he was not going back to Ashland if it meant he had to attend the same school again. His parents assured him that they would do everything they could to avoid that, including possibly homeschooling him. But when they got back to Ashland, the Naboznys learned that they could not homeschool Jamie because neither of them had a high school degree. (The only private high school in the area was a fundamentalist Christian one, and even if there had been others, the Naboznys could not have afforded the tuition.) They kept Jamie home for as long as they could, but after several weeks, they started receiving letters from the school district informing them that Jamie had to return to school. Much to their frustration and despair, the Naboznys had no choice but to send their boy back to the Ashland high school.

▲

Bob and Carol hoped that things would improve for Jamie when he returned to school. The harassment, however, grew worse as the months progressed. A few months before the end of ninth grade, Bob and Carol once again took their oldest son out of school. This time, they convinced the department of social services to put Jamie in a foster home in a nearby school district so that he could attend another public high school.

When Jamie arrived at his new school, he was harassed by a boy there. Jamie reported the incident and school officials acted swiftly to discipline the harasser. He was never bothered again while at that school. Jamie's grades, which had been declining for several years under the weight of the constant harassment, began to improve. He also seemed happier and more self-confident. He was doing so well, in fact, that when he was halfway through tenth grade his social worker demanded that he return home. Jamie missed his parents and was happy to be back with them, but living at home, unfortunately, meant going back to the local school.

The harassment started again almost immediately at the Ashland high school. This time around, some of the worst incidents took place on the school bus. Carol complained to school officials about the harassment that was occurring on the bus, and they told her that she had to speak to the bus company operators, who, in turn, suggested that Jamie sit in the front of the bus with the elementary school students. This only led his tormentors to further ridicule Jamie and to warn the younger children not to sit next to him because he was a pervert who would sexually molest them. While on the bus, the harassers constantly tripped, shoved, and punched Jamie as he tried to make his way down the aisle. In addition, they spat on him, threw pencils and bolts at him, and shot paper clips out of rubber bands at him. After a few weeks of this relentless abuse, Jamie refused to get back on the bus, choosing instead—when his parents could not drive him—to walk the two and a half miles between his home and the school.

At school, the most dangerous places for Jamie were the hallways and bathrooms. Eventually, a sympathetic teacher allowed him to use a private bathroom. She also told Jamie that he could spend time in her classroom when it was not being used. At least the harassers could not bother him there.

The same teacher introduced Jamie to a new high school counselor, who took an interest in Jamie's ordeal. The counselor spoke to principal Davis and assistant principal Thomas Blauert about the harassment that Jamie was experiencing on an almost daily basis, but neither official investigated any of the incidents of harassment, much less disciplined the perpetrators. In fact, Blauert told Jamie several times during the spring of tenth grade that if he was being harassed, it was because he was provoking the other boys in some way. And on one occasion, after Jamie told Blauert about how his tormentors had pushed and tripped him as he was walking down the hallway, the assistant principal actually laughed at him.

The lack of action by school officials led Jamie to wonder if the nightmare he was living through was all his fault. He would later testify at the trial that "I felt like I was doing something wrong . . . and that what was happening to me somehow was right or that I deserved it. After people [harass you] for so long you start thinking that there's something really wrong with you and that [the school officials] are supposed to protect you and they don't."

Despite the many pleas for help by Jamie and his parents, no Ashland school official ever took any action to discipline or sanction any of the students who verbally and physically harassed Jamie for more than four years. The school records would eventually show that during this same period, a female student was suspended for a day for calling another female student a "bitch." Another was suspended for scratching, and pulling the hair of, a fellow student. One of the same boys who tormented Jamie for years with impunity was suspended for calling his girlfriend a bad name. (This student was also suspended several times for smoking on school property.) Most of the harassment suffered by Jamie was much worse than any of these incidents and yet no student was ever punished for any of it.

▲

For Jamie, eleventh grade began in the same way that tenth grade had ended, with constant harassment. One fall day, he arrived at school early and went straight to the library to hide. The lights were off, and there was no one around. For several days now, Jamie had been hiding in an out-of-the-way corner of the library, waiting for his first class to begin. He felt relatively safe in that spot. But on that particular morning, a pack of about ten boys loudly stormed into the library looking for him. When they found him, they pushed him to the floor and started taunting him. One of the boys, who was wearing leather cowboy boots, started kicking Jamie in the stomach as the other boys watched and cheered. This went on for several minutes. The attacker only stopped when the school librarian walked in and turned on the lights, causing the gang of boys to flee. Jamie slowly got up from the floor, holding his stomach in pain. He found a telephone, called his parents, and waited for them to pick him up.

Jamie had recurring stomach cramps and pains for several weeks after the school library incident. It turned out that he was suffering from internal bleeding and bruising as a result of the beating, a condition that eventually required abdominal surgery.

Not surprisingly, given the horrific nature of the latest beating, Jamie's school attendance became sporadic. He repeatedly told his parents that he was going to run away from home if he had to continue attending the same school. One night in early December 1992, Jamie sat in his room for several hours planning his escape from Ashland. He did not have any money, but he did have a checkbook. Early the next morning, as the diners in town started opening, he walked into the center of town. He went to several different diners, writing a check in each for more than the amount owed. After he had collected more than one hundred dollars in cash, he went to the bus station and took the first bus back to Minneapolis.

▲

Jamie never returned to Ashland permanently. Instead, with his parents' permission, he stayed in Minneapolis, living in the home of a gay deacon and his partner, who took him in as their foster child, and eventually earned a GED. While in Minneapolis, Jamie was diagnosed as suffering from depression and posttraumatic stress disorder as a result of what had happened to him in the Ashland public schools. He spent several years in therapy, requiring treatment for anxiety and loss of self-esteem.

Jamie's treatment was successful and by the end of the decade he had enrolled at the University of Minnesota, pursuing a degree in psychology. He also spoke frequently at schools and to community groups across the country, telling audiences about what had happened to him as a teenager in the Ashland schools. During his presentations, Jamie eloquently implored school administrators, teachers, and parents alike to take the problem of antigay harassment in schools seriously. Jamie was committed to doing everything he could to make sure that what had happened to him did not happen to other LGBT students. It was for this reason that he decided to sue.

## The Lawyer

It so happened that when Jamie, almost three years after moving to Minneapolis, called Lambda seeking help with his lawsuit against the Ashland school district and several of its administrators, the organization was looking for a test case involving a student who had been subjected to antigay harassment in school. Prior to the mid-1990s, Lambda, like other gay rights groups, had largely avoided tackling LGBT youth issues because of the particularly controversial nature of same-sex sexuality among young people. In fact, of the almost two hundred cases that Lambda participated in during its first twenty years of existence (between 1973 and 1993), only two involved LGBT youth.[1] Starting around 1995, however, Lambda decided there had been enough progress made on LGBT rights issues generally that the time was right to start paying more attention to the plight of LGBT adolescents, including their treatment in schools.

Unfortunately, what had happened to Jamie was happening to many other LGBT adolescents in schools across the United States. A study conducted for the federal government in the late 1980s found that 45 percent of gay males and almost 20 percent of lesbians had experienced verbal abuse or physical assault in high school. Almost a third of those students dropped out of school. Another study found that 41 percent of girls and 34 percent of boys who reported gay-related violent assaults attempted to commit suicide.[2] It seemed, in fact, that every week Lambda received a new report from somewhere in the country of a student who was being subjected by schoolmates to antigay harassment. The time was now right for Lambda to take action. The organization's attorney who took the lead in Jamie's case was Patricia Logue, the head of its midwestern office.

Logue, who was born in 1960, grew up in the Philadelphia suburb of Swarthmore. Her father, a political science professor at Villanova University, was a self-acknowledged idealist who called for the formation of a world government and who made five quixotic and ill-fated efforts to be elected to Congress. Her mother, a reporter for the *Dela-*

*ware County Daily Times*, was the pragmatist of the family, responsible for running a large household of six children.

Logue attended Brown University and from there went on to study at the Northwestern University School of Law. When she arrived at law school in the fall of 1983, Logue had little interest in becoming a practicing attorney; instead, she viewed a law degree as a means to land a public policy position. Her father's three brothers were all lawyers, and two of them were heavily involved with public policy issues, one as an urban planner and the other as a community organizer who served as mayor of New Haven in the late 1970s. While in law school, Logue represented clients through Northwestern's legal clinic and interned for the Chicago Committee for Civil Rights Under Law, an organization that provided free legal services to the poor. These experiences exposed Logue for the first time to the ways in which litigation can be used as a tool of social reform by improving the lives and opportunities of poor people and other marginalized groups in society.

She also, in law school, fell in love for the first time—with a woman. Her physical and emotional attraction to another female law student was at first confusing for Logue, but it ended up explaining a lot, including her modest track record of unsatisfying relationships with boyfriends. Although the new relationship lasted only a few months, it made Logue realize that she was—and perhaps had all along been— a lesbian.

After earning her law degree, Logue worked for the corporate law firm of Jenner & Block and for a nonprofit organization representing poor and minority tenants in housing cases before Lambda hired her in 1993 to open its Chicago office—the organization already had offices in New York and Los Angeles—and to manage its cases originating in the Midwest.

In her first case with Lambda, Logue persuaded the organizers of Chicago's Bud Billiken Parade—the largest African American parade in the country—to reverse their original decision prohibiting a black LGBT group from marching under its own banner. A few months

later, voters in Cincinnati approved an amendment to that city's charter depriving the city council of the authority to enact laws protecting
lesbians and gay men from discrimination. A group of attorneys, including Logue and Cincinnati civil rights lawyer Alphonse Gerhard-
stein, quickly went into action by filing a motion for a preliminary
injunction in federal court seeking to stay the implementation of the
new law. At a hearing a few days after the election, Logue argued to
the court that the ballot initiative violated the rights of free speech and
equal protection of Cincinnati's gay and lesbian residents. The court,
after concluding that it was likely the plaintiffs would ultimately prevail in their constitutional challenge, issued the injunction.[3]

On the evening after the injunction was issued, Logue was on a
plane heading back to Chicago when she read a newspaper article
about Tim Hollis, a man with AIDS who had been literally dragged
off of an American Airlines airplane because several passengers complained that he had self-medicated during a long delay. Logue ended
up representing Hollis, threatening to sue the airline for the way in
which it had treated her client. A monetary settlement was eventually
reached, one that Hollis signed two days before he died. (The money
went to his nephews and nieces.) The airline also agreed to train its
employees not to discriminate against passengers with disabilities in
general, and with HIV in particular.

A few months later, Jamie Nabozny filed a lawsuit against the Ashland school district and several of its administrators for failing to protect him from the antigay harassment and violence to which he was
subjected for four years. As soon as Logue heard about Jamie's suit,
she suspected that the litigation might serve as a test case through
which to protect LGBT students across the country from being harassed in their schools.

### The Law

In the fall of 1993, following the recommendation of a counselor at a
Minneapolis gay community center, Jamie contacted Rae Randolph,
a solo practitioner in town. Randolph had recently filed a lawsuit on

behalf of a young woman after she was repeatedly harassed by a male student during three years of high school, making it one of the first cases in the country brought against a school district for failing to prevent one student from sexually harassing another.

After meeting with Jamie, Randolph filed a similar complaint on his behalf in federal court, naming as defendants the Ashland school district, principals Mary Podlesny and William Davis, and assistant principal Thomas Blauert. The complaint's primary legal claim was that the defendants had violated Jamie's constitutional right to equal protection. Specifically, the complaint alleged that school officials had refused to take the necessary steps to protect Jamie from harassment because he was gay. It also alleged sex discrimination by contending that school officials would have responded differently to the harassment had Jamie been a girl. Given the years of physical and emotional abuse that Jamie had suffered at the hands of his tormentors, the complaint asked that he be awarded $50,000 in compensatory damages and $300,000 in punitive damages.

The school district's insurance company, which had issued a policy protecting it from lawsuit-related liability, hired Timothy Yanacheck, a forty-seven-year-old lawyer from Madison to represent the defendants in the lawsuit. After familiarizing himself with the legal and factual aspects of the case, Yanacheck filed a motion for summary judgment, contending that there was no need for a trial. In support of his motion, Yanacheck argued that Jamie's claim had no merit because school employees had not themselves participated in or authorized the harassment.

The case was assigned to district court judge John Shabaz, a former Republican state legislator who had a reputation for controlling his courtroom with a firm hand. Lawyers all over Wisconsin knew him as the judge who once ordered that a man who suffered a heart attack in his courtroom be moved out quickly so that the proceedings could continue.

In October 1995, Shabaz granted the defendants' summary judgment motion, concluding that there was no evidence suggesting that Jamie had been treated differently because of his sex. Interestingly, although Shabaz's ruling ordered that Jamie's case be dismissed in its entirety, the judge failed to address a crucial issue raised in his complaint, namely, the allegation that the defendants had treated him differently because he was gay.

Even though Jamie did not blame Randolph for Judge Shabaz's disappointing ruling, he had disagreed with some of her strategic decisions. Randolph, for example, had advised Jamie not to seek public attention for the case. In particular, Randolph did not want the case described in the media as a gay rights lawsuit. She believed that Jamie's chances of succeeding were greater if the case was viewed as a harassment case rather than as an *antigay* harassment case. Jamie, on the other hand, wanted to bring as much attention to the litigation as possible. In fact, his main objective in bringing the lawsuit was to educate people about the problem of antigay harassment in the schools and the failure of many school officials to combat it. Just as Jamie had refused to hide his sexual orientation when asked during his school years, he now chafed against the idea of publicly minimizing the gay aspects of the case.

Jamie's disagreements with Randolph, coupled with Judge Shabaz's ruling dismissing his claim, led him to seek another lawyer for the appeal. Lambda, which had recently opened its midwestern office headed by Logue, was a logical choice. After receiving Jamie's inquiry, Logue consulted with other Lambda lawyers about whether to take the case. One of the attorneys with whom she spoke was David Buckel, who had recently been hired by the organization to work on LGBT youth issues. Logue and Buckel knew that no student had ever succeeded in suing school officials for failing to protect him or her from antigay harassment perpetrated by other students. But the facts in Jamie's case were so compelling—the abuse he had suffered was so severe and the pattern of neglect on the part of the school officials seemed so clear—that the lawsuit might serve as an important test case through which to provide LGBT youth across the country with protection from harassment in schools. Lambda, therefore, took the case, naming Logue as the lead attorney.

The first order of business was to appeal Judge Shabaz's ruling to the U.S. Court of Appeals for the Seventh Circuit. Logue thought that if the case ever went to trial, Jamie had a good chance of succeeding. A jury, after all, was likely to be sympathetic to a young man who had endured years of harassment and abuse as school officials stood by and did nothing. It would not be possible, however, to bring the case before a jury unless Logue could first convince the appellate court that Judge Shabaz had erred in granting the defendants' summary judgment motion.

▲

The federal statute under which Jamie sued, which is known as Section 1983, was originally called the Ku Klux Klan Act. Congress enacted that law after the Civil War in response to the failure of government officials in southern states to protect black citizens from violence and harassment perpetrated by whites. The new law opened the federal courts to former slaves who were seeking the same legal protections afforded by state and local governments to white people. Although Section 1983 originated in the nation's deeply troubled racial past, the language used by Congress in that statute did not limit its applicability to cases involving racial discrimination. Instead, the law is broad in scope, offering protection to any person who is deprived of a federal constitutional right as a result of government representatives acting in their official capacities.

Logue argued in her brief to the Court of Appeals that Jamie's lawsuit raised a quintessential Section 1983 claim. Jamie's principal argument, after all, was that government officials, for discriminatory reasons, had failed to provide him with the protection from violence and harassment to which he was entitled under state law. Wisconsin was one of the first states in the country to enact a statute prohibiting schools from discriminating against students on the basis of sexual orientation. That same law required school boards to develop written policies and procedures to investigate allegations of discrimination, including harassment, against students. The very crux of Jamie's claim, Logue argued in her brief, was that the defendants had failed to protect him from harassment as they were required to do under Wisconsin law.

The defendants discriminated against Jamie, Logue told the court, both because he was gay and because he was a boy. Although Judge Shabaz, in his summary judgment ruling, had inexplicably failed to address the allegation of sexual orientation discrimination, Jamie had offered evidence of such discrimination, including his contention that school officials had told him on several occasions that he was to blame for the harassment because he insisted on being openly gay in school. The proffering of this evidence should have been enough to permit Jamie to proceed to trial so that he could establish the veracity of his allegations.

Furthermore, Logue pointed out to the Court of Appeals that there was evidence in the record showing that school officials had acted with great speed and concern in investigating allegations of harassment against girls. Indeed, it was difficult to imagine that the defendants would have ignored the level of abuse and harassment to which Jamie was subjected if he had been a girl. The defendants' dismissal of Jamie's complaints of harassment with retorts like "boys will be boys" showed that they did not take male-on-male harassment seriously.

For purposes of equal protection doctrine, it often makes a difference whether the government's differential treatment that is subject to challenge was based on an individual's sex or sexual orientation. Courts generally subject differential treatment on the former ground to a more searching form of judicial scrutiny than the latter. At the very least, however, a rational explanation must exist *whenever* the government treats similarly situated individuals differently. In Jamie's case, Logue told the court, the defendants had failed to articulate *any* rational justification for affording Jamie less protection from assaults and harassment merely because he was a gay boy.

▲

The composition of the three-judge panels that hear cases in the federal Courts of Appeals is not usually disclosed until the day of oral argument. As a result, it was not until a few minutes before Logue had to make her presentation to the court in late March 1996, that she learned the identity of the three judges—William Bauer, Jesse Eschbach, and Joel Flaum. Logue was, on the whole, pleased with the panel that was randomly assigned to Jamie's case. Although all three men had been appointed to the appellate court by Republican presidents—Bauer by President Ford in 1974, and the other two by President Reagan in 1981 and 1983, respectively—they were members of an older generation of judges who seemed to be less ideological (and therefore more open-minded) than some of the judges who would later be appointed by Republicans.

Logue believed that she had the law on her side, but, as often happens with test cases, the lawsuit's facts were as compelling as the legal arguments arising from them. Logue therefore spent some time early on in her oral argument letting the court know just how prevalent and severe the abuse that Jamie suffered had been. "We're talking about four years of abuse," she explained, "daily abuse, clearly escalating in severity with the ages of the abusers." And then, with a truly felt sense of outrage in her voice, she told the judges, while pointing at the defendants' table in the courtroom, that "the abuse occurred on their school grounds and on their watch. They had the power to stop it," and they never did.

The equal protection argument based on sexual orientation discrimination was relatively simple, and Logue kept it that way, telling the court that it is unconstitutional for government officials to "deny protection because a person is gay." But Jamie had been treated differently not only because he was gay but also because he was a boy. Logue was able to convey the dismay that her client felt over the way school officials treated him when she told the court that "if a girl student was subjected to a mock sexual assault in a classroom, was kicked so hard in the stomach she had to be hospitalized, or urinated on, I don't think school officials would have been standing idly by."

In his remarks, Yanacheck, the defendants' lawyer, wisely chose not to minimize what had happened to Jamie in Ashland's schools. Instead, he expressed regret that "we were not able to stop the harassment." Nonetheless, he contended that the Constitution did not provide what he called "special protection" to gay people and that, in any event, school officials should not be found constitutionally liable for the actions of students.

By the end of the forty-minute argument, it seemed that Logue had done a better job than Yanacheck in getting her points across emphatically and persuasively. A few days later, Logue heard that one of the judges on the panel had been so impressed with her advocacy skills that he commented to a lawyer that she was close to being to the gay rights movement what Thurgood Marshall had been to the civil rights movement. There can, of course, be no greater praise for a civil rights lawyer than that.

▲

Four months later, the Court of Appeals, in a unanimous opinion written by Judge Eschbach, concluded that Jamie was entitled to proceed to trial on both of his equal protection claims. On the issue of sex discrimination, the court focused on the fact that when Jamie complained to principal Podlesny about the mock rape, she dismissed the incident by saying that "boys will be boys." The court accepted Logue's contention that, as Eschbach noted, it was "impossible to believe that a female lodging a similar compliant would have received the same response." Furthermore, Eschbach pointed out that the defendants, while not denying "that they aggressively punished male-on-female battery and harassment," claimed that they had pursued Jamie's allegations with the same degree of aggressiveness. Given that Jamie was disputing the latter point, a trial was required to determine who was correct.[4]

Eschbach also rejected Yanacheck's attempt to reframe Jamie's equality claim as one based on the notion that school officials had to treat every student who alleged harassment at the hands of other students in precisely the same way. The Constitution clearly did not require that school officials provide *identical* treatment to every aggrieved student. Instead, the Constitution required that the officials provide "male and female students *equivalent* levels of protection." As for the sexual orientation discrimination claim, Eschbach ruled that the differential treatment of individuals on the basis of their sexual orientation violated the Constitution unless the defendants provided a rational reason for that treatment. The judge added that there was a basic factual disagreement between the parties, necessitating a trial, since Jamie alleged that he had been treated differently than other students because of his sexual orientation, an assertion that was denied by school officials.

▲

Now that the case was going to trial, it was important that Logue add to Jamie's legal team a lawyer who, unlike her, had extensive trial experience. She decided, therefore, to ask David Springer, a partner at the Chicago office of the corporate law firm of Skadden Arps, to take the lead in the trial. Although Logue had never met Springer, she was aware of his reputation among Chicago lawyers as a skilled trial advocate. Logue also knew that he was deeply committed to the cause of gay rights, having been a generous financial contributor to Lambda for several years.

When Logue called Springer in the summer of 1996 to ask whether he would be interested in helping to represent Jamie, the Skadden Arps partner, who was HIV positive, was about to complete a five-month medical leave of absence. It did not take much to convince Springer to join Jamie's legal team. Springer, who had mostly worked on behalf of corporations during his career as a litigator, was immediately intrigued by the possibility of representing a sympathetic young gay man who had clearly been wronged by school officials.

Springer officially signed on to represent Jamie in early September 1996, giving him about ten weeks to prepare the case for trial. One of the first things he did was to send two Skadden Arps lawyers to Ashland to find witnesses and gather documents. While in Ashland, the two attorneys learned that Roy Grande, one of Jamie's worst tormentors, was serving a prison term for assault. They visited Roy in prison and asked him whether he might be willing to testify at the trial. Roy, apparently wanting to atone for the physical and mental pain that he had inflicted on Jamie, agreed to testify. The lawyers also contacted Mary Grande, Roy's mother, who was similarly willing to help with Jamie's case. The mother and son eventually offered crucial testimony that supported Jamie's version of events, the credibility of which was bolstered by the fact that they were associated with neither Jamie nor the defendants.

One of the biggest concerns that both Springer and Logue had going into the trial was the jury pool. The prospective jurors would be drawn from within a ten-mile radius around Eau Claire, Wisconsin, where the trial was to be held, a rural and conservative area where most people had little exposure to LGBT rights issues or, for that matter, to openly gay people. If Jamie was going to prevail in his lawsuit, it was crucial to select jurors who could be impartial in a case involving homosexuality. Springer and Logue prevailed on Judge Shabaz to ask prospective jurors whether they were gay, or had a gay family member or friend. Both lawyers were aware of research showing that those who know someone who is gay are more likely to be open minded about homosexuality than those who do not. In the end, four out of the seven jurors chosen to hear the case knew at least one gay person, which Jamie's lawyers believed boded well for his chances of receiving a fair hearing.

The trial started the week before Thanksgiving. Springer's opening remarks to the jury were centered around the idea that each successive failure by school officials to stop the harassment of Jamie encouraged the harassers to increase the frequency and severity of the abuse. For his part, Yanacheck signaled in his opening remarks that the defense would be built around the notion that the defendants were good and decent school administrators. These highly qualified professionals, who were responsible for educational institutions with hundreds of students, had no recollection of having known or heard of Jamie while he was in school, much less that he was gay. Yanacheck told the jury that they would find the testimony of the school administrators, all of whom had years of experience coping with student disciplinary issues, more credible than the "pack of lies" that Jamie had been telling about them.

The trial, however, was not about whether the defendants were good or bad people. It was not necessary, therefore, for Jamie's lawyers to portray the defendants as homophobic individuals. Instead, the case was about whether the defendants had failed to address antigay harassment against a gay boy in the same way that they had in the past treated harassment against heterosexual girls. It was relevant, in answering that question, that none of the defendants had had much experience with LGBT people. In fact, two of them acknowledged on the stand, in response to Springer's questions, that they had never known anyone who was gay and that they had never, prior to Jamie's lawsuit, given much thought to LGBT issues. The defendants did testify repeatedly that they had no memory of Jamie or of any of the incidents that he and his parents complained about for more than four years. However, the defendants' apparent inability to recall *anything* related to what had happened to Jamie while he attended their schools, including several incidents in which serious physical assaults were perpetrated against him, was simply not credible.

It also helped Jamie's case that Roy Grande and his mother Mary corroborated some of the testimony proffered by both Jamie and Carol Nabozny. Roy, who was permitted to leave prison in order to testify at the trial, admitted that he had called Jamie names and that he had tripped, pushed, kicked, and punched him repeatedly throughout middle school and high school. After he acknowledged this long history of harassment, Roy told the jury that school officials never disciplined him for terrorizing Jamie while once suspending him for calling his girlfriend "a very bad name."

For her part, Mary Grande supported Jamie and Carol's contention that Podlesny—the middle school principal—had said Jamie was being harassed because "he was going around expressing his sexual preference." This was a key moment in the trial because Podlesny vehemently denied that she had ever made such a statement. The fact that Mary Grande, who had no vested interest in the case, testified to the contrary, significantly bolstered Jamie's version of events. It also helped that a high school counselor told the jury that Jamie had come to her on several occasions to tell her that he was being physically and verbally harassed. She further testified that she had passed that information on to principal Davis and assistant principal Blauert, who did nothing in response.

Although Yanacheck attempted to portray the defendants as serious and responsible administrators, the evidence introduced at trial suggested otherwise. The jury learned, for example, that Podlesny kept suspension records in her office for years, even though school policy required her to destroy them after the students in question left her school. Even worse, Blauert inexplicably and illegally stored thousands of pages of old suspension records at his principal home and at his summer home. While vacationing at the latter, he even burned some of those records in order to fuel up a sauna stove.

The trial lasted two full days. After the close of evidence, Judge Shabaz told the jury that their first task was to determine whether the defendants had intentionally discriminated against Jamie because of his sex and sexual orientation. If they were to answer that question in the affirmative, then the trial would proceed to a damages stage in which Jamie would be allowed to introduce evidence of the physical and mental harm that he suffered as a result of the defendants' discriminatory conduct.

After deliberating for a little less than four hours, the jurors notified the court that they had agreed on a verdict. As the jurors— five women and two men—walked back into the courtroom, Jamie reached under the plaintiff's table to hold Logue's hand. When the foreman announced that the jury had unanimously found that the three school officials had intentionally discriminated against Jamie, the young man began to cry. So did his parents, who had watched the entire trial from the front row of the courtroom's spectator area.

This jury in rural Wisconsin—in the middle of the country's heartland—had concluded that school officials treated Jamie with indifference and neglect because he was a gay boy. Although nothing could make up for the suffering that Jamie and his parents had for years endured unnecessarily, the verdict constituted an official recognition that what school administrators had done to Jamie was wrong.

▲

After the Court of Appeals, earlier that summer, reversed Judge Shabaz's granting of the defendants' summary judgment motion, Logue
had told Yanacheck that Jamie would consider settling the case. At one
point, the figure of $50,000 was discussed, but the school district and
its insurance company, apparently believing that they would prevail
at trial, never made a firm settlement offer. Now, a few minutes after
the jury's verdict, it was Yanacheck who approached Logue looking to
settle the case. The defendants' lawyer knew that his clients' potential
liability exposure was significant, especially given that Jamie was asking not only for compensatory damages but also for punitive ones.

When Logue told Jamie that the other side was now interested in
settling the case, he was not sure whether he wanted that outcome.
There was a part of him that wanted to see the case through to the end
by allowing the jury to hear what the abuse cost him physically and
emotionally. Although Logue made clear that the decision whether
to settle the lawsuit was entirely his, she also told him that, if the trial
proceeded to the damages phase, his entire life would be subject to
scrutiny. There was no doubt that Yanacheck would do everything
he could to try to convince the jury that most of the emotional harm
that Jamie had suffered through the years was the result of incidents
that took place outside of school, many of them related to his difficult
childhood at home.

During the conversation, Jamie told Logue, as he had done several times during the litigation, that what he cared about most was
that other young LGBT people not have to go through the same ordeal that he went through while attending public schools. Logue replied that if the school district could be persuaded to settle the case
for a large amount of money, the settlement could then be used to
bring considerable attention to the plight of LGBT youth in schools
throughout the country. After wrestling with the issue for more than
an hour, Jamie instructed Logue to try to settle the case.

The damages stage of the trial was scheduled to begin the following morning. The lawyers negotiated past midnight, with the par-

ties eventually agreeing to settle the case for $900,000, plus $62,000 to cover Jamie's medical expenses. During the following twenty-four hours, most major news outlets in the country published or broadcasted stories on this first-of-its-kind jury verdict.

The abuse that Jamie repeatedly suffered for four years in the Ashland schools had not been enough to get the attention of administrators. To put it simply, school officials could hardly be bothered by the fact that a boy under their charge was being continuously and seriously harassed by other boys because he was gay. Now, however, Jamie, with the help of Logue, Springer, and the other lawyers who worked on the case, had not only gotten the attention of Ashland school officials but also of school districts across the country. As Logue put it the day after the trial ended, "countless gay kids have paid a high price for abuse. Now the tables have turned, and it is prejudice that is costly."[5]

## The Impact

Several studies conducted in the 1990s attempted to bring attention to the prevalence of antigay harassment and violence in American public schools. A 1993 survey of Massachusetts high school students reported that 98 percent had heard homophobic remarks at school and that more than half had heard *school staff* make such comments. Two years later, another Massachusetts study found that LGBT students were five times more likely to have missed school due to safety concerns and four times more likely to have attempted suicide than straight students. In 1997, the Vermont Department of Health issued a report finding that LGBT students were seven times more likely to have been injured or threatened with a weapon and four times more likely to have attempted suicide than straight students.

Another study published by the Washington (State) Safe Schools Coalition reported over one hundred antigay violence and harassment incidents in the state's public schools between 1993 and 1998. Eight of those cases involved the gang rape of eleven different students, two of whom were sixth-graders. Also included in the list were thirty-nine instances of physical assault and harassment, as well as thirty-eight instances of long-term verbal harassment. Ten of the victims of antigay harassment and abuse attempted suicide, with two of them succeeding.[6]

Despite the prevalence of antigay harassment in schools, few of the nation's school districts, at the time Jamie brought his lawsuit, were doing anything about it. In fact, a 1998 survey of the nation's forty-two largest school districts conducted by the Gay, Lesbian and Straight Education Network (GLSEN) found that half of them did not have in place a single policy or program aimed at protecting the rights of LGBT students. A further indication of the lack of interest shown by many school officials in the issue of antigay harassment was that when David Buckel, the Lambda lawyer who for most of the 1990s led the organization's efforts on behalf of LGBT youth, called administrators to discuss serious incidents of antigay harassment at their schools, most of them refused to even take his calls.

It is not an exaggeration to say that the *Nabozny* lawsuit changed much of that. In the days after the media reported the almost $1 million settlement in the case, Buckel received calls from school officials around the country wanting to know what they could do to prevent what had happened to Jamie from being repeated in their schools. In the weeks and months that followed, many more officials contacted Lambda and other organizations like GLSEN seeking advice about how to prevent and discourage student-on-student antigay harassment. Not surprisingly, some of these calls were spurred by insurance companies that were now insisting that their policy-holding schools implement programs and procedures to avoid future million-dollar claims in antigay student harassment lawsuits.

The advice that LGBT rights advocates gave school officials who sought their help was that they adopt comprehensive harassment policies that specifically included antigay harassment as a separate category of prohibited conduct. The advocates also suggested that schools adopt formal grievance mechanisms that would allow victims of antigay harassment to report incidents that could then be investigated by school officials. Finally, it was essential that school administrators educate staff and students about the need to make sexual orientation harassment as unacceptable as racial or sexual harassment.

The core of the legal claim in *Nabozny* was that it was unconstitutional for school officials to have treated Jamie differently than how they treated other victims of harassment. By the mid-1990s, most educators in the country were prepared to respond aggressively to instances of racial and sexual harassment. Many of them, however, deemed harassment on the basis of sexual orientation to be of lesser importance, not meriting the same type of firm institutional response. The *Nabozny* litigation made it clear that such differential treatment was unconstitutional. As the federal Court of Appeals noted in its ruling, there was no justification for treating severe instances of student-on-student antigay harassment any less seriously than episodes of racial or sexual harassment.

▲

The success of the *Nabozny* lawsuit empowered other LGBT students across the country to pursue legal claims against school officials who had ignored repeated complaints of physical and verbal harassment. One of them was Jesse Montgomery, a gay student who attended public schools in Duluth, Minnesota, during the 1990s.[7] As in Jamie's case, verbal harassment, left unaddressed by school officials, eventually led to physical abuse. And, as had happened to Jamie, there came a point when the attacks took on a sexual component. One particular male student on several occasions in middle school grabbed Jesse's thighs, chest, crotch, and buttocks. Another student did the same to Jesse in high school. This latter student eventually went further by on several occasions standing behind Jesse and rubbing his penis against Jesse's backside. Finally, this same student once threw Jesse to the ground, jumped on top of him, and pretended to rape him while other students watched and laughed. When Jesse sued the school district for failing to protect him from the harassment, the defendant argued that the Constitution did not protect individuals who had been treated differently because of their sexual orientation. The trial court, citing *Nabozny*, rejected that argument. A few months after the court's ruling, the school district agreed to settle the case with Jesse for an undisclosed amount.

The precedent set in *Nabozny* also helped in a lawsuit brought by Alana Flores against the Morgan Hill Unified School District in northern California. For Alana, the harassment began one day in tenth grade when she asked some boys to stop calling one of their classmates a "faggot." One of those boys then turned to her and angrily called her a "dyke." Shortly after that, Alana began to find notes in her locker with messages such as "dyke bitch," "die, dyke bitch," and "we'll kill you."[8]

One day, a student approached Alana in school with a picture of a man and a woman engaged in intercourse and told her that "this is the way that you should be doing it." A few weeks later, someone left a photograph in Alana's locker of a bound and gagged woman, whose legs were spread apart and whose throat had been slashed. When a tearful Alana took the picture to the school's assistant principal, she reprimanded the girl for bringing her this "trash" and ordered her to return to her classes. At one point during the conversation, the assistant principal asked Alana whether she was gay. When the girl answered that she was not, the woman replied that she then had no reason to be so upset.

The harassment of Alana continued unabated for many more months. In the fall of 1996, at around the same time that Jamie's case was heading for trial, Alana tried to kill herself at a party by overdosing on LSD. She was taken to a hospital where doctors pumped her stomach. As she lay strapped to a gurney in the emergency room, Alana realized that she wanted to live and that it was time to tell others that she was a lesbian.

When she returned to school, a friend recommended that she go speak to Ron Schmidt, an openly gay teacher who had taught in the district's middle schools for fifteen years. As Alana recounted to Ron her experiences at the high school, he remembered reading about Jamie's case and how he had won a $900,000 settlement in a lawsuit against a school system that had also failed to protect him from antigay harassment and abuse. Ron suggested to Alana that she might want to sue the school district and several of its administrators, and she eventually agreed.

Other students who had also been subjected to antigay harassment in the district's schools agreed to join the lawsuit. One of them was a boy who had been hospitalized in the seventh grade after being beaten by other boys screaming antigay epithets at a bus stop as a school bus driver watched without so much as getting up from his seat.

In Alana's case, the U.S. Court of Appeals for the Ninth Circuit concluded that she and the other plaintiffs had presented sufficient evidence that the defendants discriminated against them based on their actual or perceived sexual orientation. Relying on *Nabozny* as a precedent, the court noted that there was evidence in the record that school administrators had acted with deliberate indifference in failing to respond to the numerous instances of harassment, perpetrated by students under their charge, of Alana and the other plaintiffs.

A few months after the court ruled in Alana's lawsuit, the school district agreed to settle the case. As part of the settlement, the defendant paid the plaintiffs $1.1 million. The district also agreed to institute a mandatory staff training program for all school administrators, teachers, and counselors that focused on harassment and discrimination based on sexual orientation and gender identity. In addition, the district agreed to change its policies and student handbooks to state explicitly that harassment and discrimination based on actual or perceived sexual orientation and gender identity were prohibited, while making it clear that antigay harassment would be treated as a separate category of proscribed conduct, rather than as a subset of sexual harassment. Finally, the district agreed to provide training sessions on preventing antigay harassment to all seventh- and ninth-grade students.

▲

In the decade following *Nabozny*, school districts across the country agreed to pay over $4 million to LGBT students who sued them for refusing to take the necessary steps to stop harassment against them.

In addition to Jesse's and Alana's cases, other notable lawsuits followed. In 2002, the Washoe County School District in Nevada agreed to pay a gay student $450,000 in damages after he had been harassed in its schools for years. In one particularly nasty incident, a group of students surrounded the plaintiff in a school parking lot, threw a lasso around his neck, and threatened to drag him on the road behind a truck. In 2005, after losing a jury trial in federal court and while the case was on appeal, the Tonganoxie School District in Kansas entered into a settlement agreement that paid $440,000 to a teenager—who happened to be straight but was thought by some of his fellow students to be gay—for antigay harassment that started when he was in middle school and eventually led him to drop out of high school. Also in 2005, a California jury awarded a gay student and a lesbian student a combined $300,000 after it concluded that school officials failed to protect them from harassment and abuse (which included repeated threats of harm, plus being spat on, kicked, punched, and having one of their cars vandalized). The two teenagers ended up being home-schooled during their last year of high school because they could no longer tolerate the constant harassment.

It is clear that *Nabozny*, then, laid the legal foundation that has permitted many other victims of antigay harassment and abuse in schools to turn to the courts for help. In addition, the settlement agreements that have sometimes been reached in those lawsuits have required school districts to adopt policies, procedures, and training programs specifically aimed at addressing and preventing harassment of LGBT students.

None of this is to suggest, of course, that the lawsuits and the accompanying changes in the policies of some schools have completely solved the problem of antigay harassment in America's public schools. A recent nationwide survey of LGBT students found that three-quarters of them still frequently hear derogatory antigay remarks at school. In addition, a third of the students experience physical harassment because of their sexual orientation while nearly one-fifth are physically assaulted for the same reason.[9]

Although a great deal of work remains to be done to stop the harassment of LGBT students in America's schools, *Nabozny* and its legal progeny have played a significant role in bringing greater attention to the problem. Many schools today would not have sexual orientation harassment policies and programs in place but for the series of legal cases that have challenged long-lasting patterns of neglect and indifference by school officials toward LGBT students. And most of those cases can be traced back to Jamie Nabozny's courageous decision to sue.

The harassment suffered by Jamie Nabozny was, sadly, only too typical of what many LGBT students had experienced in American public schools. What set Jamie's case apart was not the extent of the harassment, as severe as it was. Instead, Jamie's case became as important as it did because his was the first to succeed. With the assistance of Logue and the other attorneys who worked on the case, Jamie was able to hold the school officials who for years had ignored his plight accountable for their actions (and omissions). Jamie refused to play the role of the passive victim and fought back, not verbally or physically, but by seeking the protection of the law and, in particular, that of the U.S. Constitution.

# CHAPTER 3

# Discrimination

## The Facts

Angela Romero, who joined the Denver police department in 1978, loved being a cop and working with children. After a few years on foot patrol duty, Romero was thrilled when she was assigned by her department to be a liaison to the city's public schools, a job that allowed her to work directly with students. One day in 1986, her supervisor went to a school where she was giving a lecture and told her ominously that he had disturbing information about her. The supervisor refused to elaborate, but Romero later learned that someone who worked for the department had seen her go into a lesbian bookstore. A few days later, she was transferred out of the school liaison position and assigned back to patrolling the streets. Although she never received an official explanation for the transfer, she was told unofficially that her superiors now believed that it was inappropriate for her to work with children.

After Romero returned to street patrol, there were several incidents during roll call in which other officers made disparaging comments about lesbians and about her. In addition, she sometimes found herself being followed around town by unmarked police cars in an apparent effort to intimidate her. Even more disturbingly, on a couple of occasions, her fellow officers ignored her requests for backup while dealing with dangerous people on the street, making Romero fear for her life.

All of these incidents led Romero to come out of the closet as a lesbian and to begin agitating within the department for the adoption of a policy prohibiting discrimination on the basis of sexual orientation. For the next four years, Romero led a mostly lonely fight to change the pervasive homophobia that was seemingly part of the department's culture. She also joined other Denver LGBT rights activists in lobbying the city council to enact an ordinance protecting employees from discrimination on the basis of sexual orientation. The activism by Romero and others paid off when Denver enacted a gay rights ordinance in 1990. A few weeks later, the police department instituted a policy prohibiting antigay harassment.

These measures made Romero, who had experienced firsthand the harmful impact of discrimination, feel safe and secure in her job. That feeling, however, was short-lived because less than two years later, a majority of Colorado's voters approved a state constitutional amendment—known as Amendment 2—that repealed all existing laws and policies (such as those of Denver and its police department) that protected lesbians, gay men, and bisexuals from discrimination.[1] At the same time, and more controversially, Amendment 2 prohibited all state and local governmental entities from *ever* providing such protection in the future.

▲

In hindsight, it is clear that 1991 was a crucial year for LGBT politics in Colorado. During that year, Denver voters rejected a proposed repeal of their city's gay rights ordinance. Counterbalancing that LGBT rights victory, conservative activists succeeded in convincing the Colorado Springs city council to reject a similar law.

Frustrated by their defeat in Denver but emboldened by their victory in Colorado Springs, anti–gay rights forces formed an organization called Colorado for Family Values (CFV). This new group was led by three social conservatives: Tony Marco, David Noebel, and Kevin

Tebedo. Marco was a right-wing activist in Colorado Springs who had led the charge against the proposed antidiscrimination ordinance in that city. Noebel was the head of Summit Ministries, a conservative Christian organization whose primary focus was to fight what it perceived to be the twin evils of communism and homosexuality. He was also the author of a book called *The Homosexual Revolution*, which warned that the toleration of homosexuality encouraged pedophilia, atheism, and nihilism. Tebedo was the son of a Republican state senator who had used his mother's connections to form extensive political relationships throughout Colorado. After founding the group, the three men reached out to Will Perkins, a wealthy Colorado Springs car dealer active in conservative politics. Perkins bankrolled the group in its early days, and eventually served as its chairman.

The CFV leaders had two main political goals when they formed the organization. First, they wanted to repeal the gay rights laws that were already in place not only in Denver but also in Aspen and Boulder. Second, they hoped to prevent the state government, as well as municipalities across Colorado, from enacting such laws in the future. The CFV leaders knew that they could not achieve their first goal by working only at the local level; Denver residents, after all, had only recently rejected an effort to repeal the city's gay rights measure. In addition, Boulder citizens had made their tolerant views clear, five years earlier, when they voted to approve their municipality's gay rights law.

There were also obstacles to the attainment of CFV's second objective, that of preventing new gay rights measures. Two years earlier, for example, Colorado governor Roy Romer had issued an executive order prohibiting state agencies from discriminating on the basis of sexual orientation. And only the year before, the Colorado Civil Rights Commission—the state agency whose responsibility it was to enforce Colorado's civil rights laws—had recommended that the state's antidiscrimination laws be amended to include sexual orientation as a protected category. Finally, although CFV leaders believed that they could prevail in efforts to convince some Colorado municipalities—outside of liberal enclaves like Aspen and Boulder—not to enact gay rights laws, they worried that it would be expensive and time-consuming to engage LGBT rights activists in community-by-community political battles all over the state.

It quickly became clear to the CFV activists that the easiest and most efficient way of achieving their political goals would be through a state constitutional amendment that would (1) retroactively repeal all gay rights laws then on the books in Colorado and (2) prospectively deny the state and local governments the authority to enact such laws in the future. For advice on how to draft such an amendment, the CFV leaders turned to lawyers working for the National Legal Foundation, a conservative organization founded by Pat Robertson. The result of this collaborative effort was a proposed constitutional amendment that read as follows:

> NO PROTECTED STATUS BASED ON HOMOSEXUAL, LESBIAN, OR BISEXUAL ORIENTATION. Neither the State of Colorado, through any of its branches or departments, nor any of its agencies, political subdivisions, municipalities or school districts, shall enact, adopt or enforce any statute, regulation, ordinance or policy whereby homosexual, lesbian, or bisexual orientation, conduct, practices, or relationships shall constitute or otherwise be the basis of or entitle any person or class of persons to have or claim any minority status, quota preferences, protected status or claim of discrimination.

Before Amendment 2, most anti–gay rights ballot measures—such as the one successfully promoted by Anita Bryant in Miami in the late 1970s—aimed only at overturning the enactment of a particular gay rights law by a particular municipality. Amendment 2 was a different legal beast altogether because it applied not only retrospectively by repealing previously enacted laws, but also prospectively by stripping all governmental bodies (both state and local, as well as legislative and executive) of the authority to protect lesbians, gay men, and bisexuals from discrimination. If Colorado voters approved Amendment 2, and if it survived legal challenges, it would render lesbians, gay men, and bisexuals, as a matter of state constitutional law, unprotectable from discrimination by employers, landlords, and places of public accommodation. And it would mean that, in the absence of a change in the state constitution, legislators would be barred forever from providing sexual minorities with the legal right to challenge such discrimination.

▲

Amendment supporters collected over eighty-five thousand signatures, thirty-six thousand more than were needed to place the measure on the ballot. After that initial step was completed, CFV turned its attention to orchestrating a political campaign on behalf of the measure. An important part of that work entailed coordinating the efforts of social conservative groups and individuals from both inside and outside of the state. Christian organizations, such as James Dobson's Focus on the Family and Lou Sheldon's Traditional Values Coalition, as well as antifeminist groups like Eagle Forum and Concerned Women for America, joined in the effort to secure passage of Amendment 2. Former U.S. senator Bill Armstrong and University of Colorado football coach Bill McCartney also worked hard on behalf of the initiative.

By the 1970s, most Americans had come to accept the notion that racial minorities and women were entitled to the protection afforded by civil rights laws. That consensus began to break down in the 1980s when civil rights supporters, frustrated with the slow progress in achieving racial and gender equality, began pressing for the increased implementation of affirmative action programs. Although supporters of these programs defended them as essential remedial steps required to effectively address the pervasive consequences of long-lasting and deeply entrenched discrimination, many Americans came to view them as problematic examples of government-approved reverse discrimination that granted special rights to (what they understood to be) increasingly privileged minorities. Amendment 2 supporters claimed that gay rights laws provided LGBT people with special rights and preferential treatment, and in doing so they astutely tapped into the discomfort that many voters felt about affirmative action. In fact, the supporters went so far as to claim that Amendment 2 was a *pro-equality* measure because it prevented the government from awarding special rights to a discrete segment of the population.

In their political campaign in favor of the Amendment, conservative activists repeatedly distinguished LGBT people from African Americans. Blacks were entitled to antidiscrimination protection because the legacy of slavery and segregation had led to their political and economic disempowerment. Sexual minorities, on the other hand, had not suffered a similar history of discrimination, nor were they politically or economically marginalized. Indeed, Amendment 2 supporters told the public that the opposite was true: LGBT people, primarily because of their (supposed) relative wealth, had political power that went beyond their relative small numbers. Conservtive activists portrayed legislators who supported laws prohibiting sexual orientation discrimination as "elites" who were out of touch with the wishes of the majority of citizens. The Amendment was sold as a needed mechanism for the people, in effect, to take back their government.

Opponents of Amendment 2 tried to respond to these claims by stressing that the antidiscrimination laws at issue did not provide an unfair advantage to sexual minorities. Instead they leveled the playing field by requiring employers, for example, to make hiring decisions based on the qualifications of applicants rather than on personal traits like sexual orientation. Rather than treating lesbians, gay men, and bisexuals in a special or privileged manner, the laws in question provided them with the same protections afforded by Colorado law to many other groups, including racial minorities, women, and the disabled.

These types of arguments against Amendment 2 failed to gain much political traction, in part because opponents were unable to capture their essence in a catchy slogan. Amendment supporters, on the other hand, built their entire political campaign around a simple mantra: "equal rights—not special rights." That phrase was plastered in advertisements all over the state; it was also repeated constantly by conservative activists whenever they spoke to the media.

It is important to note, however, that CFV did not limit itself to a rhetoric of special rights in promoting Amendment 2. It also sought to portray lesbians and gay men as pedophiles who threatened the well-being of children. In fact, the organization distributed 750,000 copies of a pamphlet in support of Amendment 2 which stated that "sexual molestation of children is a large part of many homosexuals' lifestyle" and that a failure to approve the constitutional measure would "destroy the family."

In the weeks leading up to the election, LGBT rights supporters were heartened by some polls which suggested that Amendment 2 would be defeated. But there were also warning signs. In a *Denver Post* poll taken a few days before the election, for example, nearly three out of five respondents agreed with the proposition that "When homosexuals talk about gay rights, what they really mean is that they want special rights." Colorado for Family Values's strategy of linking gay rights laws to special rights legislation seemed to be working. And sure enough, when the vote counting ended late on the evening of November 2, 1992, it turned out that 53.4 percent of Colorado voters supported the Amendment.

▲

A few days after the election, a lawsuit was filed to stop the enforcement of Amendment 2. The complaint listed several plaintiffs, including Richard Evans, the Denver mayor's liaison to the LGBT community, and Angela Romero, the police officer who had been prohibited by her superiors from working in the public schools.

The lead plaintiffs' attorney in the case was Jean Dubofsky, a solo practitioner from Boulder who a few years earlier has stepped down from the Colorado Supreme Court after serving as its first female justice. The Amendment 2 lawsuit is unusual in the annals of LGBT rights litigation in the United States because a case of this importance and magnitude has usually been led by an organization, such as the ACLU or Lambda, with a great deal of experience litigating LGBT rights lawsuits. Community leaders in Colorado, however, wanted to retain as much control over the legal challenge as possible, and they believed, not unreasonably, that they would be better able to do so if they selected a lead attorney from Colorado rather than turning the lawsuit over to one of the national legal organizations. While the local activists chose Dubofsky to serve as lead attorney, they also recognized that the national legal organizations, with their extensive experience litigating LGBT rights cases, also had an important role to play in the lawsuit. Although many attorneys from different organizations ultimately contributed in important ways to the lawsuit, it was the ACLU's Matthew Coles and Lambda's Suzanne Goldberg who ended up playing leading roles in advising and assisting Dubofsky (as well as the other Colorado attorneys who worked with her) during the years that it took to litigate the case.

## The Lawyers

Matthew Coles's father, Albert, was a prominent Connecticut lawyer-politician who served as state senate majority leader in the 1930s and as attorney general in the 1960s. After his father died, Coles learned from his mother that during the early 1950s, when Coles was a boy growing up in Bridgeport, his father had supported the candidacy of a former law partner even after the latter was arrested for having sex with another man in a public bathroom. As a gay man who never spoke to his father about his sexual orientation, Coles to this day wonders whether his father, a committed liberal, may have been years (if not decades) ahead of his time in thinking that being gay should not disqualify a person from running for office.

Coles attended Yale University as an undergraduate, arriving in New Haven in 1969, arguably the apex of political radicalism and unrest on America's campuses. Coles looked the part of the student radical—with scraggly hair that flowed down to his shoulders—but he would turn out to be more of an observer than a participant in the activities of the student left. For most of his time at Yale, he wrote for the college newspaper, covering historic events such as the massive May 1, 1970, antiwar protest on campus and the trial, held later that year, of Black Panther Party members who were charged with the murder of an alleged police informant.

Coles, who was closeted in college, decided in 1974 to attend law school at the University of California's Hastings Law School in the hope that living in San Francisco would help him come out. Coles's plan worked, and in his second year of law school he joined a street advocacy group called the Bay Area Gay Liberation.

In the mid-1970s, there was a growing divide among gay activists in San Francisco. On one side were the members of the Alice Toklas Democratic Club, which had been formed by gay leaders closely associated with the city's political establishment. On the other side were more progressive gay activists who criticized the Toklas club leadership for repeatedly endorsing seemingly sympathetic straight candidates for political office who then paid little attention to the LGBT community once they were elected.

Coles felt more comfortable with the more progressive activists, especially after the Toklas club refused to endorse Harvey Milk, the openly gay candidate who was trying to get elected to the city's Board of Supervisors. In 1976, after Milk lost a board election for the second time, a group of gay activists—including both seasoned ones such as Harry Britt and new ones such as Coles—formed the San Francisco Gay Democratic Club. The founders of the new organization believed that it was time for LGBT people to have a direct impact on the policies adopted by city hall that affected them.

One of the new political club's objectives was the passage of a gay rights law, with members turning to Coles to draft the law because, as a third-year law student, he was the only one among them who had legal training. Once Coles came up with a draft, he and other activists circulated it among the Supervisors. The bill hit several bumps on its way to passage, including an effort by the city attorney to strip its provisions prohibiting discrimination by employers and places of public accommodation, leaving only a proscription against housing discrimination. Coles, who was furious that the city attorney had rewritten "his" law in this way, visited Milk at his camera store to share his concerns. Milk had by this point been elected to the Board, becoming the first openly gay male candidate to be elected to a government position in the United States. After thanking Coles for coming, Milk told the young man that he would take care of the problem. A few weeks later, Milk publicly challenged the city attorney's authority to rewrite the law. Faced with a possible rebuke by the Board, the city attorney backed down. In March 1978, the Board approved the gay rights law. With minor exceptions, the language in the ordinance, still on the books in San Francisco today, was the same that Coles drafted.

After he received his law degree in 1977, Coles opened up a law practice on Castro Street, the main thoroughfare that runs through the largest gay neighborhood in San Francisco. Word quickly spread throughout the community that Coles was a lawyer to whom LGBT people could speak honestly about their lives. As a result, there was soon a steady stream of LGBT clients walking through his door looking for a gay lawyer to represent them.

Coles offered several distinctive legal services to his clients, including the drafting of agreements that allowed same-sex couples to protect jointly owned property in the case of death or separation. He was also one of the first lawyers in the country to draft documents requesting that officials permit LGBT people to visit their hospitalized partners, an issue that became especially important after the onset of AIDS. In addition, Coles became an expert in representing men who had been arrested for sexually soliciting undercover police officers in public restrooms and parks.

In 1979, Coles met Robert Nakatani, a third-year law student at Berkeley. The two men quickly fell in love and started a committed relationship that lasted over twenty years. The two also became business partners when Nakatani joined Coles in his law office, converting the latter's solo practice into a two-lawyer firm. Much of the work that Coles and Nakatani did in the coming years involved representing clients who were dying of AIDS. The writing of wills and the legal planning for death became the primary focus of their practice. On occasion, Coles was able to work on matters that did not involve AIDS. In one instance, he successfully represented a young black woman in a lawsuit against the Hilton Corporation after employees at one of its hotels had her arrested because they incorrectly believed she was a prostitute. Coles also represented a gay man who had been fired by a leading art institution in San Francisco because of his sexual orientation. But it was AIDS—and in particular the legal consequences of death—that came to dominate Coles's legal practice as the 1980s progressed. It was all terribly sad and emotionally exhausting, and by early 1987, a burned-out Coles decided he needed to find another way of practicing law. A few months later, he got a position as a staff attorney with the ACLU's Northern California affiliate, and, in his first case, successfully vindicated the free speech rights of peace activists who were prohibited by the military from demonstrating near dignitaries observing a procession of naval ships crossing the San Francisco Bay.[2]

When Coles was not litigating cases, he worked on gay rights legislation. He was, for example, the main drafter of San Francisco's domestic partnership ordinance. That provision, which was adopted in 1990, required the city to offer its employees who registered as domestic partners the same legal benefits that it provided to its married employees. Coles also helped draft laws prohibiting discrimination on the basis of sexual orientation that were enacted in Los Angeles, Oakland, Sacramento, San Diego, and San Jose. Finally, Coles was heavily involved in drafting, and lobbying for, the 1992 California statute that prohibited employment discrimination on the basis of sexual orientation.

A year before the enactment of that law, Coles had helped to challenge an initiative approved by voters in Concord, California, that, like Colorado's Amendment 2, prohibited the government (in this case, the local government) from enacting a gay rights law.[3] His work on that lawsuit, when coupled with his extensive experience litigating LGBT rights cases, made Coles an obvious choice to become the leading ACLU lawyer in the lawsuit challenging the constitutionality of Amendment 2.

▲

In 1973, when Suzanne Goldberg was nine years old, she decided to play Little League baseball in her hometown of White Plains, New York. Goldberg's decision to participate in what had until then been an activity reserved only for local boys received the full support of her father—a corporate lawyer whose clients happened to include the founders of *Ms.* magazine—and her mother, a committed feminist who was a regular participant in consciousness-raising groups in Westchester County. The experience of being a Little League "gender pioneer" was a formative event for Goldberg, making her aware at an early age both of the existence of discrimination and of the possibility of confronting and overcoming it.

After attending Brown University, she matriculated at Harvard Law School. Goldberg, who did not feel an attraction to other women until about a year before she started her legal education, spent most of her time at Harvard closeted. At the end of her third year, she attended a student rally in favor of greater diversity at the law school. At that rally, the head of the gay law student organization invited other LGBT students in the audience to join him in the front of the crowd to show their support for diversity. Goldberg, along with several others, took this opportunity to come out publicly, to the boisterous applause of those present.

During the summer following her second year of law school, Goldberg spent a few weeks working for a corporate law firm in New York City. She enjoyed her brief time with the firm, but the experience confirmed that her passion did not lie in representing the interests of wealthy corporations. After her term at the law firm ended, Goldberg spent the rest of the summer working at the ACLU's Reproductive Freedom Project, primarily helping to challenge the policies of industrial employers that prohibited women, but not men, from working in lead-exposed sites.

After she graduated in 1990, Goldberg clerked for a justice on the New Jersey Supreme Court and then received a fellowship to work for Lambda. Two years after that, the gay rights organization hired her outright. One of her first cases as a Lambda attorney involved a legal challenge to an employer's reduction of maximum lifetime health benefits for employees with AIDS from $1 million to $5,000. (The employer did not reduce benefits for any other medical condition.) Another of Goldberg's early Lambda cases involved the denial by immigration officials of an orphan visa petition brought by a gay man who was hoping to adopt a child in another country and bring him back to the United States. The New York district office of the Immigration and Naturalization Service (INS) denied the petition on the ground that the gay applicant was intending to parent the child with his domestic partner. Goldberg appealed the case to the INS commissioner, emphasizing in her legal papers that her client fulfilled all of the visa requirements and that the statute did not grant the agency the authority to deny the petition simply because the child would have more than one functional parent. It was still relatively rare, in the early 1990s, for a gay man in an open relationship with another man to try to adopt a child. Somewhat to Goldberg's surprise, the commissioner stuck to the wording of the law, overruling the district office and ordering that the visa be issued.

Goldberg had been working for Lambda for fifteen months when she was tapped by the organization to be its lead lawyer in the lawsuit challenging the constitutionality of Amendment 2. The other Lambda attorneys, all of whom had greater experience than Goldberg, had a full load of cases, with little time to spare. Mary Newcombe, who was Lambda's lawyer in Los Angeles, and who in 1991 had successfully challenged an anti–gay rights initiative approved by voters in Riverside, California, was leaving the organization to go into private practice.[4] That left the twenty-eight-year-old Goldberg as the logical choice to take on the state of Colorado on Lambda's behalf.

## The Law

When Goldberg arrived in Colorado a few days after the 1992 election, she encountered an LGBT community that felt under siege. This was hardly surprising given that a majority of the state's voters had approved a law that denied LGBT people the type of legal protection against discrimination that everyone else in the state remained eligible to receive. In the years leading up to Amendment 2, LGBT rights proponents had used the democratic process in Aspen, Boulder, and Denver to convince elected officials to enact ordinances proscribing sexual orientation discrimination. Now the people of Colorado had approved a constitutional amendment that not only repealed those laws but also prohibited the enactment of similar laws in the future.

Goldberg knew that it had taken the LGBT community in South Florida many years to recover from the wounds inflicted by Anita Bryant's nasty campaign to repeal Dade County's antidiscrimination law in the late 1970s. Goldberg believed that, as a movement lawyer, she had a responsibility to help the LGBT community in Colorado work through the difficult and painful issues associated with the passage of Amendment 2. In the weeks following the election, therefore, she took it upon herself to speak at several community forums throughout the state.

At these well-attended events, Goldberg reminded her audiences that the election was only the first skirmish in what was likely to be a long and protracted fight over whether Amendment 2 would become law. She also provided a historical perspective by explaining how courts in the past had come to the aid of minorities, in particular blacks in the South, who were the victims of majoritarian oppression. While not minimizing the seriousness of Amendment 2, Goldberg sought to empower her audiences by giving them a sense of what a constitutional challenge to the new law might be able to achieve.

▲

From the early days of the lawsuit, it became Coles's responsibility to help the plaintiffs' lawyers frame the constitutional issues in the case. As Coles saw it, the fundamental constitutional problem with Amendment 2 was not so much that it deprived the legislature of the authority to enact antidiscrimination laws but that it did so selectively by rendering one group (and no others) ineligible to receive the protections provided by such laws. Amendment 2, in other words, was constitutionally flawed because it placed restrictions on the ability of an identifiable group to participate in the political process without doing the same for any other group.

When we think about the Supreme Court's civil rights cases from the 1950s and 1960s, we tend to focus primarily on the equality cases, especially *Brown v. Board of Education.* The Court during that era, however, issued as many civil rights opinions grounded in the First Amendment as in the Equal Protection Clause. Most of the First Amendment cases involved efforts by southern states to silence and harass blacks by limiting the organizational and political efforts of groups such as the NAACP.[5] As Coles reread those cases, it dawned on him that the Supreme Court, after it decided *Brown,* protected blacks primarily by making sure that they were not *excluded* from the political process. The cases helped Coles focus on what would become a crucial point in the litigation over Amendment 2, namely, that the Constitution does not guarantee groups that their participation in the political process will allow them to reach specific objectives; instead, it protects their ability to participate equally in that process.

▲

While Coles was helping to frame the constitutional arguments in the case from his base in San Francisco, Goldberg was in Colorado, helping Dubofsky and the other plaintiffs' lawyers prepare for a preliminary injunction hearing in which the plaintiffs would ask a state court judge to temporarily stop the implementation of the new law in advance of a full challenge of its constitutionality. There was not much time to get ready for the hearing, which was scheduled for January 11, 1993, four days before Amendment 2 was to take effect. The judge assigned to the case was H. Jeffrey Bayless, a former chief deputy district attorney in Denver. Bayless, who had a reputation around the courthouse for being politically conservative, grew up in Galesburg, Illinois, served in the army reserves during the Vietnam War, and earned his law degree from the University of Denver.

The most powerful witness at the preliminary injunction hearing was police officer Angela Romero, who broke down in tears as she told the story of how she had been treated by others in her department once the word spread that she was a lesbian. Romero's testimony gave the court a sense of the pain and humiliation caused by anti-gay discrimination. In addition, a clinical psychologist testified about how being a member of a stigmatized minority causes stress for many LGBT people, a problem that would be compounded if Amendment 2 became law. And a heterosexual University of Colorado professor, who had been pushing his employer to adopt a sexual orientation non-discrimination policy, testified how such a policy would be voided by the new law.

After two days of presenting this type of testimony, the plaintiffs rested their case. The state then called several witnesses, including a former member of the Colorado Civil Rights Commission who testified that legal protections based on sexual orientation were different from protections on the basis of race, sex, and disability because the traits that defined the latter categories were more easily identifiable. The state also called some of the Amendment's leading supporters, who claimed that voters had not approved it because they were prejudiced against LGBT people but because they objected to giving special rights to any group.

The preliminary injunction hearing ended at 5:25 p.m. on January 14, a little less than seven hours before Amendment 2 was to become law. A clearly annoyed Judge Bayless stated that he could not render a decision in such an important case in so little time. He therefore issued a temporary restraining order, delaying the implementation of the Amendment until 5:00 p.m. the following day.

On the following afternoon at 4:00 p.m. the lawsuit's participants congregated again in Judge Bayless's courtroom, anxiously awaiting his ruling. Shortly after he entered the room, he started reading his decision, beginning with a summary of the testimony and arguments presented by each side. It took Bayless an excruciating thirty minutes to do this, during which he gave no indication of how he might rule. When he finally got to the crucial issue for purposes of whether to issue a preliminary injunction, namely, whether he believed that the plaintiffs had a reasonable probability of eventually prevailing on the merits of the case, he answered that question in the affirmative. Relying on a 1984 Supreme Court decision in which the high court held that it was impermissible for government officials to make decisions based on the likely prejudicial response of some citizens, Bayless concluded that Amendment 2 was constitutionally vulnerable because it seemed to endorse, and give effect to, private biases.[6] As a result, he ordered, a few minutes before the 5:00 p.m. deadline, that the state not enforce Amendment 2 until explicitly permitted to do so by the courts.

Once the judge left the courtroom, LGBT rights supporters cheered and exchanged hugs, while a few shed tears. The plaintiffs' lawyers knew perfectly well that this was only the first round of what was likely to be a long and drawn-out legal battle. Nonetheless, the victory was a sweet one, coming as it did literally minutes before the Amendment was scheduled to become effective.

▲

The state immediately appealed Judge Bayless's issuance of the preliminary injunction to the Colorado Supreme Court. Coles was one of several lawyers who worked on the plaintiffs' brief submitted to that court. He also thought it was important for the court to receive an amicus brief that would address *exclusively* the one claim that Coles thought was the strongest, namely, the one related to the right to participate equally in the political process. The opportunity for such an amicus brief presented itself when the Colorado Bar Association decided to file a brief in support of the plaintiffs.

During the following months, Coles had many conversations about the constitutional implications of the case with Stephen Bomse, a friend and a partner in the San Francisco law firm of Heller Ehrman, who was recruited by the bar association to be the main author of its brief. Those discussions led Bomse to write a brief that reads like a mini-treatise on why and how the Constitution protects the right of citizens to participate equally in the political process.

The brief begins by making the point that the Founders were deeply committed to the principle of majoritarian rule. At the same time they realized that, in order to avoid a tyranny of the majority, the nation's constitutional framework had to protect the ability of relatively small groups to be heard and to have some impact on government policies. Thus the Founders understood that meaningful pluralism was impossible to achieve unless a multiplicity of social groups were provided with the opportunity to participate equally in the political process.

The brief pointed out to the Colorado court that the U.S. Supreme Court had protected the right to participate equally in the political process through several lines of cases. The first was a group of cases in which the Court had struck down laws that limited the right to vote to those who met certain qualifying criteria (such as the paying of a poll tax or the owning of property).[7] In a second line of cases, the Court rejected "reapportionment" schemes instituted by states that gave more weight to some voters (such as those in rural areas) than others.[8] As the bar association's brief put it, the constitutional value that was ultimately at issue in those cases "was participatory *effectiveness*, i.e., the right to have one's vote count the same as the votes of others."

Citizens can be denied an equal opportunity to participate in the political process not only through an outright denial of the right to vote (as in the first line of cases) or through the dilution of their votes (as in the second line of cases) but also through a restructuring of governmental decision making in ways that make it significantly less likely that certain groups will be able to attain their goals through the political process. The Court had addressed this last way of limiting participation in the political process through a third line of cases that began in 1967 with *Reitman v. Mulkey*. In *Reitman*, the Court struck down a constitutional provision approved by California voters that prohibited the government from denying property owners the opportunity to refuse to sell or rent to whomever they chose. In doing so, the Court concluded that the measure was essentially aimed at codifying into the state constitution a right to discriminate on the basis of race.[9]

Two years after *Reitman*, the Supreme Court in *Hunter v. Erikson* struck down an amendment to the Akron, Ohio, city charter which required that voters approve ordinances aimed at addressing housing discrimination. The most important principle arising from *Hunter* is found in a concurring opinion written by Justice John Marshall Harlan II. In that opinion, Harlan distinguished between laws that affect the legislative process by imposing general requirements on everyone and laws that make it more difficult for *particular groups* to achieve their political goals. Provisions that fall under the former category pass constitutional muster even if they lead to the repeal of laws that are intended to protect certain groups like racial minorities. In contrast, provisions that fall under the latter category (such as the Akron measure) are improper because, rather than being based on neutral principles that apply to everyone, they burden identifiable groups of citizens.[10]

It is a sure sign of a legal brief's effectiveness when its structure and arguments are reflected in the court's eventual opinion. If one places the Colorado Bar Association's amicus brief next to the Colorado Supreme Court's first opinion in the Amendment 2 litigation—the court would issue a second opinion the following year after the completion of a trial in the case—one finds several sections of the former directly reflected in the latter. The court's opinion, like the brief, focused entirely on what the former referred to as the "core democratic value" of equal participation in the political process. In doing so, the opinion discussed the same three lines of Supreme Court cases elaborated on in the brief. And perhaps most crucially of all, the court embraced the brief's rejection of the state's position that the precedential value of *Reitman* and its progeny was limited to cases involving the restructuring of governmental decision making that negatively impacted racial minorities.[11]

In the end, the court concluded that it was proper for the trial court to have issued the preliminary injunction because it was likely that Amendment 2 infringed on the fundamental right to participate equally in the political process. The court noted that rather than removing antidiscrimination issues as a whole from the traditional legislative process (which would have been a neutral way of restructuring governmental decision making in a manner that applied equally to all groups), Amendment 2 impermissibly altered that process by burdening only one group. Amendment 2, the court reasoned, was constitutionally suspect because, under its strictures, sexual minorities were the only group that would have to amend the state constitution in order to seek the protection afforded by antidiscrimination laws.

▲

The legal victory before the Colorado Supreme Court was a complete one. The court not only affirmed the issuance of the injunction, but it also issued a comprehensive opinion that carefully delineated the nature of the fundamental right to participate equally in the political process, the existence of which now required the state to establish a compelling interest that justified the enactment of Amendment 2 into law.[12]

During the 1980s and early 1990s, the LGBT legal rights movement frequently attempted to convince courts that laws which made distinctions on the basis of sexual orientation were constitutionally suspect under the Equal Protection Clause. This effort to persuade courts to treat LGBT people as a "suspect class" was largely unsuccessful. (Although the term suggests otherwise, when courts conclude that a group constitutes a "suspect class," that is a good thing for those who seek to challenge a law on equality grounds because the designation requires courts to strictly scrutinize whether that law's differential treatment is justified.) One of the reasons for this failure was that many courts came to understand the U.S. Supreme Court's conclusion in *Bowers v. Hardwick* that it was constitutional for the state to criminalize same-sex sodomy as precluding a finding that LGBT people were, as a class, entitled to heightened judicial protection.

Some courts also contended that LGBT litigants had to show that sexual orientation is an immutable characteristic in order to qualify as a suspect class. It is not clear that parties seeking a suspect class designation should be required to show immutability—differential treatment based on religious affiliation, for example, triggers heightened scrutiny under the Equal Protection Clause even though religious belief is obviously not an immutable trait. The ACLU and Lambda consistently took the position in LGBT rights cases that immutability was not a required component of the suspect class analysis. Nonetheless, some courts concluded that sexual orientation was a choice and that, as a result, LGBT litigants were not entitled to heightened judicial scrutiny of governmental actions that treated individuals differently because of their sexual orientation.[13]

The Colorado Supreme Court, by concluding that Amendment 2 implicated the fundamental right to participate equally in the political process, provided the plaintiffs with what they hoped to achieve in the early stages of the litigation, that is, a ruling that placed the burden on the government to defend the Amendment's constitutionality. This burden could be satisfied only if Colorado established that there was a compelling state interest that supported the passage of Amendment 2 and that the law was narrowly tailored to achieve that interest. It is difficult for the government to meet such a high burden, which is why the Colorado Supreme Court's opinion so elated the plaintiffs and their attorneys.

For some of the lawyers, that elation faded in the weeks following the court's ruling as Dubofsky, the plaintiffs' lead attorney, made controversial strategic choices. For example, Dubofsky decided that the plaintiffs would try to establish what so many LGBT litigants had failed to show in the preceding decade—that sexual orientation is a suspect classification for purposes of the Equal Protection Clause. To Coles, Dubofsky's decision made little sense because the Colorado Supreme Court had already ordered that heightened scrutiny be applied in assessing the constitutionality of Amendment 2. Even if Judge Bayless could be persuaded that LGBT people constituted a suspect class, that would only provide the plaintiffs with what they were already entitled to as a result of the higher court's ruling.

Dubofsky made another controversial strategic choice when she decided that the plaintiffs would ask Judge Bayless to rule that LGBT people constituted a suspect class through a full-blown trial rather than through motions and affidavits. Even though trials can be effective vehicles for telling stories about the discrimination that LGBT people frequently face in America, they can also be messy, especially when they address complicated issues such as whether sexual orientation is immutable and whether LGBT people are sufficiently powerless to qualify for suspect class designation. Although Coles mentioned to Dubofsky several times during their telephone conversations that he had serious reservations about going through a trial in the case, it was Goldberg, who was physically present in Colorado for most of 1993, who spent the most time attempting to convince Dubofsky to reconsider her decision to seek a trial.

As a lawyer for a national gay rights organization, Goldberg believed it important that she keep the interests of LGBT people across the country in mind as the *Romer v. Evans* litigation proceeded. Goldberg was particularly troubled about making a civil rights claim on behalf of LGBT plaintiffs that depended on a finding that sexual orientation is an immutable characteristic. The question of immutability was an exceedingly complicated one, not only as a matter of biology and genetics but also politically. There was then (as there is today) little consensus among experts on whether sexual orientation is immutable, or on whether it can be explained primarily by "nature" or "nurture." As Goldberg saw it, the basic civil rights of LGBT people should not depend on the answer to those complicated (and perhaps unanswerable) questions. Furthermore, Goldberg worried that by making immutability an issue at a trial, the plaintiffs risked removing the spotlight from the state's justifications for Amendment 2 and placing it directly on LGBT people by asking the following questions: Why are LGBT people different? How do they become that way? Can they change if they want to?

Dubofsky, however, believed that both the courts and the public were likely to be more suspicious of a law that denied antidiscrimination protection to LGBT people if they were persuaded by witnesses testifying in open court that homosexuality was not a choice. And, as the lead lawyer, she had the final say on issues of strategy.

▲

The government argued throughout the litigation that one of the reasons why Amendment 2 passed constitutional muster was because it did nothing more than reflect the moral views of Colorado citizens. If the people of Colorado, the state contended, believed that homosexuality was morally wrong, they were entitled to approve laws that reflected that view.

To support this position, Colorado solicitor general Timothy Tymkovich and his staff enlisted several conservative academics who shared the state's position on the proper role of morality in questions of governance. One of those academics was Professor Robert George, a legal and moral philosopher at Princeton University. George had recently published a book titled *Making Men Moral* in which he argued that it was proper for the government to use laws to encourage individuals to behave in moral ways.[14]

Lawyers in civil cases are allowed to "depose" their opponents' witnesses prior to trial, that is, to ask questions under oath, the answers to which are transcribed. This permits attorneys to learn what the other side's witnesses will testify to in court. Dubofsky assigned to Goldberg the responsibility of deposing George.

Going into the deposition, Goldberg's primary aim was to test just how far Professor George was willing to go to defend his view that it was proper for the government to enact laws in order to enforce a particular understanding of sexual morality. Early on in the deposition, the professor made it clear that he believed that homosexuality is immoral. When Goldberg asked why he thought that was the case, George provided the following answer:

> I believe that the wrong that is inherent in [homosexual acts has] to do with introducing a kid of disintegrity into the person, so that such acts share what I believe to be a crucial element of masturbatory sex which has to do with the alienation of the person, considered as a conscious subject, from the person's body and the instrumentalization of the body in the service of a conscious self which is now considered as something separate.

Although the answer was wrapped in dense, philosophical language, what George was essentially saying was that LGBT people, regardless of personal circumstances, engage in sex for no reason other than to experience physical pleasure and that this instrumental use of the body and its sexual functions alienates people from their true selves.

Goldberg then proceeded to explore how far George's views on sexual morality would take him. The only type of sex that passed George's moral standards was procreative sex within the institution of marriage. According to George, all other forms of sex, including sex between unmarried people, sex with the aid of contraception (regardless of marital status), and masturbation, were immoral and harmful.

Under Goldberg's questioning, George also revealed that he thought it was proper for landlords, for example, to refuse to rent to LGBT people who intended to engage in sexual conduct in the leased premises. George further opined that landlords should be free to refuse to rent to straight people who intended to use contraceptives. The professor added that it would be proper for landlords to make the necessary inquiries of prospective tenants to determine the nature of their sexual proclivities. The bottom line, George stated with conviction, was that he believed that the people of Colorado would be better off if its citizens were free to discriminate against all sexually active LGBT people, as well as against all heterosexuals who engaged in sex outside of marriage. As the professor put it, "it would be a better state of affairs if [the people of Colorado] had the freedom to act on their moral judgments about the immorality of those acts than if they didn't have that freedom."

By the end of the deposition, Goldberg had achieved her goal of establishing just how radical George's views were. Carried to their logical conclusion, George's political and moral views would allow employers and landlords to discriminate in ways that most Americans, even many who did not support LGBT rights positions, would find highly problematic.

▲

The trial in *Romer* began on October 12, 1993, and lasted for nine days. There was no jury, which meant that Judge Bayless would be responsible both for making factual findings and for reaching legal conclusions.

Although much of the trial would get bogged down on the question of whether sexual orientation was a suspect classification, the more important legal issue, given the Colorado Supreme Court's ruling, was whether the state had a compelling interest that justified the voters' approval of Amendment 2. The state's lawyers, led by Solicitor General Tymkovich, argued that the government had limited resources to fight discrimination, and that as a result, it had a compelling interest in providing protection only to groups, like racial minorities, who were economically and educationally disadvantaged as a result of discrimination. Part of the state's trial strategy, in other words, was to show that LGBT people were not victims of real discrimination.

With this goal in mind, the government called Wilford Perkins, the chairman of Colorado for Family Values, to testify. Although it was not clear why Perkins, the owner of a car dealership in Colorado Springs, was particularly qualified to testify about the status of LGBT individuals in our society, he nonetheless proceeded to assure the court that discrimination on the basis of sexual orientation was not a problem worth addressing. The state also called Ignacio Rodriguez, a former member of the Colorado Civil Rights Commission, who testified about the kind of employment discrimination that many Latinos in Colorado faced. Gay people, he contended, did not confront similar obstacles. Rodriguez also testified that adding sexual orientation to civil rights statutes was a "drastic departure" from the historical aims of civil rights laws because "it would weaken and dilute those civil rights protections that had been earned by minorities ... over the years."

There was, of course, an internal inconsistency in the positions taken by the state's witnesses. On the one hand, they argued that discrimination against gay people was not a problem and therefore did not have to be addressed through the enactment of laws. At the same time, they contended that fighting sexual orientation discrimination would take such a large share of the state's limited antidiscrimination resources that it would leave other (more deserving) groups largely unprotected.

In order to undermine the state's contention that Amendment 2 was needed because gay rights laws, in effect, diluted the state's antidiscrimination efforts, the plaintiffs' lawyers called to the stand Denver mayor Wellington Webb, as well as a compliance officer charged with enforcing Denver's antidiscrimination ordinance. Both witnesses testified that enforcing the section of the city ordinance that covered sexual orientation did not detract in any way from the enforcement of the other sections aimed at protecting other groups. In the same vein, the director of the Wisconsin Civil Rights Bureau testified that the relatively small number of cases of alleged sexual orientation discrimination investigated by her office under the state's gay rights law did not impair the enforcement of other civil rights laws.

To counter the charge that laws which prohibited discrimination on the basis of sexual orientation conferred "special rights" on LGBT people, the plaintiffs called Jerome Culp, a Duke University law professor, and Joseph Hicks, the executive director of the Southern Christian Leadership Conference of Greater Los Angeles, to testify. Both men explained how antidiscrimination laws prohibit employers and landlords, for example, from taking into account traits that are irrelevant to decisions related to jobs and housing. Laws that prohibit discrimination on the basis of sexual orientation are, in this way, no different from laws that prohibit discrimination on the basis of race or sex. All three types of laws protect *all* individuals because everyone has a sexual orientation, a race, and a sex.

Another argument made by Colorado's lawyers during the trial was that the state had a compelling interest in protecting the integrity of its political processes. In the context of the case, this argument essentially amounted to the contention that LGBT rights advocates had somehow hijacked the political process by convincing elected officials that sexual orientation discrimination was a problem that had to be addressed through civil rights laws. To establish this point, the state called Tony Marco to the stand. Marco, one of the leaders of Colorado for Family Values, testified that Amendment 2 "was necessary because it was obvious that the aggression of gay militants through the legislature was not going to cease." He added that "the only way to insure that this kind of activity would stop [was] through passage of [a] constitutional amendment."

It is not particularly surprising that conservative activists like Marco believed that LGBT rights advocates had somehow impermissibly influenced the political process. It is common for those who object to particular pieces of legislation, such as sexual orientation antidiscrimination laws, to assert that the legislature was unduly influenced by "special interest" groups. What is more surprising is that the state of Colorado was willing to defend the constitutionality of Amendment 2 on the basis of the heated rhetoric—"special rights" and "gay militants"—used by conservative social activists in the political arena. The state's lawyers seemed to have been operating under the assumption that the same arguments that had succeeded in the political arena would also prevail in the courtroom. Those lawyers, however, would soon learn that what works in the former is not necessarily effective in the latter.

▲

While Colorado's lawyers tried to establish that there was a compelling state interest which justified the voters' approval of Amendment 2, the plaintiffs' attorneys attempted to show that sexual orientation should be deemed a suspect classification for purposes of the Equal Protection Clause. As part of that effort, the plaintiffs called on George Chauncey, a historian at the University of Chicago, who testified to the long history of discrimination that lesbians and gay men in the United States have endured. The plaintiffs' lawyers then moved to the task of showing that LGBT people were a sufficiently powerless group in political matters, relying primarily on the testimony of Kenneth Sherrill, a political science professor at Hunter College. Sherrill testified about the difficulties that LGBT people, as a small segment of the population, have had in attaining crucial and long-standing goals such as the enactment of federal antidiscrimination protection and the repeal of the military's ban on gay service members.

As Coles and Goldberg suspected, however, it was the attempt to resolve the question of whether sexual orientation is an immutable characteristic that presented the greatest difficulty. The first complication arose from the fact that there was no established way of determining who is gay or lesbian. Should a married man who has sex with other men but does not identify as gay nonetheless be deemed gay? What about a woman who is sexually attracted to other women but never acts on that attraction and instead has sex only with men? It was possible, in other words, to define sexual orientation in terms of sexual behavior, sexual attraction, or self-identification, and there was little consensus among the experts as to which criterion should prevail.

Much of the immutability-related testimony presented by the plaintiffs addressed a handful of scientific studies suggesting that gay people may share genetic or physiological traits. For example one of the plaintiffs' witnesses on the immutability issue was Dean Hamer, a molecular biologist and leading scientist at the National Cancer Institute. Hamer had looked at the DNA of gay brothers, finding that about two-thirds of the set of brothers whom he studied shared the same DNA in a particular region of the X chromosome.[15] Although Hamer's study showed a closer genetic link to sexual orientation than previous studies, he conceded on the stand that it did not establish that sexual orientation can be explained solely as a result of genetics.

In the end, the scientific testimony, which took about seven hours (out of a total of thirty-five hours of testimony for the entire trial), raised about as many questions as it answered. The issue of what makes people gay (or straight) seemed too complicated, and the state of knowledge too limited, for anyone listening to the testimony to be able to reach any firm conclusions on the subject.

▲

The Amendment 2 trial ended in late October 1993. When Judge Bayless issued a decision six weeks later, he refused to opine on "whether homosexuality is inborn, a product of 'nature,' or a choice based on life experiences, a product of 'nurture.'" That question, he concluded after reviewing the conflicting and disputed evidence, is one "for another forum." The judge, however, then proceeded to reject *all* of the claims made by Colorado that it had a compelling interest which justified the voters' approval of Amendment 2, including the notion that having to provide antidiscrimination protection to lesbians, gay men, and bisexuals made it less likely that the state would be able to effectively deter discrimination against racial minorities and women. As a result, Bayless ordered that the temporary injunction, which he had issued eleven months earlier, be replaced with a permanent injunction barring the state from enforcing Amendment 2.[16]

In the end, Coles and Goldberg were proven correct in their belief that there had been no need to fully litigate at a trial the issue of whether LGBT people constituted a suspect class. The issue turned out to be an unnecessary distraction, although one that fortunately (for the plaintiffs) did not change the outcome of the case. In late 1994, the Colorado Supreme Court affirmed Judge Bayless's ruling.[17] The state's defeat, in its own courts, was now complete. The only option remaining to Colorado and its lawyers was to appeal the case to the U.S. Supreme Court.

▲

As we have seen, Coles played a crucial role in framing and articulating the political process argument that won in the Colorado courts. It was that issue that would serve as the basis for Colorado's request that the nation's highest court hear the case. The state argued in its certiorari petition to the U.S. Supreme Court that the Colorado court's ruling that Amendment 2 violated the fundamental right to participate equally in the political process was untenable because it meant that the federal Constitution was violated every time a state amended its constitution to remove an issue from the traditional political process. The state noted that its constitution, for example, placed term limits on certain elected officials and restricted government funding of abortions. Both provisions, the state contended, were now suspect under the federal Constitution because the state constitution removed both issues from the traditional political process.

As Coles had realized early on in the litigation, the constitutional problem with Amendment 2 was not that it excluded *issues* from the political process. Instead, as the plaintiffs argued in their brief to the U.S. Supreme Court urging it not to take the case, Amendment 2 was unconstitutional because it excluded an *identifiable group* from the political process. Although it was true that the Colorado constitution made it more difficult for opponents of term limits and for proponents of state-funded abortions to have their views enacted into law, those constitutional provisions, unlike Amendment 2, did not "fence out" a distinct group of individuals.

Despite the best efforts by the plaintiffs' lawyers to try to convince the Supreme Court not to grant the appeal, however, the Court announced in February 1995, that it would review the case.

▲

Up until now, all of the plaintiffs' lawyers, under Coles's constitutional guidance, had been committed to defending the legal position that Amendment 2 violated the fundamental right to participate equally in the political process. But Coles suspected that if the Supreme Court was going to rule on behalf of the plaintiffs, it would not do so based on the violation of a fundamental right. For several decades, particularly since *Roe v. Wade*, the Court seemed loath to decide cases on fundamental rights grounds. The fundamental right at issue in *Romer* was quite different from the one recognized in *Roe* and other privacy cases (such as those involving restrictions on the availability of contraceptives). The privacy cases had addressed what is known as the substantive component of the Due Process Clause, one that protects certain personal and intimate decisions from governmental interference. In contrast, the right recognized by the Colorado Supreme Court in *Romer* had its roots in a line of equal protection cases (guaranteeing, for example, the equal weighing of votes) that were, by the 1990s, considerably less controversial.

Nonetheless, the recognition of a fundamental right, whether under the Equal Protection Clause as it relates to the political process or under the Due Process Clause as it relates to considerations of privacy and personal autonomy, has important implications for questions of democratic theory. The application of such a right requires that courts begin their analysis with a presumption that laws approved by a majority of voters or legislators are constitutionally impermissible. Although the courts' exercise of this countermajoritarian function has been an important part of our democracy since the early days of the republic, such an exercise nonetheless makes judges vulnerable to the criticism of judicial activism, that is, of placing their personal views on controversial issues ahead of those of the majority of citizens.

Even though there were hurdles to winning the case on the basis of the existence of a fundamental right, Coles had believed that such a claim provided the plaintiffs with their best chance of succeeding before the Colorado courts. It was considerably less likely, however, that the U.S. Supreme Court would hold that the case implicated a fundamental right. Coles surmised, therefore, that if the Supreme Court was going to affirm the Colorado's court ruling, it would do so by applying the "rational basis" test. (Courts applying this test, which is highly deferential to the government, will uphold a law that makes distinctions among classes of individuals if there is any legitimate governmental interest at stake and if the means chosen by the government are rationally related to the achievement of that interest.) This would permit the Court to strike down Amendment 2 without having to explicitly hold that there was a fundamental right to participate equally in the political process.

Since Coles believed that the plaintiffs' chances of prevailing before the nation's highest court depended on the strength of their rational basis argument, he asked the American Bar Association to submit an amicus brief that explained in considerable detail why Amendment 2 was constitutionally impermissible even under the rational basis test. Coles hoped that the Court, which would undoubtedly be inundated with amicus briefs from many different organizations supporting one or the other side in the case, would pay particular attention to a brief filed by the largest and most prestigious organization of lawyers in the country, one that had never before filed a brief with the Supreme Court on behalf of gay litigants in an LGBT rights case.

In its brief, the ABA told the Court that Amendment 2 lacked a rational basis because the sole purpose of the law was to disadvantage lesbians, gay men, and bisexuals. The Amendment, the brief argued, was nothing more than an effort to codify into law the fact that a majority of Coloradans apparently disapproved of homosexuality. While individuals are free to believe what they want about homosexuality, it is a different matter altogether when prevailing attitudes about gay citizens are used to justify a law that denies them (and no others) the opportunity to seek legal protection from discrimination.

▲

When Goldberg was in law school at Harvard, her favorite professor was Laurence Tribe, one of the leading constitutional scholars in the country. A year before Goldberg started law school, Tribe had unsuccessfully argued before the Supreme Court in *Bowers v. Hardwick* that it was unconstitutional for states to criminalize consensual sodomy. Tribe's loss in that case was a devastating one to him, both because he was personally committed to LGBT rights and because he was sure that the Court had misinterpreted the Constitution.

Goldberg got to know Tribe well when she was in law school, and the two remained in touch after she started working for Lambda. Goldberg knew that Tribe was eager to approach the Supreme Court again in another important LGBT rights case. When the Supreme Court agreed to hear *Romer*, Goldberg contacted Tribe to discuss the possibility of his writing an amicus brief on behalf of the plaintiffs. It so happened that Tribe, who had been following the case closely, had developed a fascinating and novel theory as to why Amendment 2 violated the Equal Protection Clause. As Tribe saw it, Amendment 2 constituted a per se violation of that provision because it literally denied the protection afforded by an entire category of laws (relating to discrimination) to a particular class of individuals. Tribe believed that the highly unusual character of Amendment 2 required the Court to dispense with its usual analytical approach under the Equal Protection Clause of assessing the state's justifications for a law. Instead, Tribe contended that Amendment 2 was antithetical to the very idea of constitutional equality because, by its own terms, it rendered an entire class of people ineligible to receive a distinct form of legal protection.

Goldberg worked closely with Tribe in the writing of an amicus brief in which he elaborated on these points, going over more than a dozen drafts written by her former professor, helping him to sharpen and crystallize his arguments. In the end, the Tribe brief (which was also signed by several other leading constitutional scholars), was not only a masterful and creative exegesis on equal protection jurisprudence but it also ended up having a profound influence on the Court's understanding of the case.

In addition to working with Tribe on his brief, Goldberg was responsible for coordinating the writing of several other amici briefs. This effort was an important part of her responsibility as a movement lawyer because it involved reaching out to other organizations, most of which were not LGBT rights groups, in order to build a broad coalition of support for the plaintiffs' case. In the end, many organizations, including the NAACP Legal Defense Fund, the American Association of Mental Retardation, the General Assembly of the Presbyterian Church, the American Psychological Association, and the National Education Association, committed themselves to writing briefs. The support that the plaintiffs received from this broad coalition of groups sent a strong message to the Court and to the public that the *Romer* litigation was about more than just LGBT rights. The case ultimately was about the basic rights of all Americans not to be excluded from the democratic process based on their membership in any particular group.

▲

The oral arguments before the Supreme Court in *Romer* took place on October 10, 1995. From the moment the Court had granted review in the case several months earlier, there was speculation in LGBT rights legal circles that it might be best if the argument on behalf of the plaintiffs was conducted by a lawyer who, unlike Dubofsky, had experience appearing before the Supreme Court. The plaintiffs, however, following the advice of Colorado LGBT rights activists, refused to consider having anyone else argue the case. They had stuck with Dubofsky through thick and thin for the previous three years, and they would allow her to see the case through until the end.

On the day of the argument, Timothy Tymkovich, Colorado's solicitor general, got up first. A few seconds into his opening statement, Justice Anthony Kennedy, sounding slightly annoyed, asked Colorado's lawyer whether there had ever been a law that, like Amendment 2, seemed to create a classification for its own sake. "I've never seen a case like this," Kennedy complained. In response, Tymkovich pointed to an amendment to the California constitution—upheld by the Supreme Court in 1971—that prohibited public agencies from building low-income housing without the approval of local voters.[18] That provision, Tymkovich argued, also involved a classification of an identifiable group, namely low-income persons. That was true, Kennedy replied, but the Court in that case had been able to weigh the government's objective of controlling the growth of low-cost housing in certain areas against the interests of low-income people. When it came to Amendment 2, Kennedy suggested, there seemed to be no reason for the law other than to deny one group the protections of the law.

This initial exchange led to an extended colloquy between the Court and Colorado's lawyer over the precise scope of Amendment 2. While Tymkovich argued that the provision only barred explicit antidiscrimination laws based on sexual orientation, several of the Justices were not so sure. Justice Sandra Day O'Connor, for example, suggested that the expansive language of Amendment 2—which covered not only statutes, regulations, and ordinances, but also governmental policies—might not permit legal redress if a public library were to deny the opportunity to borrow books based on a patron's sexual orientation. Tymkovich seemed unsure about how to answer that question, leading conservative Justice Antonin Scalia to lend a helping hand. Scalia asked whether it was not in fact the case that the hypothetical library policy could be struck down through a law of general applicability that prohibited government officials from acting arbitrarily. But Scalia's point only led to the further question of whether laws of general applicability, that is, laws that did not single out any particular category (such as race, sex, or sexual orientation) for explicit protection, were indeed beyond the scope of Amendment 2. Justice John Paul Stevens, for example, asked whether the common law principle that prohibits innkeepers from turning guests away—which was presumably a rule of general applicability because it protected any potential patron regardless of membership in any particular class or group—could be interpreted, after Amendment 2, in a way that afforded protection to gay people. Tymkovich did not have an answer to that either, except to repeat the state's long-held position that what Amendment 2 sought to do was to prevent gay people from receiving "special preferences" under the law.

None of the Justices at any point during Tymkovich's argument (or Dubofsky's, for that matter) seemed interested in discussing the fundamental right to participate equally in the political process, the ground on which the Colorado Supreme Court had decided the case. Instead, the Justices were interested in whether the Amendment could survive rational basis review. Justice Stevens at one point explicitly asked Tymkovich what the rational basis was for Amendment 2. The state's lawyer responded by saying that it was reasonable for the people of Colorado to have decided that they wanted certain issues addressed, not by local or state legislators, but by themselves directly through the constitutional amendment process. It was entirely permissible, Tymkovich argued, for the people of Colorado to decide which issues were to be decided by what level of government.

Tymkovich's assertion led Justice Kennedy to remind him that the plaintiffs were not arguing that they were entitled to have antidiscrimination laws that provided protection on the basis of sexual discrimination considered at any particular level of government. Instead, the plaintiffs were making an *equality* argument, that is, they were contending that a majority of Colorado voters had targeted gay people by relegating them (and no others) to seeking antidiscrimination protection at one level of governmental decision making while all other groups were free to seek that protection at whatever level of government decision making they chose. This was a crucial point in the plaintiffs' argument against the constitutionality of Amendment 2 for which Tymkovich did not have much of a response.

Dubofsky did not fare much better during her thirty minutes at the podium. Justice Scalia specifically asked her whether she was asking the Court to overrule *Bowers v. Hardwick*, the case in which the Court had held that states could criminalize same-sex sodomy. When Dubofsky said that she was not, Scalia then asked the following: if the state can constitutionally criminalize sodomy, why could it also not take the lesser step of prohibiting "special preferences" for the group of people who engage in that conduct? When Dubofsky seemed unsure in her answer, it was the liberal Justice Stevens's turn to provide a helping hand by asking whether it was not in fact the case that Amendment 2 covered not only those who engaged in *conduct* that was proscribable by the state but also those who had a gay sexual *orientation* without engaging in sodomy. That was correct, a relieved Dubofsky answered, before adding that the measure would also apply to straight people who were perceived to be gay and who were discriminated against on that basis.

At the end of the one-hour argument, neither lawyer had been particularly effective in responding to the Justices' questions. As sometimes happens in arguments before the Supreme Court, the most salient points were made by the Justices themselves through the asking of questions in ways that answered earlier questions posed by other Justices who seemed to be on the other side of the issue.

▲

On the morning of May 20, 1996, eight months after the oral argument in *Romer*, Coles was in his office at the ACLU's New York headquarters, when a friend who worked in the ACLU's communications department came in to ask him a question about a minor issue. As Coles answered the query, he noticed that his friend seemed to be holding back a smile. After the brief conversation ended, the other man, before proceeding to leave Coles's office, said matter-of-factly: "Oh, by the way, we won *Romer v. Evans.* The vote was 6–3." After Coles got over his momentary shock at hearing such monumental news, he jumped out of his seat, grabbed his cheeky friend in a bear hug, and demanded all the details.

A few minutes later, Coles closed his office door and sat down to read a faxed copy of the Court's decision. Three sentences into the opinion, Coles became so moved by what he was reading that he had to momentarily stop. Justice Kennedy had opened the Court's ruling with the following language:

> One century ago, the first Justice Harlan [in his dissent in *Plessy v. Ferguson*] admonished this Court that the Constitution "neither knows nor tolerates classes among citizens." Unheeded then, those words now are understood to state a commitment to the law's neutrality where the rights of persons are at stake. The Equal Protection Clause enforces this principle and today requires us to hold invalid a provision of Colorado's Constitution.[19]

The fact that Kennedy had chosen to begin the opinion by citing Justice John Marshall Harlan's dissent in *Plessy* was imbued with a deep symbolic meaning that was immediately clear to Coles. The Court in *Plessy*, much to its later embarrassment, made it possible for segregation to remain firmly entrenched for decades by giving its constitutional stamp of approval to the notion of "separate but equal" racial policies. Among members of the *Plessy* Court, only Justice Harlan had had the moral courage and vision, thirty years after the end of the Civil War, to defend the principle of equality in the face of racist policies seemingly supported by a majority of Americans.

Exactly one hundred years later, Justice Kennedy, in his opening paragraph in *Romer*, was stating unequivocally that the Court would not make the same mistake twice. In deciding between the will of the majority and the basic right to equality of all citizens, the Court this time around would choose the latter. After he read the opinion's first three sentences, Coles knew that he had in his hands a momentous judicial ruling, one that for the first time held that LGBT people were entitled to the rights and opportunities of citizenship on an equal basis with everyone else. As Coles later wrote in a law review article, "I choked up when I read [the Court's opening words] because I never really believed I would read them in a U.S. Supreme Court opinion. The message could not have been clearer. To the Court, sexual orientation discrimination [was] the moral (if not the legal) equivalent of race and sex discrimination."[20]

▲

Justice Kennedy's opinion, which was joined by Justices Stephen Breyer, Ruth Bader Ginsburg, Sandra Day O'Connor, David Souter, and John Paul Stevens, flatly rejected the claim that supporters of Amendment 2 had been making for years both inside and outside courtrooms, that is, that the Amendment did nothing more than deny LGBT people special rights. Kennedy made clear that the case was not about special preferences; instead, it was about denying one group of citizens the "protections taken for granted by most people either because they already have them or do not need them."

The Amendment, Kennedy added, categorically disqualified lesbians and gay men from receiving the types of protection against discrimination provided to many groups under Colorado state and local law, including not only those—like racial minorities and women— that were entitled to receive heightened judicial protection under the Equal Protection Clause but also many others—such as members of the military and the disabled—that were not. The opinion held that Amendment 2 "fails, indeed defies" even the "conventional" and lenient rational basis standard of equal protection analysis. There were, Kennedy noted, two distinct reasons for that. First, he wrote, Amendment 2 was "unprecedented" in its scope and inconsistent with "our constitutional tradition"; identifying persons by a single trait, Amendment 2 denied them protection "across the board." Following the reasoning of Professor Tribe's amicus brief, Kennedy added that "[a] law declaring that in general it shall be more difficult for one group of citizens than for all others to seek aid from the government is itself a denial of equal protection of the laws in the most literal sense."

Second, Kennedy wrote, Amendment 2 failed to pass constitutional muster under the rational basis standard because there was no legitimate governmental interest that could possibly justify the imposition of such a broad denial of legal protections to only one group. Indeed, the classification was so disconnected from the purposes offered for it that the Court was compelled to conclude that only animus toward the targeted group could explain the law's adoption. In the end, Amendment 2 had to be struck down because it created a classification "for its own sake," which unacceptably rendered lesbians and gay men strangers to the state's laws.

Three Justices dissented from the Court's opinion: Justice Antonin Scalia (who wrote the dissenting opinion), Chief Justice William Rehnquist, and Justice Clarence Thomas. Justice Scalia's dissent was as long as it was angry. As far as he was concerned, Amendment 2 was nothing more than an effort by the "seemingly tolerant" people of Colorado to defend their mores against a "politically powerful minority." He therefore accused the Court of presumptuously disregarding the views of Colorado voters in matters related to homosexuality in order to impose on all Americans the views "favored by the elite class from which the members of this institution are selected."

For Scalia, the constitutionality of the Amendment was clear for two reasons. First, it prohibited the "special treatment of homosexuals, and nothing more." And second, the fact that Colorado could criminalize same-sex sodomy meant that it could also "deny special favor to those with a self-avowed tendency or desire to engage in the conduct." Scalia complained that the majority's categorization of Amendment 2 as being driven by animus was "so false as to be comical." As Scalia saw it, Amendment 2 was simply a reflection of the same type of moral disapproval apparent in laws that prohibit murder, polygamy, and cruelty to animals. He added that it was entirely reasonable for those who disapprove of homosexuality to amend the state constitution to counteract gay rights proponents who, because they "reside in disproportionate numbers in certain communities[,] . . . possess political power much greater than their numbers." In the last sentence of his blunt dissent, Scalia charged that the striking down of the Amendment was "an act, not of judicial judgment, but of political will."

▲

A few hours after the Court issued its opinion in *Romer,* Coles and Goldberg spoke before hundreds of LGBT people in the West Village of Manhattan, first at the Gay Community Center and then at a street rally in Sheridan Square, a few feet away from the Stonewall Inn, the birthplace of the modern LGBT rights movement in the United States. At these events, both lawyers were cheered as heroes by a community that was clearly appreciative of their efforts.

In many ways, *Romer* dealt with fairly abstract issues about the meaning of equal citizenship in a constitutional democracy. The case also raised the related question of what it means, quite literally, for the Constitution to guarantee the equal protection of the laws. Although most of the LGBT people celebrating the Court's opinion that night in New York and elsewhere around the country may not have fully understood the complex legal issues that had arisen during the course of the litigation, they all knew that the case could be boiled down to one simple but powerful concept: equality. When all was said and done, the Supreme Court, for the first time, had held that LGBT people, acting as citizens in our constitutional democracy, were equals and that the government had an obligation to treat them accordingly.

## The Impact

The success of *Romer v. Evans,* which at the time was the greatest judicial victory in the history of the American LGBT rights movement, came a decade after the movement's greatest judicial defeat in *Bowers v. Hardwick.* Interestingly, although *Hardwick* upheld the constitutionality of sodomy laws, that opinion had little impact on the *criminal* regulation of homosexuality. This was the case for two reasons. First, criminal prosecutions for consensual sodomy in private places were rare before the case and remained so after it. Second, in the years after the opinion was issued, several state appellate courts struck down sodomy laws on state constitutional grounds, while legislatures in several other states repealed sodomy statutes on their own. The move across the country toward the decriminalization of sodomy, which had been under way for several years before *Hardwick*, became even more pronounced after that opinion was issued.

*Hardwick* had a severe negative impact on LGBT rights, then, not in matters related to the criminal law, but in civil law issues instead. It is no exaggeration to state that *Hardwick* became a significant obstacle in almost every important civil LGBT rights case litigated in the decade between it and *Romer*. This was particularly true in cases, most of them employment related, where litigants challenged government policies that treated individuals differently because of their sexual orientation.

Several of these employment cases turned out to be particularly important because they raised the question of whether lesbians and gay men constitute a "suspect class" for purposes of equal protection, meaning whether courts should apply a rigorous form of judicial scrutiny when the government makes distinctions on the basis of sexual orientation. At first glance, it would seem that *Hardwick*, a right-to-privacy case that challenged a criminal law under the Due Process Clause, would not be relevant to cases that challenged employment-related decisions under the Equal Protection Clause. In the late 1980s and early 1990s, however, several appellate federal courts held that *Hardwick* prevented courts from subjecting government classifications that made distinctions on the basis of sexual orientation to a heightened form of judicial scrutiny.[21]

These courts reasoned as follows: If the state, under the Due Process Clause, can criminalize the conduct that (ostensibly) defines the class, then, the class should not be treated as one that is entitled to special constitutional protection under the Equal Protection Clause. Under this reasoning, the fact that the state could constitutionally criminalize same-sex sexual conduct meant that it could also treat in-dividuals who engage in that conduct less punitively by, for example, limiting their job opportunities. Or to put it somewhat differently, if the government could incarcerate individuals for engaging in sodomy, then it should also be able to deny them jobs.

LGBT rights lawyers, in the wake of *Hardwick*, responded to this type of reasoning in several different ways. One approach was to dis-tinguish between conduct and status. Even if the state could criminal-ize gay sex (the conduct), the argument went, that did not mean that it was free to use gay sexual orientation (the status) to make distinctions among individuals.

A second argument emphasized the differences between the Equal Protection Clause and the Due Process Clause. The notion that the due process decision in *Hardwick* dictated the outcome in equal pro-tection cases, the lawyers noted, overlooked the different role that historical considerations play in the proper interpretation of the two clauses. For a court to consider striking down a law under the Due Process Clause, it must decide that the right in question is deeply rooted in the nation's history and traditions. A court, on the other hand, will typically strike down legislation under the Equal Protection Clause if the group it disadvantages has historically been subjected to discrimination. There was no inconsistency, the LGBT rights lawyers argued, in concluding both that no historic right to privacy protected LGBT people (as determined by the *Hardwick* Court) and that there was a history of unfair discrimination against them.

Although LGBT rights lawyers were successful in convincing some lower courts that *Hardwick* should not prevent gay litigants from pre-vailing in cases that challenged governmental policies which treated individuals differently because of their sexual orientation, those ini-tial rulings were all later reversed by higher courts.[22] By the time the Supreme Court agreed to decide *Romer*, then, *Hardwick* had become a largely insurmountable obstacle confronting LGBT people seeking to challenge governmental policies that made distinctions on the basis of sexual orientation.

▲

Interestingly, Justice Kennedy's opinion in *Romer* never explicitly addressed *Hardwick*, an omission that was criticized not only by Justice Scalia in his dissent, but also by some legal commentators. In many ways, *Hardwick* was the big pink elephant in the *Romer* room that went unacknowledged by the majority opinion.

We do not know why Justice Kennedy chose not to address *Hardwick* in *Romer*, but his opinion nonetheless implicitly but significantly limited the scope of the sodomy ruling. The argument that had frequently prevailed in the years between the two opinions, and which Justice Scalia had embraced in his bitter dissent, namely, that the Constitution allowed the government broad discretion to treat lesbians and gay men differently because it had the authority to criminalize sodomy, did not pass muster in *Romer*. The Court made clear in *Romer* that the Equal Protection Clause prohibits the government from targeting lesbians and gay men and imposing on them legal disabilities that have no justification other than majoritarian disapproval. This meant that going forward the government's differential treatment of lesbians and gay men would have to be justified on grounds other than either a majoritarian disapproval of LGBT people or the state's authority to criminalize sodomy. This was a crucial doctrinal development because governments up until that point had primarily relied on one or both of those (now impermissible) justifications to defend themselves against LGBT litigants challenging the differential treatment of individuals based on sexual orientation.

Lower courts quickly got the message that government defendants after *Romer* could no longer deploy *Hardwick* as a means to derail equality claims raised by LGBT litigants. The earliest example of this shift is the opinion by the U.S. Court of Appeals for the Seventh Circuit in *Nabozny v. Podlesny*. The Seventh Circuit issued its ruling in *Nabozny* only a month after *Romer* was decided. The defendants in *Nabozny* had relied on *Hardwick* to argue that they should not be held liable for the harm inflicted on the gay student by his harassing peers. The appellate court rejected that argument, concluding that the sodomy case presented no obstacle to the claim that school officials had failed to protect the gay plaintiff from harassment because of his sexual orientation. As the court put it, "*Hardwick* will soon be eclipsed in the area of equal protection" by *Romer*.[23]

The following year, the U.S. Court of Appeals for the Sixth Circuit, also relying on *Romer*, allowed a lawsuit to proceed in which a woman argued that police officers wrongfully arrested her for drunk driving solely because they thought she was a lesbian. The defendants, in trying to get the case dismissed, relied on *Hardwick* to defend the proposition that "it is always constitutional to discriminate on the basis of sexual orientation."[24] In hindsight, it is nothing less than disturbing that the police officers in the case, through their lawyers, argued that *Hardwick* provided them with complete constitutional immunity in a case where it was alleged that they had arrested someone solely because she was perceived to be a lesbian. The fact that the defendants had the legal temerity to make such an argument is an illustration of the extent to which *Hardwick* was understood by many to justify a broad range of government-sponsored discrimination against LGBT people.

Although *Romer* should not have been needed in order to reject the police officers' rather preposterous claim, the Supreme Court's opinion nonetheless provided the Court of Appeals with the means of defending the proposition that the government cannot discriminate against members of a group simply because many in society dislike them. This may seem to us now like an obvious constitutional point, but it took the Supreme Court's opinion in *Romer* to get the lower federal courts to accept it in cases involving lesbians and gay men.

Indeed, one of the reasons why *Romer* is such an important case is because it led the Court for the first time to acknowledge that lesbians and gay men are vulnerable to laws enacted on the basis of animus. Proponents of Amendment 2, of course, never admitted that they were driven by animosity toward sexual minorities; instead, they cloaked their arguments in notions of morality. Rather than expressing animus against LGBT people, the proponents contended, the people of

Colorado approved Amendment 2 to express their moral disapproval of conduct that they found morally problematic. For the Court, however, it did not matter whether the animus was grounded in morality or in other factors. Instead, what was ultimately dispositive for the Court was that there was no possible justification for the Amendment other than an intent to harm a politically unpopular group.

*Romer*'s animus-related holding has proven helpful in cases where plaintiffs have challenged laws that uniquely burden LGBT people. An example of such a law was a statute enacted by the Oklahoma legislature in 2004 that prohibited state courts and agencies from recognizing adoption decrees issued to same-sex couples in other jurisdictions. The law was passed in response to efforts by same-sex couples, who had adopted Oklahoma-born children in other states, to have Oklahoma issue birth certificates for those children listing the names of both legal parents. A group of LGBT parents challenged the constitutionality of the law in federal court, raising several arguments, including one grounded in the Equal Protection Clause. The state defended its law in court by contending that it was needed in order to promote the formation of "traditional families" and to protect Oklahoma children from being chosen for adoption by same-sex couples across the country. The federal district court, however, struck down the law as unconstitutional under *Romer*, noting that the Oklahoma statute, like Amendment 2, deprived LGBT people of the ability to seek government assistance, which in this case related to obtaining legal recognition of already established parental rights, solely because of their sexual orientation. The court concluded, following the Supreme Court's reasoning in *Romer*, that the state's targeting of LGBT parents, purportedly in order to protect "traditional family environments," was nothing more than an effort to harm a politically unpopular group.[25]

*Romer* also played an important role in a constitutional challenge to a Kansas statute known as the "Romeo and Juliet" law. Under that statute, Kansas punished consensual sexual conduct between different-sex teenagers significantly less harshly than it did the same kind of conduct between same-sex teenagers. The young man who challenged the statute was sentenced to seventeen years of imprisonment for having consensual oral sex with an underage male teenager. Under the Romeo and Juliet law, he would have received a jail sentence of only a year if his sexual partner had been an underage female.

In defending its law, the state argued that the difference in punishment was justified by the need to promote traditional sexual mores. The Kansas Supreme Court, relying on *Romer* (and on *Lawrence v. Texas*), concluded that while it is not generally improper for the state to take notions of morality into account in enacting legislation, it is unconstitutional for the government to impose legal burdens on a distinct group solely on the basis of moral disapproval.[26]

Kansas also tried to justify its Romeo and Juliet law by arguing that it was rationally related to its legitimate interest in reducing sexually transmitted diseases in general and HIV in particular. But the state ran straight into *Romer* with that argument as well. The Kansas court pointed out that the state's position made no sense because the risk of HIV transmission in male/female vaginal or anal intercourse is much greater than the risk in male/male oral sex or any type of female/female sex. The lack of any discernable relationship between, on the one hand, the harsh consequences of the distinction between straight sex and gay sex codified in the statute and, on the other, the protection of public health, led the Kansas court to conclude, following the reasoning of *Romer,* that the distinction was inexplicable except as an expression of animus toward the targeted group. As a result, the Kansas court ordered that the state, when penalizing consensual sex between teenagers, treat same-sex sexual conduct in the same way that it treats different-sex sexual conduct.

The impact of *Romer* has been felt not only in cases that have challenged laws that explicitly treat lesbians and gay men differently than heterosexuals but also in ones involving more individualized decision making by government officials. In one instance, a federal court ordered that a teacher be reinstated as her school's volleyball coach after administrators removed her from that position because parents expressed displeasure with her being a lesbian. The administrators' decision, the court reasoned, violated the teacher's equal protection rights under *Romer* because it was based solely on the objections expressed by the parents to her sexual orientation.[27]

In another case, a federal district court was called upon to review the harassment and abuse of a gay police officer by his straight peers. The court first found that the officer's supervisors encouraged or allowed this type of conduct to take place. It then concluded, citing *Romer* as precedent, that the department violated the gay police officer's constitutional rights to equality because the actions of the officers and their supervisors was "motivated by irrational fear and prejudice towards homosexuals."[28]

It is clear that after *Romer*, government officials must provide reasons that go beyond mere dislike or disapproval of lesbians and gay men in justifying policies that place unequal burdens on LGBT people. This is a tremendously important legal development given that much, if not all, of the state-sponsored differential treatment of lesbians and gay men is grounded in dislike or disapproval of those with a same-sex sexual orientation.

▲

Not all LGBT litigants with seemingly compelling equality claims have succeeded in deploying *Romer* to their advantage. One area where *Romer* has failed to make a difference is in legal challenges to the military's "Don't Ask, Don't Tell" policy. Under that policy, thousands of gay service members have been discharged from the military solely because they have been open about their sexual orientation. The government has defended its policy primarily by arguing that permitting openly gay service members to serve alongside heterosexuals threatens military preparedness and unit cohesion. The contention, in effect, is that many heterosexual members of the armed forces will be made so uncomfortable by the mere presence of openly gay people in their units that they will become less effective warriors.

Many commentators, including former military officials, have argued that the presence of openly gay service members presents no threat to military preparedness or effectiveness. Aside from the merits of the government's justification for its exclusionary policy, it seems clear that it is treating gays differently than straights because some in the military do not like or approve of gay people. This is precisely the type of justification for the differential treatment of lesbians and gay men that the Court rejected in *Romer.*

*Romer* also proved insufficient in supporting a constitutional challenge to a Florida law that bans all lesbians and gay men from adopting children. In rejecting the challenge, the U.S. Court of Appeals for the Eleventh Circuit concluded that the adoption ban was not based on animus toward LGBT people. Instead, it accepted the government's argument that it was rational for the legislature to believe that children are better served when they are raised by married heterosexual couples.[29]

There is a closer link, however, between the Florida adoption ban and Colorado's Amendment 2 than the Court of Appeals was willing to recognize. The Florida legislature enacted the adoption ban one day after Anita Bryant and her supporters—at the end of an ugly and divisive political campaign—convinced voters to repeal Dade County's gay rights law. That repeal effort was a direct predecessor to the efforts by conservative activists in Colorado to overturn gay rights laws by alleging, among other things, that LGBT people constituted a threat to children. The same type of hostile rhetoric used to garner support for Amendment 2 in Colorado in the 1990s was deployed by social conservatives in their efforts in Florida during the 1970s both to repeal the Dade County gay rights ordinance and to enact the adoption ban.

It seems clear that the adoption ban was intended to send a majoritarian message of disapproval of lesbians and gay men. As a Florida legislator who supported the ban argued in 1977, the law was meant to say to gay people, "We're really tired of you. We wish you would go back into the closet." The same legislator added that "the problem in Florida is that homosexuals are surfacing to such an extent that they're beginning to aggravate the ordinary folks, who have rights of their own."[30]

Amendment 2 and the Florida adoption ban share similarities that go beyond the rhetoric adopted by their respective supporters. Both laws also target only one group of citizens for differential treatment. In fact, under Florida law, there is no other class of individuals, including convicted murderers and child molesters, that is categorically banned from adopting. This singling out of one group only for the imposition of a significant legal disability is precisely the type of targeted burdening that troubled the Court in *Romer*.

Some judges have contended that *Romer* requires that both the federal government's military policy and Florida's adoption ban be struck down as unconstitutional. Unfortunately for LGBT litigants, those judges have been in the minority, limited as such to writing dissenting opinions. As frequently happens in civil rights cases, however, dissenting opinions, with the passage of time, eventually become the law. There is perhaps no better example of this phenomenon than Justice Harlan's dissent in *Plessy v. Ferguson*, the case that upheld the constitutionality of the "separate but equal" doctrine. It is likely that future courts will reconsider the constitutionality of laws that, like the military and adoption bans, categorically exclude LGBT people from government-provided jobs, benefits, and opportunities.

▲

The impact of *Romer* has not been limited to issues of legal doctrine. The case has also had a significant political impact by ending the efforts of social conservatives to use the ballot box to repeal existing gay rights laws and to prevent the enactment of future ones. In the five years before *Romer*, conservative activists succeeded in placing fifty-three initiatives on voting ballots addressing the question of whether lesbians and gay men should be afforded antidiscrimination protection. Thirty-seven (or 70 percent) of those measures were approved by voters. In contrast, only one such measure has been placed on a ballot since *Romer* was decided. That was in 2004, when opponents of gay rights in Maine unsuccessfully attempted to have voters repeal a sexual orientation antidiscrimination law enacted by the state legislature.

The disappearance from the American political landscape of anti–gay rights initiatives aimed at denying antidiscrimination protection to LGBT people cannot be explained solely by the doctrinal impact of *Romer*. Clearly, after *Romer*, it is impermissible for a state to amend its constitution in a way that deprives state and local governments of the authority to provide discrimination protection to LGBT people. At least one court has suggested, however, that *Romer* does not prohibit an initiative at the local level (i.e., one that does not implicate state constitutional or statutory law) that limits the ability of one municipal government to enact an antidiscrimination ordinance on the basis of sexual orientation.[31] In addition, the LGBT rights movement has never taken the position that a simple referendum to repeal a specific gay rights law—such as the one called for by gay rights opponents in Maine in 2004—is unconstitutional.

Conservative activists could have continued, even after *Romer*, to use the ballot box to repeal specific gay rights laws (at the state or local level) or to approve local initiatives prohibiting individual municipalities from enacting gay rights laws in the future. The fact that LGBT rights opponents chose not do so demonstrates how that case rendered suspect all ballot initiatives that seek to deny discrimination protection to lesbians and gay men. The Court's strong denunciation of efforts to target lesbians and gay men in Colorado for differential treatment under the auspices of Amendment 2 made it politically impossible for social conservatives to continue to argue that their ballot initiatives had nothing to do with a raw dislike of LGBT people.

The fact that *Romer* put an end to efforts by social conservatives to undo or prevent the passage of gay rights laws allowed the LGBT rights movement to put its energies and resources elsewhere. In the twenty years preceding *Romer*, the movement was forced to use a large proportion of its resources to try to derail, defeat, or strike down ballot measures that sought to deprive LGBT people of discrimination protection. These efforts required the movement to play defense, that is, they required it to focus on preserving legislative victories that had already been achieved rather than to focus on expanding the rights and opportunities of LGBT individuals. *Romer* permitted the movement to go back on offense by seeking to have additional states and municipalities enact antidiscrimination provisions protecting LGBT people.

The progress in this area has been nothing short of remarkable: since *Romer* was decided, twelve states (including, in 2007, Colorado) and dozens of municipalities have enacted laws prohibiting discrimination on the basis of sexual orientation.[32]

Matthew Coles had argued early on in the Amendment 2 litigation that what was ultimately at issue in the case was whether conservative activists were going to succeed in pushing thousands of LGBT people in Colorado back into the closet. Once sexual minorities become vulnerable to losing their jobs and their housing solely because they are open about their sexual orientation, and once they realize that the law offers them no hope of relief, then the incentive to deny that orientation becomes significantly stronger. There can be little doubt that if the Court had upheld Amendment 2, several additional states, especially those in which social conservatives have significant political clout, would have adopted similar legal provisions. The approval of such laws would have contributed in powerful ways to rendering invisible the lives of countless LGBT people across the country. Instead, the Court, through its decision in *Romer*, made the opposite result possible by allowing more LGBT people to be more open about who they are without fearing that such openness will lead to their being rendered second-class citizens who are strangers to the law.

# CHAPTER 4

# *Marriage*

## The Facts

Genora Dancel and Ninia Baehr were born in Honolulu in 1960, four days and five miles apart—but they did not meet and fall in love until thirty years later.

Dancel, the daughter of a Filipino father and a native Hawaiian mother, had known since she was a young girl that she was a lesbian. While playing "house" with other girls in elementary school, she liked to pretend that they were her wives and that she worked outside the home in order to pay the family's bills. Before meeting Baehr, Dancel had dated women on and off but had not met a soul mate with whom she wanted to spend the rest of her life. Like Dancel, most of the women she dated were closeted; unlike her, they eventually wanted to marry a man and have children. By the time Dancel turned thirty, she was beginning to think that she might never find a partner, and that instead her life would mostly revolve around her career as a television equipment engineer and her passion for motorcycles.

Baehr is the daughter of two schoolteachers. When young, her parents moved constantly, seeking new experiences and adventures; before she reached the age of fifteen, Baehr had lived in Hawaii, Tennessee, American Samoa, and Norway. After graduating from Montana

State University with a degree in sociology in 1981, Baehr moved to New York, where she pursued a master's degree in women's history at Sarah Lawrence College. Her graduate school thesis, eventually published as a book, explored the history of abortion politics in the United States.[1]

In the early 1980s, Baehr served as the regional director of the National Abortion Rights Action League in Albany, New York. Later that decade, she moved to New York City, where she became vice president of Eve's Garden, the first mail-order and sex-shop business aimed exclusively at the sexual needs of women. (The company was founded in 1974 by Dell Williams, a feminist activist, after she was humiliated by department store employees when she attempted to buy her first vibrator.) After working at Eve's Garden for several years, Baehr left to become acting director of New York Women Against Rape, an advocacy group that worked on behalf of the just and humane treatment of sexual assault victims.

In 1990, after breaking up with her lesbian partner of several years, Baehr decided to return to Hawaii, where she had lived as a young girl, to become a doctor. Her initial plan was to live with her mother, C.J., take some premed classes, and then attend medical school. Shortly after arriving back in Honolulu, Baehr met Dancel and her plans changed.

▲

It was C.J. who first suggested that Baehr might want to meet Dancel. During the 1980s and early 1990s, C.J. and Dancel worked together at KHET, Honolulu's PBS television. One day when C.J. pointed her coworker out to her daughter at the station's parking lot, Baehr thought that Dancel, with her light brown skin and dark hair, was just about the most beautiful woman she had ever seen.

The following day, Baehr visited the station and asked to see Dancel. Some of the male equipment engineers with whom Dancel worked snickered when the receptionist's voice squawked through the station's intercom system announcing that C.J.'s daughter—who was widely known around the office to be a lesbian—was in the lobby looking for Dancel. After a brief and somewhat awkward conversation, Baehr asked Dancel whether she wanted to have coffee sometime, and Dancel said yes. When Dancel went back to work, she had a hard time getting Baehr out of her mind. She had been struck by how pretty Baehr was, and, although she had initially been embarrassed by her showing up unannounced at the station, the more Dancel thought about it, the more she liked Baehr's take-charge attitude. Dancel was also impressed by how comfortable Baehr seemed in her own skin, including with the fact that she was a lesbian.

That night Dancel called the Baehr household, ostensibly to ask C.J. a question, but really to speak to her daughter. When the latter answered the phone, the two women giggled nervously, before settling into a long conversation telling each other about their lives and interests. Their first date lasted more than eight hours. It started with drinks and dinner, and ended with a long walk along the beautiful Mana Kai beach on Maui. After that, the two women became inseparable, spending most of their free time together. At the time, Dancel had full-time jobs at two different television stations, but she juggled her schedule as best she could to maximize her time with Baehr.

In early September 1990, three months after they first met, Dancel was scheduled to go on a work-related trip to the mainland that would take her to San Diego and Washington, D.C. A few days before leaving Hawaii, Dancel realized she loved and wanted to marry Baehr. Dancel knew she could not marry another woman in the United States but thought perhaps they could get married if they traveled to another country. Truth be told, however, she did not spend too much time pondering the practical aspects of marriage. As Dancel saw it, she was deeply in love and wanted to spend the rest of her life with Baehr. Marriage simply seemed like the natural next step in their relationship.

While on the business trip, Dancel called Baehr from California and asked if she would marry her. Although Baehr was surprised by Dancel's proposal, she was also deeply in love and said yes. Later that week, while in Washington, an ecstatic Dancel bought Baehr an engagement ring, and after she returned to Hawaii, Baehr moved in with her.

A few weeks later, Dancel had to rush her partner to the emergency room after she developed a painful ear infection. Baehr did not have health insurance, and the couple was forced to reach deep into their savings to pay for the medical treatment. The trip to the hospital led Dancel to look into adding Baehr to her employer-provided health insurance. She soon learned that such a benefit was available only to the spouses and children of employees. She also tried to buy a life insurance policy naming Baehr as the beneficiary but was told by the insurance agent that the beneficiary could only be someone related to her by blood, marriage, or adoption.

Neither Dancel nor Baehr knew much about their legal rights as a same-sex couple. Seeking assistance, Baehr called the Gay Community Center in Honolulu and spoke to an organizer by the name of Bill Woods. Baehr asked Woods whether it was possible under Hawaiian law for same-sex couples to register as domestic partners. Baehr, who was living in New York in 1989 when the city began providing limited benefits to same-sex domestic partners, thought that there might be similar benefits available under Hawaiian law. Woods informed her that domestic partnerships were not recognized under Hawaiian law. He mentioned, however, that he was planning a lawsuit challenging the state's failure to recognize same-sex marriages and asked Baehr to speak with Dancel about the possibility of the couple joining the suit as plaintiffs.

Learning that the law did not protect or even recognize their relationship in any way left the lesbian couple feeling vulnerable. If, for example, they were unable to add Baehr to Dancel's health insurance and the former got sick again, the couple might not be able to pay the medical bills. And, if either of them was hospitalized, the other might be denied the right to visit or to help make decisions about the treatment. Despite these concerns, they did not call Woods back, mostly because they felt like they had little time to dedicate to a lawsuit. Dancel was juggling full-time jobs at two different television stations and Baehr—who had by then stopped taking premed classes after deciding that medical school was not right for her—was doing the same with two part-time jobs, one of which was at the newly created Women's Center in Honolulu.

It was Woods who, two months later, forced the issue when he unexpectedly called Dancel at work one day to tell her that two other same-sex couples were planning on taking the first step in bringing a lawsuit by going to the Department of Health the following morning to request marriage licenses. Woods asked whether Dancel and Baehr would be interested in coming along. He added that he needed an answer in less than an hour because he wanted to notify the press about what was going to happen the following day.

After hanging up with Woods, Dancel immediately called Baehr, who joined her a few minutes later at the television station. Baehr told Dancel to make the decision because, unlike Baehr, Dancel was still largely closeted and had more to lose by joining the lawsuit. Dancel had not told either her family or most of her coworkers that she was a lesbian. She was also not someone who was used to being in the spotlight; she was not an activist and had never participated in any organized LGBT-related event in her life.

Dancel's biggest worry about the suit was the publicity and loss of privacy that would inevitably accompany it. She was also concerned about what the lawsuit might mean for her job security since there had been rumors of possible layoffs at one of the television stations where she worked. As the only woman in all-male departments, she already felt vulnerable to being fired. How would her employers react if it became widely known that Dancel was not only a lesbian, but that she was also a plaintiff in a gay rights case? At the same time, she wanted to marry Baehr because she was deeply in love. In addition, it rankled her that she had been unable to put Baehr on her health insurance. Most of the people with whom Dancel worked were married, and all of them had the opportunity to add their spouses to their health insurance. It was simply unfair that she was not allowed to do the same for her partner.

After weighing these issues, Dancel reached for Baehr's hand and told her that she wanted to join the lawsuit. Baehr asked several times whether she was sure. Dancel answered yes each time. To this day, Baehr describes Dancel's decision to become a plaintiff in the marriage lawsuit as the most courageous choice she has ever witnessed.

The following day, December 17, 1990, at 9:00 a.m., Dancel and Baehr joined Woods and two other couples at the offices of the Department of Health's vital records division in downtown Honolulu.[2] Since Woods had alerted the media about what would occur that day, several reporters and television cameras were waiting for the couples when they arrived. Dancel had tried to mask her identity by wearing her hair differently and putting on dark sunglasses, but she soon realized that such efforts were futile because several of the cameramen recognized her from her work for television stations around town. It seemed to Dancel that they were extremely surprised to see her in this role as a lesbian activist.

When the three same-sex couples went to the clerk's window and asked for marriage licenses, the person behind the glass, unsure of what was happening, said that she would give them the licenses. But a supervisor soon appeared and informed them that the department was unable to issue the licenses because they were same-sex couples. The whole interaction took less than ten minutes.

▲

Of the three couples who sued the state of Hawaii over the denial of marriage licenses, Dancel and Baehr seemed most willing to serve as the lawsuit's public face. In the months and years that followed the filing of the suit, the couple gave dozens of media interviews and speeches while participating in countless parades, rallies, and fundraising events.

This public role came easily to Baehr, who had been an activist for most of her adult life. In contrast, managing the public aspects of the case initially proved difficult for Dancel. When they first appeared together at public events as plaintiffs in the case, Dancel stayed largely in the background while Baehr did most of the speaking. But Dancel gradually became more comfortable in her role as an LGBT rights advocate, eventually becoming a surprisingly confident and effective public speaker and activist.

By 1993, both women were exhausted from the constant media attention and the endless public appearances. Believing that their relationship needed a respite from the pressures of the case, they decided to move to Baltimore, where Dancel hoped to attend medical school. Although they still occasionally spoke at LGBT political and fundraising events throughout the country, they were able to enjoy a modicum of privacy and anonymity in Baltimore that had become impossible to maintain in Honolulu.

By late 1996, at around the time the case finally went to trial, their relationship began showing some strain. Dancel does not think the pressures of the lawsuit led to problems with their relationship. From her perspective, it was more a breakdown in communication and a case of going separate ways in matters of the heart. Baehr is not so sure. Looking back, she believes that the demands of the high-profile lawsuit proved too much for the couple to withstand. It did not help matters that they had known each other for only six months when they joined the lawsuit.

In any event, by early 1997, more than six and a half years after they first met, Dancel and Baehr had gone their separate ways. Even though their relationship ended, their decision to bring a lawsuit challenging Hawaii's marriage law started a process that eventually led to an extended national conversation about LGBT people and their place in our society. It also eventually resulted in the legal recognition of tens of thousands of same-sex relationships across the country.

## The Lawyers

When Evan Wolfson was a third-year student at Harvard Law School in the early 1980s, he decided to write a thesis on why it was unconstitutional to deny same-sex couples the opportunity to marry. The topic seemed so outlandish at the time that none of the politically progressive professors at the law school were interested in helping with the project. In the end, he was able to write the thesis only because David Westfall, a family law professor who was not particularly political, agreed to supervise it. Years later, after Wolfson had become the leading LGBT rights lawyer in the country advocating on behalf of same-sex marriage, Westfall commented that it was refreshing to see a former student apply in the real world what he had learned in law school.

Wolfson, who was born in 1957 and is the son of a doctor and a homemaker, grew up in Squirrel Hill, the primarily Jewish neighborhood in Pittsburgh where Bill Rubenstein also spent his time as a child. Wolfson attended Yale University and was active in the Yale Political Union, the nation's oldest student debating society. As a member of the Union's Liberal Party, he regularly debated right-wing students, many of whom later became important figures in the conservative movement.[3] After he graduated from college in 1978, Wolfson spent two years as a Peace Corps volunteer in the African nation of Togo, teaching English in a small village. Interestingly, while in Togo, Wolfson was able to do something he had not allowed himself to do back in the United States: have sexual relationships with men.

Although Wolfson had known since an early age that he was gay, he did not act on his sexual orientation until he got to Togo. As an undergraduate at Yale, he had had two serious relationships with women but no intimate relationships with men. One of the reasons why Wolfson waited so long to act on his attraction to other men was that he was internally conflicted about his homosexuality, not entirely sure that it was appropriate or acceptable.

In Togo, Wolfson met men who were interested in homosexual sex but who did not consider themselves to be gay. After a while, he realized that his Togolese sexual partners did not think of themselves as gay because they had not been exposed to either the norms or the vocabulary that help to constitute a gay identity. This meant, Wolfson became sure, that they would proceed to marry women, have children, and generally lead seemingly impeccable heterosexual lives despite their sexual attraction to men. Wolfson realized that unlike these men, he had the option, after he returned to the United States, of exploring his homosexuality from within a culture that to some extent tolerated gay people.

After returning from Africa in 1980, Wolfson enrolled at Harvard Law School determined to be open about his sexuality and to experience romance and sex through an ongoing relationship with another man. As Bill Rubenstein did several years later, Wolfson used his first year of law school not only to acquaint himself with fundamental principles of legal doctrine but also to learn how to be a gay man. Like Rubenstein, Wolfson received that education in the gay bars and cafés of Boston and Cambridge.

During his third year, Wolfson read *Christianity, Social Tolerance, and Homosexuality*, a book written by the historian John Boswell that had a deep influence on him. In the book, Boswell shows how social responses to homosexuality have varied considerably through the centuries, ranging from acceptance to toleration to disapproval to persecution. Before reading the book, Wolfson had viewed homosexuality largely from a "micro" perspective, that is, from the vantage point of how he and other gay people could best lead their lives given their sexual orientation. Boswell's book led Wolfson to think about homosexuality more broadly by seeing it through the prism of politics and history. In particular, the fact that different societies had understood and valued homosexuality differently made Wolfson think seriously for the first time about the possibility of improving the lives of LGBT people through political and social change. Indeed, it was after reading Boswell's book that Wolfson decided to write his law school thesis on the question of how the institution of marriage could be reformed in ways that accounted for the existence of LGBT people.

After law school, Wolfson took a position with the Brooklyn district attorney's office, where he worked for five years. During that time, Wolfson also volunteered for Lambda, helping to write several of the organization's most important amicus briefs of the 1980s, including the one that the group filed in Michael Hardwick's challenge to Georgia's sodomy law. In 1989, after a short stint working for Bill Walsh, the independent counsel charged with investigating the Reagan administration's role in the Iran-Contra scandal, Wolfson took a position as a staff attorney at Lambda. At first, he worked primarily on AIDS discrimination cases, representing, for example, a pharmacist who was dismissed by a hospital after administrators learned that he was HIV positive. A settlement was eventually reached in the case, one that required the hospital to reinstate and compensate the pharmacist. Wolfson also represented Tom Bradley, a gay and HIV-positive Long Island high school teacher who needed a bone marrow transplant from his twin brother. (Bradley's brother was also a gay teacher in the same school district.) With Wolfson's help, Bradley successfully sued his employer's health insurance provider after it refused to pay for the procedure. Unfortunately, during the delay caused by the company's initial refusal to pay, Bradley developed an infection that made him ineligible for the treatment, and a few months later, he died of HIV-related complications.

In the years that followed, Wolfson worked on many other cases on behalf of Lambda. However, it was the Hawaii same-sex marriage case that catapulted him into the national spotlight and made him, during the 1990s, the country's leading legal advocate on behalf of marriage equality.

▲

Unlike the other lawyers profiled in this book, Daniel Foley is neither gay, nor was he—at least prior to the Hawaii same-sex marriage case—a gay rights lawyer. Like Wolfson, Foley joined the Peace Corps after college and was sent to Africa, arriving in Lesotho, a small country in southern Africa, in 1969. While there Foley worked as an agricultural extension worker helping farmers organize and run credit unions and cooperatives. But after a few months, he was expelled from the country due to political unrest.

After returning to the United States, Foley enrolled at the University of San Francisco School of Law. A few years after getting his law degree in 1974, he found himself once again abroad, this time in the Micronesian islands of the North Pacific. He lived in Micronesia for eight years, serving as legal counsel to legislatures and advising

Micronesians—who were then under the administrative control of the U.S. government—in their quest for greater self-rule.

His experience living on Pacific islands led him to decide, upon returning to the United States, to settle down in Hawaii rather than on the mainland. Shortly after he arrived in Hawaii, the local ACLU affiliate hired him to serve as its first legal director. One of Foley's most important cases during that time was a successful class-action lawsuit, brought in conjunction with the ACLU's National Prison Project, that required the state to implement a series of reforms in the operation of its then overcrowded and unsanitary prisons. Foley also successfully sued, on First Amendment grounds, the island of Maui after a local official canceled the Miss Gay Molokai Pageant out of concern that holding the parade would somehow contribute to the transmission of HIV.

In 1987, Foley left the ACLU to start his own legal practice, one that permitted him to litigate a broad range of cases from postconviction appeals to First Amendment claims to environmental lawsuits. By 1990, he was widely regarded throughout the state as a smart and effective legal advocate for progressive causes. It was for this reason that the Hawaiian same-sex couples turned to him for help in challenging the state's marriage law.

Foley spent most of the 1990s advocating for marriage equality. As he did, he frequently thought of his Uncle Joe, one of his father's two brothers, who was born in the late 1920s. Of the three siblings, Joe seemed to have the most going for him. He was a handsome man, six foot two, who when young loved books and ideas and was full of dreams about what he wanted to do when he became an adult. Unfortunately, Joe never did much with his life, in part because he lived at a time when LGBT people like him had little choice but to lead a forced life inside the closet. For a brief period during the early 1950s, he worked for a Hollywood studio escorting young starlets around town. But Joe never seemed able to hold a job for very long, and he was never able to pursue any type of career or profession, as he had dreamed of doing when he was young.

Although Joe had a male partner of almost twenty years, he never acknowledged to anyone in his family that he was gay. Indeed, Foley wonders whether his uncle's severe alcoholism—he died in 1982 of liver failure—was worsened by his despair at having to lead a closeted life.

It is likely that Joe would have had the opportunity to lead a more open and dignified life as a gay man if he had been born a few decades later. It is also likely that if Joe had lived long enough to witness Foley's advocacy on behalf of LGBT people, he would have been proud of his straight nephew.

## The Law

American laws criminalizing same-sex sexual conduct (as well as other forms of nonreproductive sex) can be traced back to the colonial era. In contrast, it was not until the mid-1990s that some states, responding to the Hawaiian same-sex marriage litigation, for the first time explicitly prohibited the recognition of same-sex relationships as marital. Indeed, when states in the early nineteenth century first enacted marriage eligibility statutes, there was no intent to exclude same-sex relationships. Although those laws (usually implicitly) required prospective spouses to be of different sexes, there was no real concept back then of a homosexual identity, much less a social awareness of the existence of ongoing and intimate same-sex relationships. As a result, it cannot be said that the early marriage statutes were aimed at condemning or discouraging same-sex relationships in the same way, for example, that anti-miscegenation laws enacted in the nineteenth century specifically and purposefully targeted interracial relationships.

The first time that the American legal system was confronted directly with the existence of same-sex relationships was in the 1970s, when plaintiffs brought a handful of cases challenging the constitutionality of denying same-sex couples the opportunity to marry. None of these challenges succeeded, primarily because the courts that entertained them concluded that the plaintiffs were seeking a remedy that was impossible to provide. As the courts saw it, the *very definition* of marriage required that two legal spouses be of different sexes. Whatever it was that the plaintiffs were seeking through their lawsuits, it could not be "marriage" as that term was defined legally and culturally. In one case from 1974, for example, a Washington appellate court reasoned that the gay male plaintiffs were denied the opportunity to marry not because of their sex, but "because of the recognized definition of that relationship as one which may be entered into only by two persons who are members of the opposite sex." For its part, a Kentucky appellate court concluded that two lesbians were "prevented from marrying, not by the statutes of Kentucky or the refusal of the [county clerk] to issue them a license, but rather by their own incapability of entering into a marriage as that term is defined."[4]

Although the reasoning of these early same-sex marriage opinions was tautological—not going much beyond the proposition that same-sex couples were not constitutionally entitled to marry because they were not eligible to marry—the cases clearly reflected a long-standing understanding of marriage which required that spouses be of different sexes. From this perspective, allowing same-sex couples to marry necessarily entailed a fundamental alteration of the very institution to which they sought admission.

This type of reasoning spilled over into the 1980s. In a Pennsylvania case from that decade, a man sought a divorce from what he asserted was a common-law marriage to another man. The court rejected the claim that a legally valid marriage between the two men had ever existed. The court also warned that to side with the plaintiff would usurp the legislature's prerogatives and would therefore constitute an "abuse [of] our judicial power." And in a federal case in which an American citizen sought to have his relationship with his Australian male partner recognized for purposes of immigration law, the court deemed a marriage between two persons of the same sex as "impossible" and "unthinkable."[5]

These early marriage cases were brought by private attorneys who had little connection to, and received little assistance from, national organizations such as the ACLU. In fact, by the time Evan Wolfson started working as a staff attorney for Lambda in 1989, LGBT rights leaders had refused to pursue marriage as a civil rights goal.

There were two main reasons for the unwillingness to pursue same-sex marriage either through constitutional challenges or legislative changes. The first reason was pragmatic. The lawsuits challenging marriage discrimination had gone nowhere in the courts, offering little hope of future success. At the same time, there was absolutely no prospect of being able to persuade elected officials that marriage laws should be amended in order to recognize same-sex relationships. From the perspective of most of the movement's lawyers and activists, therefore, it made more strategic sense to proceed in a piecemeal fashion by asking courts to recognize same-sex relationships in certain limited contexts, while lobbying legislative bodies (mostly at the local level) to first adopt and then expand domestic partnership laws.

A second objection to pursuing same-sex marriage was ideological rather than pragmatic. Some movement lawyers and activists argued that the institution of marriage was a hopelessly patriarchal one whose existence had not only been used for centuries to oppress women but had also served to justify discrimination against cohabiting couples and single people. Instead of seeking to expand a deeply flawed institution, those who raised ideological objections to pursuing marriage as a civil rights goal argued that the movement should focus on reducing the importance of marriage in our society by striving for alternative ways to legally recognize relationships, such as through domestic partnerships laws.

In the late 1980s and early 1990s, during meetings of the Gay Rights Litigators' Roundtable, lawyers like Nan Hunter and Matthew Coles of the ACLU articulated the pragmatic reasons for not pursuing same-sex marriage. The attorney who most strongly objected to the pursuit of marriage on ideological grounds was Lambda's Paula Ettelbrick. In contrast, it was Wolfson who consistently argued at these meetings that the LGBT rights movement should make marriage its top priority.

Wolfson saw the pursuit of marriage equality as the most effective way of changing the very terms of the debate over LGBT issues in this country. By pursuing same-sex marriage, the movement for the first time would have the opportunity to put the relationships and families of LGBT people front and center and, by doing so, show that there was much more to them than just an amalgamation of sexual acts and desires. Wolfson believed that the movement had for too long focused primarily on issues such as employment and housing discrimination that, while clearly important, did not address the fundamental question of what it meant to be gay or lesbian. It was possible, in other words, to advocate against discrimination in those areas without grappling directly with the personal and intimate relationships of LGBT people. Through the process of formally demanding admission into the institution of marriage, LGBT individuals would show the American public that they were capable of entering and remaining in committed relationships—and, for those who had them, of raising children—in ways that did not differ fundamentally from the experiences of heterosexuals.

From the beginning of his tenure with Lambda in 1989, then, Wolfson tried to persuade others in the organization to prioritize the issue of same-sex marriage. Although he had some allies on that front—most prominently Tom Stoddard, who was Lambda's executive director from 1986 until 1992—Wolfson's views were very much in the minority within the organization. Indeed, when Baehr, Dancel, and the other two couples contacted Lambda at the end of 1990 seeking its assistance with their planned challenge to the Hawaii marriage law, Wolfson was unable to convince his colleagues that the organization should take the case.

Similarly, the ACLU refused to represent the couples in their pursuit of marriage through the courts. In fact, the couples, after being turned away from the Department of Health, had proceeded that same day to the offices of the ACLU's Hawaii affiliate, only to be told by the group's representatives that they should consider seeking domestic partnership benefits through the legislature rather than marriage through the courts.

After being turned down by Lambda and the ACLU, the couples, following the suggestion of Bill Woods, met with civil rights lawyer

Daniel Foley in the offices of his small law firm in Honolulu. Although Foley, several years earlier, had advised Woods when the activist was seeking to persuade the Honolulu city council to enact a sexual orientation antidiscrimination ordinance, he did not have much experience with LGBT rights issues. In fact, Foley, who was married to a woman and had two children, had never before thought that marriage could be anything but the union of a man and a woman. As a result, he told the couples that, in his opinion, they had little chance of succeeding with their suit. He also knew, however, that no other attorney was interested in the case and that if he did not represent the plaintiffs, no one would. Believing that the couples were entitled to have their day in court, even if it was unlikely that they would prevail, Foley agreed to represent them.

In May 1991, after the Hawaii Department of Health, following the recommendation of the state attorney general, wrote to the three same-sex couples explaining that it lacked the legal authority to issue the marriage licenses, Foley filed a complaint in state court alleging that the denial violated his clients' rights to privacy and equal protection under the Hawaii Constitution. Four months later, trial judge Robert Klein rejected both claims and dismissed the lawsuit. Klein disagreed with the privacy argument because no court had ever held that there was a fundamental right to enter into a same-sex marriage. He dispensed with the equal protection argument by concluding that the government, through its marriage law, rather than impermissibly discriminating against same-sex couples, was instead properly promoting "the general welfare interests of the community by sanctioning traditional man-woman family units and procreation."[6]

▲

One of the trickiest questions when interpreting a constitutional (or statutory) provision is what meaning, if any, to give to the fact that the body that adopted it chose *not* to include certain language. When the members of the 1978 Hawaii Constitutional Convention adopted a provision that—in contrast to the U.S. Constitution—explicitly recognizes the right to privacy, they also considered amending the document to provide explicit protection to individuals on the basis of sexual orientation. The drafters ultimately decided not to do so because it would "be duplicative of the equal protection and due process protections already existing in the Constitution. Accordingly, [we] believe that the inclusion of a provision related to discrimination based on sexual orientation would be superfluous."[7]

Foley, who first encountered this passage several years earlier while successfully helping to represent two individuals who were arrested for selling obscene materials to undercover agents, argued in his brief to the state supreme court appealing Judge Klein's ruling that the passage showed the drafters of the 1978 constitution believed that courts were required to apply heightened scrutiny to governmental regulations that impacted on sexual orientation. That was the reason why, in the drafters' own words, adding a specific provision on sexual orientation to the constitution would have been "duplicative" and "superfluous." Foley's argument was that the language of the report, when coupled with the court's holding in the earlier obscenity case that the state constitution provided individuals with greater privacy protection than did the federal Constitution, meant that LGBT people had a fundamental right to marry under state law.[8]

In contrast, Assistant Attorney General Sonia Faust contended in her brief that the drafters' consideration, and eventual rejection, of a constitutional provision that would have specifically addressed issues of sexual orientation meant that there could be no fundamental right to enter into a same-sex marriage. In addition, while Foley relied on the obscenity case, Faust reminded the court of another earlier case in which it had rejected the notion that the 1978 privacy amendment rendered unconstitutional the application of prostitution laws to consenting adults in the privacy of the home.[9]

As for the equal protection issue, Foley contended that Judge Klein should have held a hearing to determine whether lesbians and gay men classified for heightened judicial scrutiny under the state constitution's equal protection clause. Interestingly, however, although the court eventually questioned the constitutionality of the state's marriage law on the ground that it might constitute impermissible sex discrimination, Foley did not raise that argument in his main brief. His equality-based argument was instead initially based only on the notion that the law was unconstitutional because it treated individuals differently on account of their sexual orientation.

Faust, in the state's brief, first denied that the state constitution's equal protection clause was even applicable. Specifically, she contended—in an argument that echoed the courts' reasoning in the early same-sex marriage cases discussed above—that gay and straight couples were not similarly situated because of the former's "biologic inability . . . to satisfy the definition of the [marital] status to which they aspire." The government's lawyer added that even if the court were to reject the proposition that marriage, by definition, was a heterosexual institution, and even if it proceeded to apply heightened scrutiny, the state's marriage law would nonetheless pass constitutional muster because the procreative function of marriage was "fundamental to our very existence and survival." Finally, the brief contended—in an argument that foreshadowed the state's later position when the case went to trial—that the government had a compelling interest in protecting the well-being of children and that that interest was clearly advanced by maintaining the institution of marriage as an exclusively heterosexual one.

▲

If lawyers at organizations such as Lambda and the ACLU had decided, say in 1991, to challenge prohibitions against same-sex marriage in court and had ranked the states according to their chances of succeeding, it is likely that Hawaii would have ended up neither at the top nor at the bottom of that list. Undoubtedly, Hawaii had some things going for it from an LGBT rights perspective. The state was ethnically and cultural diverse and was a largely tolerant place where, for example, interracial marriages were widely accepted. In addition, Hawaii had a tradition of enacting liberal laws. It was the first state to legalize abortion (in 1970) and the first to ratify the Equal Rights Amendment (in 1972). Hawaiian laws were also relatively gay-friendly. The state was one of the first to decriminalize sodomy, having done so in 1972. And the state legislature had recently enacted a law banning employment discrimination on the basis of sexual orientation. At the time, only a handful of other states had such laws on their books.

On the other hand, there were important considerations against choosing Hawaii as a place to bring a same-sex marriage test case. First, in contrast to states like California and New York, there was in Hawaii no legal recognition (however limited) by any governmental entity (whether at the state or local level) of same-sex relationships. Second, few LGBT rights cases had ever been litigated in the Hawaiian courts, which meant that judges there had little experience with LGBT legal issues. Indeed, the Hawaii Supreme Court had never before been asked to rule in an LGBT rights case.

What such a tallying could not have accounted for is the role of luck in winning legal cases. And luck ended up playing an important role in the plaintiffs' legal victory before the Hawaii Supreme Court. In the two years between the filing of the complaint (in May 1991) and the issuance of the court's opinion (in May 1993), there was a marked generational shift in the court's composition. In fact, of the four judges who ruled on the appeal in 1993, only one was on the court when Foley filed his complaint. The judge who wrote the main opinion in the case was not appointed to the court until 1992. The other two judges were named as temporary replacements for judges who recused themselves from hearing the appeal. All of these largely unpredictable changes in the court's composition meant that the judges who ultimately decided the case were considerably younger, and therefore generally more open-minded on matters related to sexual orientation, than those who sat on the court when Foley filed his complaint.

▲

The oral argument in *Baehr v. Lewin* was held in October 1992. Foley, who as the appellants' lawyer argued first, tried to persuade the court that the explicit recognition of a right to privacy in the Hawaii Constitution called for an expansive understanding of privacy, one that recognized the interest of all individuals—gays and straights alike—to have relationships with others of their choice. Although the judges listened respectfully to what Foley had to say on the right to privacy, they did not give any indication that they agreed. Foley then turned to equal protection, arguing that none of the state's justifications for treating gay couples differently than straight couples when it came to marriage held water. He pointed out, for example, that while the state relied heavily on procreation to defend the differential treatment, the Hawaii legislature, only eight years earlier, had amended the law to eliminate the requirement that marriage applicants be able to show that they were capable of reproducing.[10] Foley also argued that the state's contention that the well-being of children made it necessary to exclude same-sex couples from marriage was inconsistent with the lack of a legal provision prohibiting them from adopting.

The issue of sex discrimination made its first appearance in the case a few minutes after Foley ended his oral argument when one of the judges asked Assistant Attorney General Faust whether it did not in fact constitute discrimination to deny "a male and a male" a marriage license when it is provided to a "male and a female." Faust's responded that such a distinction was "permissible discrimination." She elaborated that the discrimination was the result of an entirely reasonable (and constitutional) moral judgment made by the legislature that same-sex couples should not be allowed to marry, a judgment that was similar to that which it made when it prohibited prostitution, polygamy, and incest.

▲

The court's opinion in *Baehr*, written by Judge Steven Levinson, rejected the plaintiffs' contention that the explicit right to privacy under the Hawaii Constitution required the state to recognize same-sex marriages.[11] The scope of such a right, Levinson concluded, was generally coterminous with the implicit right to privacy recognized by the U.S. Supreme Court under the federal Constitution. In the context of marriage, that Court had recognized a fundamental right to marry only in cases involving a man and a woman, therefore precluding a finding that the right protected same-sex couples under the Hawaii Constitution.[12]

The question of equality, however, was altogether different. When Judge Levinson, two days before the oral argument, first read his law clerk's memo on the case, he was struck by an idea that had never before crossed his mind: the state's marriage law likely discriminated against LGBT people because of their sex. The more Levinson thought about it, the more he became convinced that the plaintiffs' legal challenge had nothing to do with sexual orientation. As he noted in his opinion, "homosexual and same-sex marriages are not synonymous" because, under the current law, a gay person could marry someone of the opposite sex while a straight person could not marry someone of the same sex. This showed, Levinson reasoned, that Hawaii's marriage law classified individuals according to their sex and not their sexual orientation.

As Levinson saw it, the nature of the statute's classification was crucial because the Hawaii Constitution's equal protection clause (unlike that of the federal Constitution) explicitly protects individuals from being discriminated against on the basis of sex. This meant that the court had to apply heightened judicial scrutiny to the marriage law, one that required it to strike down the statute unless the state could show at trial that the law served a compelling governmental interest that was narrowly tailored to avoid constitutional violations.

Levinson rejected the government's argument that the plaintiffs were not entitled to relief because marriage, by definition, required the union of a man and a woman. Such a contention, which had been embraced by most of the courts from other jurisdictions that had decided same-sex marriage cases, was "circular and unpersuasive." Levinson noted that, in striking down an anti-miscegenation statute in *Loving v. Virginia*, the U.S. Supreme Court had disagreed with the lower courts' position that interracial marriages could not be legally binding because the state had always refused to recognize them as such. The *Loving* Court rejected the constitutional relevance of that tautological argument, setting a precedent for the Hawaii court now to do the same in the context of same-sex marriage.[13]

Levinson also relied on *Loving* to respond to an argument made by Judge Walter Heen in dissent that the marriage statute did not constitute a sex classification because it treated men and women equally by denying both the opportunity to marry someone of the same sex. Levinson pointed out that Virginia had made a similar argument in *Loving* when it noted that blacks and whites were similarly restricted in their ability to wed individuals of the other race. The *Loving* Court, however, had rejected the notion that the equal application of a statute that contained race classifications immunized it from equal protection scrutiny. Similarly, Levinson reasoned, the fact that the Hawaii marriage law treated men and women equally did not mean that it was beyond constitutional scrutiny as a sex-based classification.

In his dissent, Judge Heen concluded that the lower court's ruling on behalf of the government should be affirmed. In addition to contending that the marriage law did not discriminate on the basis of sex because it treated both sexes equally, Heen reasoned that the "legislative purpose of fostering and protecting the propagation of the human race through heterosexual marriages" justified denying plaintiffs the opportunity to marry. If the plaintiffs wanted the law changed, their only recourse was to go before the legislature. Heen added that the legislature was free to provide rights and benefits to same-sex couples through legal mechanisms other than marriage. In doing so, the dissenting judge presaged the debate that would take place in Hawaii and across the country in the years to come over whether the government should recognize same-sex relationships in ways that fell short of permitting them to marry.

It is fair to say that the *Baehr* opinion caught the LGBT rights movement unawares. With the exception of Wolfson and a handful of others, the movement's lawyers and activists had not thought it possible, at least in the short term, for same-sex couples to be offered the opportunity to marry. Now, as a result of the state supreme court's ruling, the lawsuit would proceed to a trial where the government would be forced to show the existence of a compelling state interest for denying same-sex couples that opportunity.

Although Lambda had chosen not to represent the plaintiffs in the case, Wolfson had been in touch with Foley regularly during the lawsuit's first two years, the only lawyer from a national LGBT rights

organization to have done so. During those phone conversations between New York and Honolulu, the two lawyers brainstormed on
how best to pursue a legal victory in the case. As a result of these
frequent exchanges, the two men developed a mutual respect and affection that would serve them well in the years to come.

After Foley's stunning victory before the Hawaii Supreme Court,
Wolfson was finally able to convince Lambda to offer to help represent the couples. Foley and his clients accepted the offer on the condition that the organization assign Wolfson to the lawsuit. Wolfson
was the only national LGBT rights lawyer who had supported them
from the beginning, and it was therefore Wolfson whom they wanted
on the case.

▲

More than three years went by between the issuance of the *Baehr*
opinion and the start of the trial. During that time, the struggle for
same-sex marriage shifted from the judicial arena to the political and
legislative ones.

Although the court's ruling at first received relatively little national
attention, it immediately created a political firestorm in Hawaii. Three
days after the opinion was issued, the chairman of the Hawaiian Republican Party, in calling for the enactment of a state constitutional
provision banning same-sex marriages, stated that "lovers may be lovers and have a right to privacy, but the state has a duty to continue to
foster marriage as an institution for basic family development." For
his part, during that same week, Democratic governor John Waihee
told the press that he was in favor of limiting marriage to a man and
a woman.[14]

In the fall of 1993, the state legislature, responding to public pressure to intervene, mobilized by holding hearings throughout the
islands on what should be the legal status of same-sex relationships.
Although the results of the hearings, as explained below, were a mixed
bag for LGBT rights proponents, the mere fact that the legislature
was suddenly interested in the issue of the legal recognition of same-
sex relationships was an early indication of the litigation's impact.

No other state legislature in American history had ever conducted hearings on the question of whether same-sex relationships should be legally recognized.

In an effort to offer something to both sides, the legislature, after the hearings ended in 1994, enacted a statute making it clear that marriage could only be between a man and a woman, expressing its view that the purpose of marriage is procreation, and denying that a ban on same-sex marriage was unconstitutional. At the same time, the new law created the Commission on Sexual Orientation and the Law to explore issues associated with the legal recognition of same-sex relationships and to make recommendations to the legislature. After holding hearings, the Commission recommended that the legislature allow same-sex couples to marry. As an alternative, the Commission proposed that legislators enact a comprehensive domestic partnership law that would provide couples with all of the benefits and obligations of marriage regardless of their gender.

The two houses of the state legislature responded to the Commission's report in different ways. The more conservative House eventually approved a constitutional amendment that would overturn *Baehr* by explicitly limiting marriage to a man and a woman. But that amendment was defeated on the floor of the more liberal Senate by a vote of fifteen to ten. The Senate then proceeded to adopt the Commission's second recommendation by enacting a domestic partnership law, but the House refused to approve it, meaning that by the spring of 1996, three years after *Baehr*, the legislative process in Hawaii was in a virtual stalemate over how to respond to the court's opinion.

In the meantime, the wheels of justice were grinding slowly in the courts. In 1994 and early 1995, the state filed several motions to have the trial postponed to permit the Commission to issue its report, and the legislature to act as it deemed necessary. Foley and Wolfson argued in response to the state's motions that it was imperative that the case proceed to trial as expeditiously as possible. The state supreme court, after all, had concluded that the current marriage law was constitutionally suspect; every day that went by meant a further delay in remedying what was in all likelihood an ongoing constitutional violation. The government, however, succeeded in postponing the trial, first until September 1995, and then until more than halfway through 1996.

▲

Foley and Wolfson spent most of the summer of 1996 preparing for the trial, which was finally scheduled to begin in September of that year. The lawyers divided their responsibilities geographically, with Wolfson in charge of finding expert witnesses from the mainland to testify on behalf of the plaintiffs. It was also his responsibility to depose the government's witnesses who lived outside of Hawaii. For his part, Foley was in charge of preparing or deposing the Hawaiian witnesses.

Never before in the history of American jurisprudence had there been a trial quite like this one. As soon as the proceedings began, it became clear that the trial would focus on trying to reach firm conclusions on a slew of weighty policy and empirical concerns, including questions about the meaning of marriage in our society; the reasons that many individuals get married; the types of parental configurations that work best for children; and what role, if any, gender and sexual orientation play in fostering appropriate parental nurture and care. Each side eventually called on four expert witnesses to present evidence on these highly contested issues.

Since the government had the burden of showing the existence of a compelling state interest justifying the exclusion of same-sex couples from the institution of marriage, it presented its case first. The first witness to testify was Dr. Kyle Pruett, a child psychiatrist and a professor at the Yale University School of Medicine. During his direct examination, the doctor discussed a study that he conducted in the early 1980s that investigated families, headed by married heterosexual couples, in which the father assumed the role of primary caretaker. From that study, Pruett concluded that mothers and fathers have different parenting styles. He expressed concern that children raised by same-sex couples "will have a great abundance of information about one gender and little information about the other gender as it is represented in their daily nurturing life." In addition, Pruett opined that biological parents have a predisposition toward their children that helps them be good parents. He noted, for example, that a mother's pregnancy, and a father's exposure to it, help create bonds with the child even before it is born.

Although Pruett's direct testimony seemed to help the government make its case regarding the importance of both gender and biology in parenting, it did not necessarily lead to the conclusion that the sexual orientation of LGBT parents was harmful to their children. This was the main point that Wolfson sought to make during his cross-examination of the state's witness. Did Pruett think, Wolfson asked, that lesbians and gay men were capable of raising healthy and happy children? In what was a key moment in the trial, Pruett answered that he thought they could. Did same-sex couples have the same capabilities as different-sex couples to manifest the qualities that Pruett believed were conducive to good parenting? The state's witness once again answered yes. Wolfson also got Pruett to admit that what ultimately mattered the most in establishing a good parent–child relationship was not the sex or sexual orientation of the parent but the extent to which the parent was able to establish a caring relationship with the child. By the time it was over, Wolfson's cross-examination of Pruett had significantly undermined the state's case.

The state's second witness was David Eggebeen, a sociologist and a professor of family studies at Penn State University, who testified about the connection between marriage and procreation. He contended, for example, that 98 percent of individuals who are married have or intend to have children. In contrast, the rate of voluntary childlessness among those who are not married is six times higher. During his cross-examination, however, Wolfson got Eggebeen to concede that the low rate of voluntary childlessness that he discussed during his direct examination was found only among spouses who were in their first marriages. The rate of voluntary childlessness goes up considerably when individuals are in their second and third marriages, the witness admitted, a fact that further undermined the state's effort to establish an inextricable link between marriage and procreation.

The validity of the social science studies on LGBT families was the main focus of the testimony by the state's third witness. Richard Williams, a professor of psychology at Brigham Young University, told the court that most of the studies which had concluded that the sexual orientation of LGBT parents did not harm their children were methodologically flawed and therefore unreliable. But in his cross-examination, Wolfson placed in doubt the witness's credibility by showing that he was an outlier in his own profession. Under Wolfson's pointed questioning, Williams conceded that in his view, *all* of the studies conducted by *all* psychologists and sociologists were flawed. In fact, Williams admitted that he thought that *all* of the social sciences, including the entire fields of psychology and sociology, were intellectually suspect. At one point, Wolfson even got Williams to state that he believed that there was no scientific proof that evolution occurred.

The reliability of the literature on LGBT parenting, which has uniformly concluded that the sexual orientation of LGBT parents does not harm their children, was questioned by all of the state's witnesses. It was unclear, however, whether the state's efforts to muddy the social science waters was constitutionally relevant, much less dispositive. This was a point that Foley made when he cross-examined Thomas Merrill, the state's fourth and last witness. Merrill, a Honolulu child psychologist, testified during his direct examination that children are better off when they have parental role models of each gender. And, like all of the state's witnesses, he also opined that the social science studies failed to show conclusively that children raised by lesbians and gay men were not harmed by their parents' sexual orientation. Foley, during his cross examination, asked Merrill the following question:

> Now, doctor, at one time in our country's history we didn't have a lot of data on the child development of children in interracial marriages. Do you think the lack of data in a situation like that should be the basis for prohibiting interracial marriage?

Not surprisingly, Merrill answered that the lack of evidence about the effects of interracial marriages in the 1960s was not a sufficient ground upon which to justify their prohibition. Once again, the inconsistencies in the state's position had been exposed by the plaintiffs' lawyers.

After the government rested its case, the plaintiffs called four expert witnesses of their own. Pepper Schwartz, a sociologist at the University of Washington, testified about studies which showed that same-sex couples approach intimacy and commitment in ways that make them virtually indistinguishable from different-sex couples. Charlotte Patterson, a developmental psychologist who taught at the University of Virginia, defended the validity of the social science studies which showed that there were no differences in development, self-esteem, and gender role behaviors between the children of LGBT parents and those of heterosexual parents. David Brodzinsky, a clinical psychologist with private clients who also taught at Rutgers University, testified that there was no increase in risk of behavioral or psychological problems for the adoptive children of same-sex couples. And finally, Robert Bidwell, a Honolulu pediatrician who specialized in adolescent medicine, told the court that he had counseled dozens of children of LGBT parents and that while some of them had experienced distress as teenagers caused by their being raised in families that were different from most others, the vast majority were able to work through these issues before developing into happy and well-functioning adults.

After nine days of trial, Judge Kevin Chang told the parties that he would reach a decision in the next several weeks. In the meantime, the political and legislative battles over the issue of same-sex marriage continued unabated both in Hawaii and across the country.

▲

For most of the 1990s, Foley and Wolfson worked not only on the legal aspects of *Baehr* but also on its political repercussions. In 1994, Lambda signaled its commitment to same-sex marriage by being the first organization to create a project (or unit) dedicated exclusively to that issue and naming Wolfson as its director. As the director of Lambda's Marriage Project, Wolfson became the first national LGBT rights lawyer/activist to work full-time on the struggle for marriage equality. Wolfson was also the driving force behind the creation of the

National Freedom to Marry Coalition, which coordinated the political work of more than twenty LGBT and civil rights organizations in support of same-sex marriage across the country. The Coalition came together around a simple and brief statement, known as the Marriage Resolution, which activists placed on countless pamphlets and petitions across the country:

> Because marriage is a basic human right and an individual choice, the State should not interfere with the same-gender couples who choose to marry and share fully and equally in the rights, responsibilities, and commitment of civil marriage.

For his part, Foley worked with LGBT rights activists and other progressives in Hawaii trying to defend the lawsuit's progress from ongoing efforts by opponents to amend the state constitution in order to ban same-sex marriages. Ever since the court's ruling in *Baehr*, some legislators had pushed a compromise that would amend the constitution to prohibit same-sex marriage while offering domestic partnerships to same-sex couples. Although Foley never rejected such a compromise outright, he consistently pointed out in his public statements that a domestic partnership statute, even if it offered same-sex couples all of the rights and benefits afforded under state law to married couples, still fell short of providing his clients with full equality. It was unlikely, for example, that other states would give the same degree of legal recognition to Hawaiian domestic partnerships that they gave to Hawaiian marriages. Registering as domestic partners would also not make available to same-sex couples the myriad of federal rights and benefits that accompanied marriage. As a result, Foley advised LGBT rights activists, as well as sympathetic legislators, to concentrate on trying to derail efforts to amend the constitution rather than being distracted by a domestic partnership compromise that would fail to provide same-sex couples with many of the rights and benefits afforded to married couples.

But Foley began to change his position after several of the state legislature's most prominent opponents of a constitutional amendment banning same-sex marriage were defeated at the polls in November 1996. The perception across the state was that these politicians had lost their seats largely because of that opposition. It also seemed to Foley that LGBT rights opponents—in particular an organization called Hawaii's Future Today, which had the full backing of the Catholic and Mormon churches—were only getting stronger, in part because they enjoyed support from a growing number of conservative groups from the mainland.

In contrast, the Hawaii Equal Rights Marriage Project, the largest group seeking recognition of same-sex marriage in the state, was a shoestring operation that had always had difficulty raising money. Despite Wolfson's efforts to encourage national LGBT organizations to get involved in the political skirmishes over same-sex marriage that were now routinely taking place in Hawaii, the cold reality was that few of them shared enough resources with the Hawaiian LGBT rights forces to make a difference.

All of these factors left Foley, by early 1997, pessimistic that supporters of same-sex marriage would be able to continue to defeat efforts to adopt a constitutional amendment banning same-sex marriage. As a result, he became more open to the domestic partnership compromise. Only a few months later, however, the political momentum shifted sufficiently in favor of LGBT rights opponents that even the compromise seemed out of reach. In the end, the legislature adopted a Reciprocal Beneficiaries Law, which permitted any two individuals who could not otherwise marry to receive a handful of the rights and benefits—such as hospital visitation rights, inheritance rights, joint ownership of property, and the opportunity to sue for wrongful death—that accompanied marriage. Although many LGBT rights supporters were disappointed with the limited reach of the new statute, it did provide same-sex couples with the most extensive form of legal recognition available anywhere in the country. Unfortunately for those supporters, the legislature at the same time approved a constitutional amendment that, if accepted by voters in November 1998, would reserve to it the authority to limit marriage to one man and one woman.

▲

On December 3, 1996, Judge Chang issued a ruling handing the plaintiffs a complete legal victory. Chang concluded that the government had failed to establish a compelling state interest that justified denying same-sex couples the opportunity to marry. In doing so, he made factual findings that accepted the claims made by the plaintiffs in his courtroom (and by LGBT activists elsewhere). Chang concluded from the evidence introduced at trial that same-sex couples want to marry for the same reasons as straight couples and that they can be as good parents as heterosexuals. He also noted that, far from harming children, the recognition of same-sex marriage would help the children of LGBT couples by offering them the legal benefits that come with having two parents who are married to each other. In short, Chang could not have been any more emphatic or explicit in rejecting all of the government's positions as to why it chose to deny same-sex couples the opportunity to marry.

The day after Judge Chang issued his ruling, the state asked for and received a stay pending an appeal to the state supreme court. Given that the government had lost before that court in 1993, and more recently before Judge Chang, state attorney general Margery Bronster decided to hire an experienced outside lawyer to oversee the appeal. Her choice of Charles Cooper, a prominent conservative lawyer, for the job was highly controversial. Cooper, a former law clerk to U.S. Supreme Court Justice William Rehnquist, worked for the Reagan Department of Justice in the mid-1980s. While in that position, he wrote an infamous memo—later rescinded by the government—in which he contended that it was not illegal for employers to fire HIV-positive employees based on fears that they might spread the virus, even if those fears were not justified. Cooper also filed an amicus brief before the U.S. Supreme Court in *Romer v. Evans* urging the Justices to uphold Colorado's antigay constitutional amendment. While LGBT rights supporters decried the choice of a lawyer active in the conservative movement to represent the interests of all of the state's people, Bronster contended that Cooper was hired not because of his political views but because of his expertise in litigating constitutional cases.

In his brief to the Hawaii Supreme Court appealing Judge Chang's ruling, Cooper decided to abandon the child welfare argument that had been the centerpiece of the government's case during the trial —a decision that showed the extent to which Foley and Wolfson had succeeded in undermining the state's effort to draw a link between prohibiting same-sex couples from marrying and protecting children from harm. Instead, the government's hired lawyer attempted to persuade the high court that it had erred four years earlier when it concluded that the state's marriage law was constitutionally suspect. The institution of marriage consisting of one man and one woman, Cooper wrote in his brief, was simply too old and too embedded in the nation's social fabric to be deemed unconstitutional.

In the end, for the government, the prohibition against same-sex marriage was justified because the state had a compelling interest in ensuring that its laws reflected the moral values of the people of Hawaii. The prohibition against same-sex marriage was no different from the prohibition against polygamous marriages—both proscriptions codified long-held moral views regarding the types of relationships that did not merit marital recognition.

For their part, Foley and Wolfson in their brief pointed out that there was nothing in the record to support the state's position that morality served as a valid justification for denying same-sex couples the opportunity to marry. The plaintiffs' lawyers reminded the court that proponents of anti-miscegenation laws had also used moral claims to defend the ban against interracial marriages. "To imply," they added, "that lesbians and gay men are somehow incompatible with, or incapable or unworthy of, marriage or morality is not morality; it is discrimination."

After all of the briefs were completed, Cooper filed a motion on behalf of the government asking the court to defer ruling on the appeal until the state's citizens had had a chance to vote on the proposed constitutional amendment in November 1998. As Foley and Wolfson saw it, the state's effort to have the proceedings delayed (yet again) raised fundamental questions about the responsibility of courts in our constitutional democracy. It was the judiciary's duty to interpret the constitution as then written. Although the people retained the power to amend that document in the future, there were now before the court litigants who had been playing by the rules for years by asking that the judiciary interpret the constitution in assessing their claim. The lawsuit was now not only about whether the plaintiffs were entitled to marry, but also about whether the court would exercise its constitutional duty, as a coequal branch of government, to interpret the law. To put it simply, after waiting patiently for more than six years, the plaintiffs were entitled to a judicial resolution. It was for this reason that the plaintiffs' lawyers stated in their papers opposing the state's motion to defer consideration of the appeal that the government was using this new delaying tactic "as a means [of] maneuvering the judiciary out of its role of enforcing constitutional claims," an effort that "is literally lawless."

After they filed their motion in opposition to the state's request for another delay, Foley and Wolfson stepped back to await the court's decision. Although they were worried that the voters might approve the constitutional amendment when they went to the polls in late 1998, the two lawyers felt relatively confident that the court would rule in favor of their clients well before then. This was because, as a legal matter, nothing had changed in the intervening years that should lead the court to reconsider *Baehr*'s holding that the prohibition against same-sex marriage was a form of sex-based classification. And, just as important, the government, during the trial, had completely failed in attempting to show the existence of a compelling interest that justified denying same-sex couples the opportunity to marry.

While the law had not changed since the original ruling in *Baehr*, the politics of same-sex marriage had. The 1993 opinion created a political firestorm, first in Hawaii and later across the country. By 1996, as Congress and many state legislatures were considering enacting laws prohibiting the recognition of same-sex marriages, the Hawaii Supreme Court, for the first time in its history, found itself the subject of national attention, most of which was quite negative. Conservatives now routinely accused the court of placing its political and personal views ahead of the people's will.

▲

On November 3, 1998, Hawaiian voters, by the wide margin of 69 percent to 29 percent, approved the constitutional amendment. Two weeks later, and almost two years after the state appealed Judge Chang's ruling, the court finally took an action in the case, albeit a limited one: it asked the parties to file supplemental briefs explaining their view of the constitutional amendment's effect, if any, on the state's appeal.

Despite the passage of the amendment, Foley and Wolfson still had legal arguments to make on behalf of their clients. Unlike the constitutional amendments relating to marriage that would later be passed in many states in the decade to come, the Hawaiian amendment did not explicitly *prohibit* the recognition of same-sex marriages. Instead, it simply stated that "the Legislature shall have the power to reserve marriage to opposite-sex couples." As a result, Foley and Wolfson, in a last-ditch effort to help their clients prevail, argued to the court that the amendment simply authorized the legislature to act and that, until it did so, the legal status quo remained.

The judges did not agree. After waiting (incredibly) an additional year before finally issuing a ruling, the court, in a three-page unsigned opinion, concluded that the amendment rendered the statute no longer subject to scrutiny under the constitution's equal protection clause. As a result, the court dismissed the case as moot.

Although the way in which the case ended undoubtedly constituted a legal defeat for the LGBT rights movement, the litigation played a crucial role in helping Americans to better understand the relationships and families of LGBT people. And, more concretely, the case started a process that led several states to legally recognize thousands of same-sex relationships. Indeed, as of 2009, five of those states have done precisely what the plaintiffs in *Baehr* set out to accomplish almost twenty years earlier by recognizing the right of same-sex couples to marry.

## The Impact

For a case that ultimately ended in defeat, the *Baehr* litigation has had a profound social and political impact. In 1991, when the lawsuit was first filed, most Americans had never given any thought to the possibility that same-sex couples could marry. Eight years later, when the litigation finally ended, the country had been engaged for several years in a conversation about not only the issue of same-sex marriage but also about the status of LGBT people, their relationships, and their families in our society.

The effort by the *Baehr* plaintiffs, with the assistance of their two lawyers, to seek admittance into the institution of marriage at a time when few people in the country had ever linked marriage with homosexuality was both audacious and controversial. As we will see, that effort generated a considerable amount of backlash, including the enactment of so-called Defense of Marriage laws in many states—and at the federal level—specifying that marriage was to be limited to one man and one woman. At the same time, however, the *Baehr* lawsuit, and the other same-sex marriage cases that followed on its heels, set in motion a series of events that led millions of straight Americans to recognize that LGBT people are as capable as they are of forming committed, lasting, and healthy bonds with their partners (and, when present, with their children) and that it is therefore unjust to deny same-sex couples access to the principal institution through which society validates and supports intimate relationships.

To be sure, the *Baehr* case was not solely responsible for the changes in the attitudes of many Americans toward same-sex relationships. Starting in the 1980s with the onset of the AIDS epidemic, the country saw how gay men in particular cared for their ill partners, belying the notion that gay love was somehow less strong or good than straight love. At around the same time, a growing number of lesbians and gay men (in particular the former) began to have (or adopt) children. These families, many of which were headed by same-sex couples, showed Americans that LGBT people could love and care for their children in ways that made them indistinguishable from straight parents. It was not, however, until the plaintiffs in *Baehr* demanded admission into the institution of marriage that the LGBT rights movement succeeded in placing the relationships of lesbians and gay men squarely before the American public.

Prior to *Baehr*, it was too easy for opponents of LGBT rights to trivialize and demean the lives of LGBT people by painting them as hedonists obsessed with sex. Encouraged by the *Baehr* litigation's early successes, many gay and lesbian couples began sharing their stories with interested media and the public at large. And some same-sex couples in other states—first in Vermont and then elsewhere—began to file lawsuits challenging prohibitions against same-sex marriage. As this process unfolded, the mental image that many Americans had of LGBT people gradually began to change from that of, for example, half-naked men in gay pride parades to that of same-sex couples celebrating their love in commitment ceremonies or being turned away at marriage license bureaus.

▲

Outside of Hawaii, and of LGBT rights circles nationwide, the initial response from the rest of the country to the 1993 *Baehr* ruling was muted, at least in comparison to the attention that the case received only a few years later. This initial lack of national interest in the Hawaii court's decision may have been explained by the state's geographic isolation and the fact that those in the mainland rarely pay much attention to what happens in that faraway state. Furthermore, the country in 1993 was consumed with a different LGBT rights issue altogether—that of gays in the military. Shortly after Bill Clinton became president, he attempted to make good on a campaign promise to lift the military's ban on gay service members. Clinton's plan to end the military's discriminatory policy was immediately engulfed in a firestorm of criticism and controversy, as many conservative politicians, right-wing activists, and military officials portrayed the proposal as a threat to both the nation's security and values.

Another less political and more legal explanation for why the *Baehr* case, at least initially, received little national attention may have been that the Hawaii court's decision was grounded entirely on state constitutional grounds. As a general matter, a successful legal challenge to a state law based exclusively on those grounds has little impact on the rest of the country. Even though courts from the other jurisdictions might be persuaded by the ruling's reasoning, they would obviously not be required to treat it as a binding precedent when interpreting their own constitutions.

The issue of same-sex marriage did not begin to resonate nationally until 1996, two and a half years after the Hawaii Supreme Court's first ruling in *Baehr*. In fact, by the middle of that year, same-sex marriage had become one of the most discussed political and legal issues in the country. There are several factors that help explain why this happened. One factor is that, by 1995, social conservatives were feeling increasingly emboldened politically given that not only had they succeeded in getting President Clinton to back down from his promise to end the military's ban on gay service members, but they had also played a crucial role in helping Republicans, in November 1994, capture both houses of Congress for the first time in almost fifty years.

After President Clinton and the Democrats were weakened politically by the gays in the military controversy, conservative activists began looking for other gay-related issues with which to energize their supporters. The question of same-sex marriage seemed tailor made for that purpose. As Martin Mawyer, the president of the Christian Action Network, wrote in a newspaper column that appeared in early 1996, the conservative movement was committed to making sure that gay marriage emerged as "the talk around water coolers in 1996." In urging social conservatives to pay close attention to gay marriage,

Mawyer warned that "like the issue of gays in the military, which virtually exploded overnight, government recognition of same-sex marriage may be a reality before many Americans have an opportunity to fully consider its adverse consequences."[15]

Much of the outrage that, beginning in 1996, conservatives expressed over the issue of same-sex marriage was directed at what they took to be the irresponsible judicial activism of the Hawaii court in *Baehr*. Interestingly, the term "judicial activist" was coined in 1947 by the liberal historian Arthur Schlesinger to describe conservative judges who had earlier in the century attempted to use the Constitution to block many of the government-led reforms implemented during the Progressive and New Deal eras. It would be conservatives, however, who would astutely deploy the "judicial activist" critique to great political effect beginning in the late 1960s and early 1970s as a response to what they perceived to be the excessively liberal rulings of the Warren Court.

By the mid-1990s, conservative leaders had become quite skilled at using judicial opinions expanding individual rights to mobilize their supporters. From the conservatives' perspective, the Hawaii Supreme Court's decision in *Baehr* was a particularly egregious example, as one right-wing commentator put it, "of the tyranny of judges who think nothing of overturning popular will" given that, as another commentator explained, "nowhere is public opinion more clearly in conflict with judicial dogma than in the matter of gay marriage."[16]

It is no coincidence that the year in which leaders of the conservative movement decided to make a national political issue out of the court's ruling in *Baehr* was a presidential election year. In February 1996, on the eve of the Iowa caucus, several social conservative groups—including the Christian Coalition, Focus on the Family, the Traditional Values Coalition, and the Family Research Council—kicked off a joint effort called the "Campaign to Protect Marriage" by holding an anti–gay rights rally in Des Moines. Republican presidential candidate Patrick Buchanan attended the rally while other G.O.P. candidates (including eventual nominee Senator Robert Dole) sent letters of support. After the rally, Bill Horn, an Iowa conservative activist and the chief spokesman of the Campaign to Protect Marriage, announced that his group would urge Congress and the fifty state legislatures to enact so-called Defense of Marriage laws that would prohibit the recognition of same-sex marriages.

The state of Utah in 1995, in a direct response to the *Baehr* lawsuit, was the first jurisdiction to enact a statute making it clear that a valid marriage could only be between one man and one woman and that it would not recognize same-sex marriages entered into in other states. By the time South Dakota became the second state to enact such a law, in February 1996, similar bills were pending in twenty-six other states. Although LGBT rights supporters were able to defeat several of the proposed bills—mostly by having them die in legislative committees before they were reported out to the full chambers—by the end of 1996, sixteen states had enacted laws banning same-sex marriages.

Well-organized efforts by social conservatives to have legislatures pass laws banning gay marriages were to some extent helped by the fact that some LGBT rights supporters were by now frequently asserting that once same-sex marriages were recognized in Hawaii, all the other states would be under a constitutional obligation to recognize them. This supposedly meant that if a gay couple from Omaha or Sacramento, for example, were to travel to Hawaii to get married, that marriage would be legally valid when they returned home. These claims by some LGBT rights supporters greatly simplified what was (and remains) a complicated legal issue, namely, the obligation of states, under the Full Faith and Credit Clause of the U.S. Constitution, to recognize the legal actions taken by other states. Although that clause does require that judicial judgments issued by the courts of one state be recognized by those of other states, the issuance of a marriage license is an administrative rather than a judicial act. Therefore, despite the assertions made by some LGBT rights supporters during the course of the *Baehr* litigation, the courts had never held that states were constitutionally required to recognize marriage licenses issued by other jurisdictions. In fact, courts had consistently held that states were generally permitted to refuse to recognize marriages from other jurisdictions that were inconsistent with their stated public policy. This meant that while some states might recognize same-sex marriages solemnized in other jurisdictions, others would likely not.

The simplification by some LGBT rights activists of what can be somewhat arcane points of legal doctrine under the Full Faith and Credit Clause and "choice of law" principles would not have been so damaging to the interests of the LGBT rights movement if it had not unintentionally helped the social conservatives' agenda of fanning the winds of public outrage over the notion that a Hawaii court could, to put it simply, ram same-sex marriage down the throats of all Americans. Indeed, it was ostensibly to prevent this result that, in May 1996, several prominent congressional Republicans introduced the Defense of Marriage Act. That legislation would federalize, for the first time in the nation's history, the definition of marriage. Under the Republicans' marriage bill, same-sex couples would be ineligible to receive hundreds of rights and benefits made available by the federal government to married couples even if they were legally married under state law. The proposed legislation also sought to exempt states from any obligation to recognize marriage licenses issued to same-sex couples by other jurisdictions.

Congressional hearings and debates on the bill were held in the summer of 1996. The law's supporters argued on the floor of Congress that the recognition of same-sex marriage constituted a pernicious threat to the very survival of our society. For example, Republican congressman Bob Barr of Georgia, the main sponsor of the legislation in the House, contended that heterosexual marriage was "an institution basic not only to this country's foundation and to its survival but to every Western civilization" as well. He added, rather hysterically, that the law was needed because "the flames of hedonism, the flames of narcissism, the flames of self-centered morality are licking at the very foundation of our society, the family unit." Two days later, the House approved the bill by the large margin of 342 to 67.

The debate in the Senate was more of the same. Republican Jesse Helms of North Carolina, for example, told his colleagues that the proposed law would "safeguard the sacred institutions of marriage and the family from those who seek to destroy them and who are willing to tear apart America's moral fabric in the process." For his part, West Virginia Democrat Robert Byrd, Bible in hand, gave a forty-five-minute speech on the Senate floor in which he compared the decline of the Greek and Roman empires with the decline of American society that would follow the recognition of same-sex relationships as marital. "The drive for same-sex marriage," he thundered, "is an effort to make a sneak attack on society by encoding this aberrant behavior in legal form before society itself has decided it should be legal."

On September 10, 1996, the very day that the trial in the *Baehr* case commenced before Judge Chang in Honolulu, the Senate approved the measure by a vote of 85 to 14. Ten days later, President Clinton, who opposed the enactment of the law but who did not want to risk his reelection by supporting another controversial LGBT rights cause, signed the bill in the middle of the night without the presence of the media or other elected officials.

▲

The political backlash that followed the plaintiffs' initial victory in *Baehr* is not unusual in the history of civil rights struggles in the United States. One need only look to the enactment by southern states of dozens of laws aimed at preventing the racial integration of schools following the U.S. Supreme Court's ruling in *Brown v. Board of Education* to understand that powerful backlashes can follow politically controversial judicial decisions that require majority groups to reassess in fundamental ways the manner in which they have in the past treated and understood certain minority groups. Indeed, cases like *Brown* and *Baehr*, and their aftermaths, show that civil rights struggles in this country usually consist of moments of heartening progress followed by instances of discouraging setbacks.

This type of civil rights roller-coaster ride characterized the issue of same-sex marriage during the second half of the 1990s. Between 1997 and 2000, fourteen additional states (including "blue states" like California, Minnesota, and Washington) enacted laws limiting marriages to one man and one woman and/or banning the recognition of same-sex marriages solemnized in other states. In addition, voters in Hawaii, Alaska, and Nebraska approved constitutional amendments prohibiting same-sex marriages. These considerable setbacks for the LGBT rights movement, however, were accompanied by significant victories. The Hawaii legislature in 1997 became the first in the country to enact a law that made available to same-sex couples a package of limited but important rights (including hospital visitation and inheritance rights) that had previously been denied to them. And in 1999, only two weeks after the Hawaii Supreme Court dismissed the *Baehr* lawsuit as moot, the Vermont Supreme Court issued its opinion in *Baker v. Vermont* holding that denying same-sex couples the rights and benefits that accompany marriage violated the state constitution.[17]

It is not possible to draw a tight causal link between *Baehr* and *Baker*. For one thing, the two rulings were grounded in different state constitutions. For a second, the *Baker* court rejected the argument initially accepted by the *Baehr* court, namely, that a prohibition against same-sex marriage constitutes a form of differential treatment on the basis of sex. Despite these differences, it is reasonable to think that the justices on the Vermont Supreme Court were more positively disposed to arguments about the unfairness of denying marital rights and benefits to same-sex couples after *Baehr* engendered an ongoing national conversation about the legal status of gay relationships. The Hawaii Supreme Court, by being the first court to suggest that same-sex couples were constitutionally entitled to have their relationships legally recognized, likely made it easier for the Vermont court to go second.

What took place in Vermont regarding same-sex relationships had national repercussions not only because of what the court did in *Baker*, but also because of what the state legislature did in response. The *Baker* court suggested in its ruling that it might be possible for the legislature to remedy the constitutional violation that it identified by offering same-sex couples the rights and benefits that come with marriage without having to recognize their relationships as marital. In 2000, after several months of heated debate, the Vermont legislature did precisely that by enacting a civil unions law that made available to same-sex couples the same rights and benefits enjoyed by heterosexual married couples under state law. (And, in 2009, the Vermont legislature became the first in the nation to recognize same-sex marriages without being ordered to do so by a court.)

One of the most notable developments in this area of the law since the end of the *Baehr* litigation has been the extent to which civil unions, as well as domestic partnership laws, have emerged as a moderate alternative to same-sex marriage—it is easy to forget just how controversial, both inside and outside of the state, the Vermont legislature's decision to enact civil unions seemed at the time. In fact, gay rights opponents mounted a strong campaign aimed at derailing the legislation, one that came close to succeeding. Polls at the time showed that Americans in general, and Vermonters in particular, opposed the creation of civil unions for same-sex couples. It is an indication of just how far, and how quickly, Americans have come on the issue of the legal recognition of same-sex relationships that only five years after Vermont adopted its civil unions law, polls showed that a majority of Americans supported making such unions available to same-sex couples.

It is exceedingly unlikely that civil unions (as well as comprehensive domestic partnership laws) would have the support of so many Americans today, and thus of so many elected officials, *but for* the ability of the same-sex marriage cases, starting with *Baehr*, to place the issue of the lack of legal recognition of LGBT relationships squarely before the American public. The political debate in a growing number of states is no longer *whether* same-sex couples deserve legal recognition; instead, the debate is about *what type of* legal recognition they deserve. That in and of itself constitutes a considerable achievement for the LGBT community.

▲

The recognition of same-sex relationships under American law since *Baehr* has, of course, not been limited to civil unions and domestic partnerships. The Massachusetts Supreme Judicial Court (2003), the highest courts of California and Connecticut (2008), and the Iowa Supreme Court (2009) have all held that the failure to recognize same-sex marriages violated their respective state constitutions.[18] (A few months after the California court issued its decision, voters overruled it by approving a constitutional amendment limiting marriage to a union of one man and one woman.) Like the majority opinion in *Baker v. Vermont*, the majority opinions in the Massachusetts, California, Connecticut, and Iowa cases did not follow *Baehr* in concluding that the differential treatment of same-sex couples was constitutionally suspect because it constituted a form of sex discrimination. Instead, those courts, in addressing the equal protection issue, focused on how the marriage laws treated individuals differently according to their sexual orientation.

Despite the unwillingness of later courts to adopt the *Baehr* court's legal reasoning, there is a clear historical parallel between the Hawaii ruling and a California Supreme Court decision from forty-five years earlier (*Perez v. Sharp*) that struck down the state's anti-miscegenation law as unconstitutional.[19] *Perez* and *Baehr* both show that it is often necessary for one courageous court to go first in holding that a long-standing law or practice is actually inconsistent with the nation's fundamental values and principles as codified in the federal and state constitutions.

When *Perez* was decided, thirty states still had anti-miscegenation laws on the books, a substantial majority of African Americans lived in states with anti-miscegenation laws, and an overwhelming number of Americans disapproved of marriage between whites and nonwhites. Courts had also consistently rejected challenges to those laws by pointing to their long historical pedigree and to the prerogative of legislatures to determine who was eligible to marry. Like the Hawaii court's marriage decision several years later, the California court's ruling at first seemed to be a constitutional outlier given that courts had for decades upheld laws and regulations that kept the races apart. In fact, courts prior to *Perez* consistently upheld explicitly segregationist policies in the same way that courts prior to *Baehr* consistently rejected the notion that it was unconstitutional to deny same-sex couples the opportunity to marry. When *Perez* was first decided, then, it seemed as if the California court was pushing the fringes of constitutional doctrine in ways that could be thought of as antidemocratic, arrogant, and elitist, the same charges that were later made against the Hawaii court after its initial *Baehr* ruling.

The *Perez* court, however, did not remain a constitutional outlier for very long. In the years following that ruling, several state legislatures repealed their race-based marriage statutes. By the time the U.S. Supreme Court in 1967 held that those laws violated the Constitution, only sixteen states still had them on their books. In fact, when the nation's highest court finally arrived at the same constitutional place staked out by the *Perez* court twenty years earlier, there was little opposition or resistance.

There is, of course, still much opposition and resistance to same-sex marriage. In fact, in the last decade, more than half of the states have adopted constitutional amendments banning same-sex marriages. Nonetheless, in the aftermath of *Baehr*, as in the aftermath of *Perez*, several jurisdictions across the country began paying closer attention to the injustice and unfairness that inhere in the state's refusal to recognize certain relationships as marital. This has led (as of 2009) to the recognition of same-sex marriages in Connecticut, Iowa, Massachusetts, New Hampshire, and Vermont, and of civil unions, domestic partnerships, or reciprocal beneficiaries in California, Hawaii, Maine, Nevada, New Jersey, Oregon, Vermont, Washington, and Wisconsin. Indeed, more than one-fifth of Americans currently live in a state that legally recognizes same-sex relationships.

At the same time, there has also been a slow but steady increase in the percentage of Americans who believe that same-sex couples should have the opportunity to marry. In 1988, five years before *Baehr*, the General Social Surveys found that only 12 percent of respondents thought same-sex couples should have the right to marry, while 73 percent disagreed. In 1996, three years after *Baehr*, a poll conducted by the Pew Research Center found that the number of respondents who supported same-sex marriage had more than doubled to 27 percent, while those who opposed it went down to 65 percent. A decade later, a Pew poll found that support for same-sex marriage had increased by another third to 39 percent, while opposition decreased to 51 percent. The clear trend in the polls shows that the debates about LGBT people and their relationships engendered by *Baehr* and the other same-sex marriage cases have led to an increase in the percentage of Americans who believe that same-sex couples should be offered the opportunity to marry.

▲

The impact of *Baehr* has not been limited to the legal recognition of same-sex relationships. It is likely that the case, and the national conversation about the lives and relationships of LGBT people that followed it, has also had a positive impact on LGBT rights issues that do not specifically involve relationship recognition. Even though the question of same-sex marriage continues to strongly divide the country, other gay-related policy matters have become considerably less controversial. For example, since 1993—the year in which the Hawaii Supreme Court issued its initial *Baehr* decision—fourteen states have enacted laws prohibiting discrimination on the basis of sexual orientation (bringing the total number of states with such laws to twenty-one), while thirty have passed laws addressing hate crimes motivated by sexual orientation. There has also been progress in the area of parent–child relationships, with New Hampshire repealing its ban against adoption by lesbians and gay men and several states, including California, Connecticut, Illinois, New Jersey, New York, and Oregon, explicitly permitting same-sex couples to adopt jointly. It is reasonable to believe that the national debate engendered by *Baehr* and the other same-sex marriage cases has contributed to progress in all of these areas because the marriage issue has increased the visibility of LGBT people in ways that no other LGBT rights issue had done before.

The same-sex marriage litigation has required citizens and elected officials alike to think through and articulate their views on the lives and relationships of LGBT people. Although those views, of course, do not always correspond with the views of LGBT rights proponents, the important point is that many Americans have been forced to take a position on these important issues rather than continue to pretend that LGBT people either do not exist or that their interests are not worth considering in setting public policy. In this sense, *Baehr* and the other same-sex marriage cases have had a positive impact on the status of LGBT Americans that is similar to that which *Brown v. Board of Education* had on the status of African Americans. Black people after *Brown* may still have been hated by some and feared by others, but they were no longer invisible. After *Brown*, it was no longer tenable to reject out of hand the claims by African Americans to equal citizenship.

The same applies to LGBT people and their position in society today. The same-sex marriage cases, and the national debate that they have engendered, have made it impossible for Americans to ignore the reality that some of their co-citizens are LGBT individuals who are entitled to some rights and protections under the law. By increasing the social visibility of LGBT people and by drawing attention to the problems and burdens associated with their status as second-class citizens, the same-sex marriage cases have made the claims by the LGBT rights movement more morally compelling and politically powerful.

No important civil rights goal is ever won through one legal case alone. Not even the Court's decision in *Brown*, by itself, achieved the civil rights movement's goal of racially integrating schools (and other institutions) throughout the country. It would take further rulings by the Court, as well as resolute action by the executive and legislative branches of the federal government, to achieve that goal. Similarly, it cannot be said that the *Baehr* litigation, by itself, led to the legal recognition of thousands of same-sex relationships in several states either through the institution of marriage or through alternative legal mechanisms such as civil unions and domestic partnerships. What the litigation accomplished instead was to force the country as a whole to grapple with the question of whether denying legal recognition to the relationships of LGBT people is consistent with the basic values and principles that we hold dear as a nation. For the vast majority of Americans before *Baehr* that question was not even worth asking because for them homosexuality was intrinsically incompatible with marriage. Although many Americans today remain firm in their objection to same-sex marriage, many others have come to see that, in the end, there is no valid justification for denying same-sex couples the opportunity to enjoy the type of full and equal citizenship that comes with being permitted to participate in the institution of marriage.

CHAPTER 5

# Sex

## The Facts

On the evening of September 17, 1998, the Harris County sheriff's office received a phone call about a black man who was wielding a gun inside an apartment in an east Houston neighborhood. Four deputies were dispatched to the scene. About an hour later, the officers arrested John Lawrence, the owner of the apartment, and his guest Tyron Garner for engaging in consensual sex in violation of Texas's Homosexual Conduct Law.

Unlike Miguel Braschi and Leslie Blanchard, and Genora Dancel and Ninia Baehr, John Lawrence and Tyron Garner were never in a long-term relationship. The two had been acquaintances since the early 1990s, having been introduced by Robert Royce Eubanks (who played a crucial role in the events that took place on the night of the men's arrest). Lawrence was a fifty-five-year-old white man who worked as a laboratory technician at a nearby hospital and who had known that he was gay all of his life. As a navy hospital corpsman stationed in Virginia in the early 1960s, he had visited gay bars and dated men in Norfolk and Virginia Beach without incident. After he received an honorable discharge, he went back to live in the small southeastern Texas town where he was born to be near his mother and stepfather. In 1971, he moved to Houston and settled down to lead a quiet life. Although Lawrence periodically dated men, he largely led a closeted life, never telling his family or his coworkers that he was gay. He was also not a politically engaged person and was not known by LGBT rights activists in Houston.

Tyron Garner was considerably younger than Lawrence, having been born in 1967. A black man, he grew up in a poor Houston neighborhood. He worked sporadically, sometimes as a waiter and sometimes as a street vendor. In the months leading up to his arrest, he had dated Eubanks, a forty-one-year-old gay white man from Pasadena, a working-class suburb of Houston. Although his immediate family knew that he was gay, Garner (like Lawrence) was not politically active. He had never, for example, attended a gay rights or pride event prior to his arrest.

On September 17, 1998, Lawrence, Garner, and Eubanks went to a Mexican restaurant for dinner and drinks. The three men had spent the day moving new furniture into Lawrence's apartment and were planning on moving Lawrence's old furniture to Eubanks's place the following day. After dinner, the three returned to Lawrence's home and had more drinks. At around 10:30 p.m., Eubanks announced that he and Garner were leaving. Garner replied that he did not want to leave with Eubanks. Lawrence then stated that Garner could stay if he wanted. Eubanks, clearly agitated by the fact that Garner wanted to stay with Lawrence rather than go with him, abruptly got up and announced that he was going to go buy some snacks and would be back soon.

Once on the street, Eubanks, rather than looking for a place to buy food, instead searched for a pay phone. When he found one, he called the sheriff's department, claiming, according to the dispatcher, that "a black man was going crazy in the apartment and that he was armed with a gun." Eubanks, who was likely inebriated at the time of the call, later admitted to the police that he phoned them because he was jealous that Garner seemed interested in spending the night with Lawrence.[1]

Four deputy sheriffs, including Joseph Quinn and William Lilly, arrived at Lawrence's apartment building shortly after Eubanks's call. As they made their way into the lobby, they saw Eubanks at the base of the stairs. When Quinn—the first deputy to arrive, and therefore, the one who was in charge—asked Eubanks where the man with the gun was, the latter pointed to Lawrence's second-floor apartment. The officers quickly ran up the stairs with their guns drawn.

Quinn entered the apartment first, announcing the officers' presence by yelling "Sheriff's deputies!" Immediately before them was an empty living room. One of the other officers went into a bedroom to the left of the apartment's entrance but found no one there. Quinn and the other deputies proceeded to make their way into the kitchen. The officers, who still had their weapons drawn, then noticed that there was another bedroom behind the kitchen area. The door to that bedroom was open, but there was no light inside. Deputy Lilly was the first to enter it, but he apparently became so startled after seeing two men on a bed, that he actually lurched back out of the room. Quinn, once again taking charge, moved around Lilly and entered the room in a crouched position holding his gun in front of him, with his finger on the trigger.

Quinn would later claim that he observed Lawrence and Garner engaging in anal sex and that the two men continued to have sex for about a minute despite his yelling at them to stop. Lilly, the only other deputy who claimed to have seen the two men having sex, contradicted Quinn by stating that the sex stopped as soon as the deputies entered the room.[2]

In any event, after the deputies barged into his bedroom, an obviously distraught Lawrence began screaming at them, asking why they were in his apartment and demanding that they leave immediately. For his part, the adrenaline-infused Quinn yelled back at Lawrence complaining that he could have been shot. Quinn then handcuffed Lawrence and led him, wearing only his underwear, into the living room. Garner, who remained silent during the verbal confrontation between Lawrence and Quinn, was permitted to pull up his pants and to walk into the living room of his own accord.[3]

In the living room, the deputies sat Lawrence and Garner down.

They were soon also joined there by Eubanks. It was at this point that the latter admitted that he had called the police out of jealousy, but Quinn seemed more troubled by the fact that Lawrence and Garner had, in his view, refused to stop having sex after he had ordered them to do so. In the meantime, Lawrence remained livid at the deputies' conduct, accusing them of acting like the "Gestapo" and as "jackbooted thugs," while complaining that the officers were "harassing" Garner and him because they were gay.[4]

A few minutes later, Sergeant Kenneth Adams of the sheriff's department arrived at the scene. Quinn told Adams that he wanted not just to give a citation to Lawrence and Garner for having violated the Homosexual Conduct Law, a Class C misdemeanor (punishable by a fine and not imprisonment), but also to arrest them. An arrest was justified, Quinn claimed, because the whole incident almost led to someone being shot.

Quinn then called the district attorney's office and spoke to a prosecutor. The deputy explained what had happened and asked whether it mattered, under the law, that the sex that Lilly and he observed had taken place in the bedroom of a private home. The prosecutor looked up the statute and a few minutes later returned to the phone to explain to Quinn that the location where the sodomy took place was legally irrelevant.

At around 11:10 p.m., Quinn placed Lawrence and Garner under arrest. (The deputies also arrested Eubanks, charging him with filing a false report.) Garner was handcuffed and led down to the police car without incident, but Lawrence refused to accompany the deputies out of his home. The officers then dragged Lawrence down a set of concrete steps, causing parts of his legs to bruise and bleed.

The men were driven in separate patrol cars to the police station. While there, they were fingerprinted, booked, and taken to a large cell that held dozens of male prisoners. Lawrence and Garner remained in that cell for twenty-four hours, after which they were arraigned and released without bail.

## The Lawyer

On the morning of July 1, 1986, Ruth Harlow opened the door of her apartment to pick up her copy of the *New York Times*. When Harlow, who had graduated from Yale Law School a few weeks before, unfolded the newspaper, she saw the following headline emblazoned on its front page: "HIGH COURT, 5–4, SAYS STATES HAVE THE RIGHT TO OUTLAW PRIVATE HOMOSEXUAL ACTS." As Harlow read the article about the *Bowers v. Hardwick* opinion, she felt as if someone had kicked her in the stomach: not only had the Supreme Court held that people like her could be arrested simply for having sex in the privacy of their homes, but it had also summarily dismissed the claim—deeming it to be "at best, facetious"—that the Constitution recognized the right of LGBT people to choose their sexual partners.

Harlow, who would spend much of her professional life as a lawyer for the next two decades working to limit the impact of *Hardwick*, was born in 1961 in Midland, a small city in central Michigan. For over a century, life in Midland has been dominated by the Dow Chemical Company, by far the town's largest employer. Harlow's father and paternal grandfather both worked for Dow, the former as a lawyer (and eventual general counsel) and the latter as a chemist (and eventual chief analytical chemist).

Harlow attended Stanford University and then Yale Law School. It was not until her second year at Yale that Harlow, who had had a serious relationship with a male graduate student while in college, realized that she was a lesbian. One night, she and her roommate—Susan Sommer, who later became a Lambda lawyer and helped Harlow litigate the *Lawrence* case—hosted a party in their New Haven apartment. As the evening progressed, Harlow found herself drawn by the physical attractiveness of a female law student. By the time the party ended, she was experiencing the most intense crush that she had ever felt in her life. The morning after the party, Harlow woke up convinced that she was a lesbian, a realization (or revelation) that literally took place overnight.

After the fateful party, Harlow tried to learn as much as she could about homosexuality by looking for books on the subject in the cavernous Yale University library. During her third year of law school, she wrote a seminar paper on lesbian identity and its impact on the law. That same year, she helped to organize the country's first conference on AIDS and the law. In addition, she co-wrote one of the first student articles published in a law review on LGBT issues.[5] By the time she graduated from law school—only eighteen months after she first realized that she was a lesbian—Harlow had become entirely comfortable with her sexual orientation.

After receiving her law degree in 1986, Harlow clerked for a federal appellate judge. While in that position, she came out to her coworkers after another judge on the court commented in her presence that he did not think gay people would make very good law clerks. After the clerkship, Harlow became an associate at a small New York City labor law firm before moving on to the ACLU, first working for its New Jersey affiliate and then for its Lesbian and Gay Rights Project. For the next five years, Harlow worked on several important cases, including one in which the ACLU, along with the Center for Constitutional Rights, successfully challenged content restrictions imposed by federal regulations on AIDS educational materials paid for with government money.[6]

Another precedent-setting case involved a lawsuit against an Ohio hospital for failing to provide medical treatment to a gay man with AIDS. In April 1992, Fred Charon and his partner Bruce Howe left their home in Maine for a vacation in Wisconsin. While driving through Ohio, Charon, who had AIDS, experienced a severe allergic reaction to a new medication. Howe drove Charon to the nearest hospital, which was in Fremont, Ohio. The emergency room doctor, after examining Charon, concluded that he should be admitted for immediate treatment. The supervising physician, however, refused to approve the admission, stating that "if you get an AIDS patient in the hospital, you will never get him out."[7] As a result, Charon was transported to a hospital in Toledo, forty-five minutes away, his condition worsening significantly because of the delay in receiving medical treatment. Charon eventually sued the Fremont hospital and its supervising physician for refusing to provide him with medical treatment in violation of several federal laws. Charon died during the course of the litigation, but his partner Howe continued with the lawsuit. In the end, Harlow, working alongside local lawyers, persuaded a jury to award Charon's estate $62,000 in compensatory damages and $450,000 in punitive damages.

While at the ACLU, Harlow also worked on a lawsuit brought against two Drug Enforcement Agency officers who became incensed when a gay couple's motorcycle nicked their parked car.[8] The officers jumped out of their automobile and proceeded to scream antigay epithets as they slammed the head of one of the plaintiffs against the hood of the car and kicked the other one while he lay on the ground. The case was eventually settled for tens of thousands of dollars.

Harlow, of course, was not successful in every case. One of the most difficult defeats came in a lawsuit against Michael Bowers, the Georgia attorney general who had successfully defended the constitutionality of his state's sodomy statute when it was challenged by Michael Hardwick in the 1980s. Harlow's client was Robin Shahar, a graduate of Emory University School of Law who in 1990 accepted a position as an assistant attorney general in Bowers's office. A few weeks before Shahar was scheduled to begin work, Bowers rescinded the job offer after he learned that his employee-to-be was in an open relationship with another woman.

Harlow filed a lawsuit on behalf of Shahar. The case took several twists and turns, but eventually the U.S. Court of Appeals for the Eleventh Circuit ruled in favor of Bowers, with a majority of the judges concluding that it was constitutional for the attorney general—who was responsible for legally defending statutes such as the state's sodomy law and its ban against same-sex marriage—to refuse to hire an openly lesbian attorney because the public might perceive that she was not committed to enforcing all of the state's laws.[9]

Two days after the U.S. Court of Appeals issued its opinion, Bowers, still basking in the glory of his legal victory over the lesbian attorney, resigned to campaign full-time for the Republican nomination for governor. The basking, however, was short-lived. Less than a week after Bowers's resignation, the media revealed that he had had a long adulterous relationship with a former employee. The same man who had once said that he could not "separate the way someone does their job from the way they respect the law" was forced to admit publicly that he had violated Georgia's law against adultery for more than a decade.[10] Although Bowers had been considered a favorite to win the Republican gubernatorial nomination, the revelation of his affair doomed his chances for higher office.

During the course of the *Shahar* litigation, Harlow had learned from trustworthy sources that Bowers had been having an affair with an employee for many years. At the time, Harlow was tempted to highlight publicly the hypocrisy of a man who seemed to have no qualms about violating Georgia's adultery law while, first, defending the constitutionality of prosecuting LGBT people for consensual sodomy before the U.S. Supreme Court, and then later arguing in court that Shahar, as an open lesbian, could not be trusted to enforce all of Georgia's laws. Harlow eventually decided to take the high road and respect Bowers's privacy interests, even though the man had never seemed particularly interested in respecting the privacy of LGBT people.

After the story of Bowers's adulterous relationship appeared in the newspapers, Harlow asked the Court of Appeals to reconsider its decision. Unfortunately for Shahar and her lawyer, the court refused to do so. In the end, however, it was Harlow who would have the last laugh, so to speak, in her legal feud with Bowers. By the time Shahar's case came to an end, Harlow had left the ACLU to become managing attorney of Lambda's national office in New York. From that position, she steered the litigation that would eventually lead the Supreme Court to admit that upholding the constitutionality of sodomy statutes in *Bowers v. Hardwick* had been a terrible mistake.

## The Law

Sodomy statutes in the United States can be traced back to the English Reformation Parliament of 1533. It was that body which transformed the religious proscription against sodomy into a secular crime (known in England as "buggery"). Although the American colonies enacted laws against sodomy/buggery, those provisions were not aimed at homosexual conduct as such—the statutes prohibited men from having anal intercourse not only with other men, but also with women, children, and animals. Colonial sodomy laws in the seventeenth and eighteenth centuries, in other words, reflected society's strong disapproval of nonreproductive sex rather than a targeted condemnation of those who had sex with individuals of their own sex.

After independence, the original thirteen states, as well most of the states that followed, adopted sodomy statutes. Although a few of those statutes proscribed specific sexual conduct (in particular anal sex), the language of most of the laws simply prohibited "crimes against nature," leaving it to judges to determine the meaning of that vague phrase. Until the end of the nineteenth century, courts for the most part permitted prosecutors to apply the statutes only in cases involving alleged instances of anal sex (both homosexual and heterosexual) or bestiality.

Beginning in the late nineteenth century, and continuing through the early twentieth century, sodomy laws were expanded (either through the enactment of new laws or the judicial interpretation of old ones) to include not just anal intercourse but also oral sex. (In addition, a handful of jurisdictions, in particular some that had large urban populations, for the first time specifically prohibited sexual conduct between women.) Although the category of proscribed sexual acts was enlarged in this way, the statutes were also, as a practical matter, narrowed because when it came to consensual sex, officials began to limit the enforcement of sodomy laws to same-sex sexual partners. In fact, by the middle of the twentieth century, prosecutors and judges, as well as the general public, had come to understand the word "sodomy" as a synonym for homosexual sex.

The first step toward the elimination of sodomy laws in the United States was taken by the American Law Institute (ALI), an organization composed of highly influential judges, lawyers, and law professors. The ALI's principal mission since its founding in 1923 has been to promote the clarification and simplification of American law, as well as its adaptation to changing social needs and circumstances. In 1951, the ALI launched one of its most ambitious projects to date: the writing of a Model Penal Code that would attempt to bring order and reform to the criminal laws of the then forty-eight states.

The Model Penal Code was drafted during the 1950s and officially promulgated in 1962. One of the Code's recommendations was that consensual sexual behavior between adults in private be decriminalized. The first state to follow the ALI's recommendation was Illinois, which repealed its sodomy statute in 1961. Ten years would go by before a second state (Connecticut) did the same. The pace of decriminalization quickened considerably after that—by the end of the 1970s, nineteen other state legislatures had voted to repeal their sodomy laws.

Gay rights activists, of course, welcomed these legislative repeals. At the same time, they grew concerned that, starting in the late 1960s, other state legislatures amended their sodomy laws by decriminalizing different-sex sodomy, while simultaneously (and for the first time) explicitly proscribing same-sex sodomy. These "gay only" sodomy statutes were unprecedented in American history. Although the word "sodomy" by then was almost exclusively associated with gay sex, the actual language of sodomy laws going back to the colonial era had never explicitly made reference to same-sex sexual conduct.

In 1973, Texas became the second state—Kansas was the first in 1969—to narrow its sodomy statute by proscribing only same-sex sodomy while renaming it the Homosexual Conduct Law. In the years that followed, the legislatures of Arkansas, Kentucky, Missouri, Montana, Nevada, and Tennessee also decriminalized different-sex sodomy while, for the first time, explicitly prohibiting the same-sex variety.

The 1970s also saw the first lawsuits challenging the constitutionality of sodomy laws. Some of these challenges were brought against the new "gay only" sodomy statutes; other challenges were brought against sodomy laws that, at least in theory, applied to anyone who engaged in anal or oral sex.

By the time sodomy laws became the targets of constitutional challenges, it was relatively rare for prosecutors to charge individuals for engaging in consensual sodomy in private. Even in the most conservative of jurisdictions, the police rarely arrested gay men for having sex in their homes. Instead, prosecutions beginning in the 1970s were largely limited to sexual conduct or solicitation in public places.

For LGBT rights activists, sodomy laws became problematic not so much because of their actual enforcement against consensual sex in private but because of the ways in which they were used to justify laws and policies that discriminated against LGBT people. The mere existence of the (now largely unenforced) sodomy laws branded them as criminals, permitting the government to defend its firing of LGBT employees, landlords to explain their refusal to rent to LGBT tenants, courts to justify their refusal to award custody of children to LGBT parents, and so on. As a result, there was a wide consensus among activists that meaningful equality for LGBT people in the United States would be impossible to achieve until sodomy laws were abolished. If state legislatures refused to repeal their sodomy laws—and indeed, by the end of the 1970s, the pace of legislative repeals had slowed down considerably—then activists were prepared to turn to the courts.

Many of the early judicial challenges to sodomy laws were brought against those that prohibited "crimes against nature." At the time, lawyers believed that these statutes were particularly vulnerable to constitutional challenges because of their vagueness. A fundamental principle of procedural due process is that laws must provide sufficient guidance to citizens regarding the actions that they prohibit. The early due process challenges to sodomy laws, however, proved unsuccessful. The U.S. Supreme Court in 1973, for example, concluded that the Florida statute, which defined sodomy as an "abominable and detestable crime against nature," was not unconstitutionally vague because the state supreme court had previously interpreted the law specifically to prohibit anal and oral sex.[11]

After these initial judicial defeats, those interested in challenging sodomy laws turned to the substantive due process right to privacy. That right was first recognized by the U.S. Supreme Court in *Griswold v. Connecticut*, a case in which it struck down a law prohibiting the use of contraceptives on the ground that it violated the privacy rights of married couples. For the next decade, the Court further elaborated on the constitutional right to privacy by including within it the right of unmarried couples to use contraceptives in *Eisenstadt v. Baird* and, most (in)famously, of women to decide whether to have an abortion in *Roe v. Wade*.[12]

It seemed clear from these opinions that the Court was determined to protect from governmental intrusion certain personal and intimate decisions made by individuals. Yet, all three of the rulings involved issues associated with procreation, making it possible for some to argue that the constitutional right to privacy in matters related to sexual conduct was limited to that context. Such a limited reading of the right to privacy seemed illogical to others. For example, if heterosexual couples (whether married or unmarried) had a constitutional right to use contraceptives, did they not also have the right to engage in anal and oral sex? And, as LGBT rights activists began asking in the 1970s, if heterosexual couples had a constitutional right to engage in nonprocreative sex, why not same-sex couples?

This last question was raised in several cases challenging the constitutionality of sodomy laws brought in both federal and state courts between 1976 and 1982. Although all of the federal cases eventually failed, some of the state court lawsuits succeeded.[13] By the time Michael Hardwick was arrested in his Atlanta apartment in the summer of 1982 for engaging in consensual oral sex, courts across the country had been grappling for several years with the constitutionality of sodomy statutes. It was Hardwick's case, however, which would lead the nation's highest court to weigh in on that issue.

Despite the fact that Hardwick was arrested for engaging in oral sex in the privacy of his bedroom, the Supreme Court ultimately rejected his constitutional challenge. The Court did not accept the argument made by Hardwick's lawyers that its privacy rulings applied to a case involving oral sex between two men. The majority reasoned that its earlier cases had all involved marriage, family, and procreation, and that none of those were implicated by the type of conduct for which Hardwick was arrested. Furthermore, the Court concluded that the long history of sodomy criminalization in the United States meant that there could be no fundamental right for two individuals of the same sex to be sexually intimate with each other.[14]

After *Hardwick*, LGBT rights lawyers began to map out a legal strategy in response to the decision. It was clear that the Court had closed the door, at least for the time being, to challenges of sodomy laws based on the Due Process Clause of the federal Constitution. There remained, however, at least two other sources of law upon which to ground future challenges. First, it was still possible to argue that sodomy laws violated *state* constitutional provisions protecting privacy and equality. Second, the Court in *Hardwick* had not addressed the issue of whether the "gay only" sodomy statutes (or the broader sodomy laws, which in theory applied to everyone, but which were as a practical matter enforced only against LGBT people, albeit rarely) violated the Equal Protection Clause of the U.S. Constitution.

The promise of the first source of law—that of state constitutions—became evident in October 1986 (only three months after *Hardwick*) when a state trial judge in Kentucky concluded that the Commonwealth's sodomy law violated the due process clause of the state constitution. This ruling was the first indication to LGBT rights litigators that it was possible to successfully challenge sodomy statutes in state courts even after such a challenge had failed before the U.S. Supreme Court. In 1992, the Kentucky Supreme Court affirmed the trial court's ruling, becoming the first post-*Hardwick* state appellate court to strike down a sodomy law.[15] And, in the years that followed, several other state appellate courts—including, ironically, the Georgia Supreme Court in a case involving the very same statute upheld by the U.S. Supreme Court in *Hardwick*—struck down sodomy statutes on the ground that they violated their state constitutions.[16]

The promise of the second source of law—that of the Equal Protection Clause of the federal Constitution—became evident after *Romer v. Evans.* One of the most important principles arising from *Romer* was that the government could not constitutionally single out lesbians and gay men for the imposition of burdens because of animus or moral disapproval. It seemed to LGBT rights activists that "gay only" sodomy laws did precisely that. When the Texas legislature, for example, abolished its old sodomy statute and replaced it with the Homosexual Conduct Law in 1973, it decided that all Texans, except for gay ones, were entitled to engage in consensual anal or oral sex. This was analogous to the decision made by Colorado voters in 1992 that all citizens of the state, except for gay ones, were eligible to receive the protection afforded by antidiscrimination laws.

▲

One day in the fall of 1998, Suzanne Goldberg, one of the lawyers in the *Romer* case, spoke on the phone with Mitchell Katine, a gay lawyer from Houston. Goldberg had met Katine several years earlier when they worked together on an AIDS discrimination case. Katine had founded (and later served as president of) the Houston Bar Association for Human Rights, an organization of LGBT lawyers. He had also, several years earlier, received an award from the Texas Bar Association for his representation of indigent individuals, many of whom had AIDS.

Katine was known by members of the LGBT community in Houston as the "go to" lawyer whenever they needed legal assistance. It was not surprising, therefore, that friends advised Lawrence and Garner to hire Katine to defend them in the sodomy prosecution.

The first thing that Katine—who had first been contacted by Lawrence and Garner two days earlier—asked Goldberg was whether she was sitting down. When Goldberg replied that she was, Katine proceeded to tell her that he had two male clients who had been arrested the previous week by Harris County deputy sheriffs for allegedly engaging in sodomy in the apartment of one of them. As Goldberg listened to Katine tell the story, she quickly recognized that this might be *the* case that the LGBT rights movement had been waiting for ever since *Hardwick*. The arrest of two individuals for engaging in consensual sex in the home, while rare, was undoubtedly the best possible factual scenario for a substantive due process challenge. In addition, the arrest took place in one of the handful of states that had a "gay only" sodomy law, providing the best legal setting for an equal protection challenge.

As soon as Goldberg finished her conversation with Katine, she walked down the hallway to speak with her supervisor and colleague Ruth Harlow. Harlow, who was then Lambda's managing attorney (the second-highest legal position in the organization), agreed that the case sounded extremely promising. They also agreed that Goldberg needed to speak in person with Lawrence and Garner to learn how they wanted to proceed.

The two defendants, early in the case, were confronted with the crucial decision of whether to fight the charges. It was possible that the District Attorney's office might be persuaded to dismiss the charges, but if the prosecutors did so, the LGBT rights movement would likely be deprived of a golden opportunity to challenge the constitutionality of the Homosexual Conduct Law in the Texas courts. From a legal ethics perspective, it was important that Lawrence and Garner make the decision of how to proceed without any pressure from the lawyers. Only the two clients could decide whether they wanted to take the risk of ending up with a sodomy conviction on their records in return for the possibility that their case might serve as a vehicle through which to invalidate the statute.

A few days after receiving Katine's call, Goldberg met with Lawrence and Garner in Houston to go over their options. She explained to the two men that the litigation could potentially have wide implications because if the case reached the Supreme Court, it could lead to the elimination of criminal laws across the country that were used to justify all sorts of discriminatory policies and practices against LGBT people. At the same time, Goldberg told them, they needed to be aware that if they decided to proceed with the constitutional challenge to the Texas statute, they would not only be taking the risk of ending up with a sodomy conviction on their records but would also be opening up their lives to considerable scrutiny by the media and the public.

Neither Lawrence nor Garner were active in LGBT rights and had not considered the connection, explained to them by Goldberg, between sodomy laws and discrimination against LGBT people. Undoubtedly, for them as individuals, the safer choice was to try to have the charges dismissed. To challenge the constitutionality of the sodomy law would probably mean that the case would remain open for years, exposing them to the uncomfortable glare of unwanted public attention. Indeed, it was ironic that in order to have the courts potentially rule that the sodomy law violated their constitutional rights to privacy, Lawrence and Garner would first have to subject their lives (and their night of intimacy together) to the scrutiny of others.

In the end, the two men repeated to Goldberg what they had told Katine a few days earlier: They felt strongly that it had been wrong for the police to barge into the apartment brandishing guns and then lead them away in handcuffs. They were prepared to do what they could to make sure that other LGBT people were not subjected to the same type of harassment and humiliation at the hands of the police. If they had to sacrifice their privacy in order to help rid Texas (and potentially the country) of these harmful laws, then that was a price they were willing to pay.

▲

When Lawrence and Garner were released after being held in jail for twenty-four hours, they were ordered to appear in a few weeks before a justice of the peace. (Texas law gives justices of the peace jurisdiction to hear traffic violations and minor crimes that are punishable by fines rather than imprisonment.) If the two men pled "not guilty," the prosecution would have to prove the facts of the case at a trial by calling on the police officers to testify that they had observed Lawrence and Garner engaging in sodomy in the former's bedroom. Goldberg and Katine did not want a trial because they were not interested in challenging the facts as alleged by the prosecution; instead, their legal position was that the government lacked the constitutional authority to enforce the statute. The lawyers therefore advised their clients to plead "no contest" to the charges. Although such a plea would have the same legal effect as a guilty plea, it would not require either that the government prove its case or that the two men admit their guilt.

On November 20, 1998, when Lawrence and Garner, accompanied by their lawyers, walked up to the government building where justices of the peace hear cases, they were met by a throng of reporters. Also present that day were activists on both sides of the issue, some holding signs hailing Lawrence and Garner as heroes while others had posters accusing them of being sinners and criminals.

The two defendants and their lawyers politely and quietly made their way around everyone and once inside found seats in the back of a big courtroom. Given the large volume of cases that were on the docket that day (the majority of which were traffic violations), the room was loud and chaotic, without the usual decorum of a court of law.

By this point in her career, Goldberg was an experienced LGBT rights lawyer who had been practicing in the field for seven years. She had worked on many different types of cases, including several that challenged the constitutionality of sodomy laws. At an intellectual level, Goldberg had always understood why sodomy laws were unconstitutional (they violated basic principles of equality and privacy) and immoral (they caused harm to LGBT people without preventing harm to others). But in many ways, it was not until that morning, as she sat in a crowded Houston courtroom, that she grasped the full extent of the injustice behind sodomy laws. Her clients, after all, would soon be forced into the demeaning position of having to stand in a packed courtroom and be asked by the government to account for their private and consensual sexual lives. It was clear to Goldberg that for all of the complex constitutional issues that the litigation was likely to raise in the future, the case came down to the seemingly indisputable proposition that it was simply outrageous, in contemporary America, for two adults to have to publicly defend their right to be sexually intimate with each other.

When their case was finally called, Lawrence and Garner, accompanied by Goldberg and Katine, went before the justice of the peace.

After the two men pled "no contest," the justice fined them $125 each. A month later, Lawrence and Garner exercised their right to have the case heard de novo (or anew) by a state criminal court judge. It was all, however, a formality; after that judge also accepted their plea of "no contest" and imposed a fine, the constitutionality of the sodomy statute could now be determined by the appellate courts.

▲

By the time the case was ready to be heard by the Texas Court of Appeals, Goldberg was on maternity leave, so the responsibility for arguing the case fell to Harlow. (The following year, Goldberg left Lambda to take a position as a law professor at Rutgers University.) Katine and the other Texas lawyers who were assisting Lambda with the case warned Harlow that the judges were likely to be openly hostile to the suggestion that the state's sodomy statute was unconstitutional. As a result, when Harlow entered the Houston courtroom of the Court of Appeals in November 1999, she expected the three judges—Chief Justice Paul Murphy, Justice J. Harvey Hudson, and Justice John Anderson—to be highly skeptical of Lambda's legal positions. To her surprise, however, the judges seemed to take her arguments seriously.

In her prepared comments, Harlow stuck to the main themes contained in Lambda's brief, emphasizing the way in which the law targeted one group of individuals based on their sexual orientation (raising equal protection concerns) for engaging in consensual sexual conduct in the home (raising privacy concerns). But to Harlow's surprise, the judges seemed mostly interested in a third argument raised by Lambda's brief—that the sodomy law constituted an impermissible form of sex discrimination because whether it applied depended on the gender of the parties: if Lawrence and Garner had engaged in consensual sodomy with a woman—instead of with each other—on the night of their arrest, they would not have been subject to prosecution under Texas criminal law.

The state's argument was presented by William E. Delmore III, the chief appellate lawyer for the Harris County district attorney's office. During his oral presentation, Delmore argued that the sodomy statute did not single out gay people because it applied to any person, regardless of sexual orientation, who engaged in homosexual acts. This led Harlow to reply during her rebuttal that such a statement could not be taken seriously. The state's position, she told the court, was akin to arguing that a law that prohibited people from attending Catholic Masses did not target Catholics because it applied to everyone regardless of religious affiliation.

The court issued its opinion in June 2000, eight months after the oral argument. Given that the argument seemed to have gone well, Harlow was not completely surprised when two of the three judges voted to strike down the statute. What did surprise her was that the two judges in the majority—Justice Anderson (who wrote the opinion) and Chief Justice Murphy—concluded that the statute was unconstitutional because it was an impermissible form of sex discrimination under Texas's equal rights amendment. The court reasoned that once the Texas legislature made sodomy illegal only when engaged in by individuals of the same sex, "the distinction between legal and illegal conduct was not the act [of sodomy itself], but rather the sex of one of the participants."[17]

By concluding that the state's sodomy statute amounted to an impermissible form of sex discrimination, the court did not have to grapple with issues related to discrimination on the basis of sexual orientation or with the question of whether there was, under the state constitution, a fundamental right to engage in (gay) sex. If the judges in the majority, however, thought that their ruling would somehow be less controversial because it focused on Lawrence and Garner's sex rather than on their sexual orientation, they would soon learn otherwise.

The panel's opinion was greeted with howls of protest from social conservatives throughout the state. In response to the ruling, the Texas Republican Party, a month after the decision was issued, amended its platform to criticize "activist judges who use their power to usurp the will of the people." (The document already stated that "homosexual behavior is contrary to the unchanging truths that have been ordained by God.") The platform also explicitly rebuked Anderson and Murphy—two lifelong Republican judges—for striking down the sodomy law. In addition, party leaders called on members to oppose the judges' reelection. The Harris County Republican Party chairman went even further by circulating a letter asking that Judge Anderson either resign or retract his ruling. The letter chastised the judge for writing an opinion that "blatantly defies the Republican Party and creates potential for further damage to our society."[18]

While state Republican leaders were working themselves into a frenzy over the court's ruling, the Harris County district attorney's office filed a motion to have the case reconsidered by all nine judges who sat on the Court of Appeals for the Houston area appellate district. The court granted the motion, which meant that Harlow now had to try to persuade the full court that the panel's decision was legally correct.

Harlow's biggest concern with the reasoning adopted by Justice Anderson was that it might require, if followed to its logical conclusion, the striking down of the state's ban against same-sex marriage. The argument could be made, for example, that if a law which allowed men to have consensual sodomy with women but not with other men constituted sex discrimination, then so did a law that permitted men to marry women but not other men. Harlow knew that the judges on the full Court of Appeals would never agree to strike down the sodomy statute if they thought that doing so would render Texas's ban on same-sex marriage constitutionally vulnerable.

In her brief opposing the reconsideration of the case, therefore, Harlow noted that when the state affirmatively seeks to exercise its coercive powers through the criminal regulation of adult consensual sexual intimacy, it by necessity implicates constitutional concerns not present in civil law matters (such as regulations pertaining to who is entitled to marry). Harlow also focused on the circumstances surrounding the adoption of the state's equal rights amendment in 1972 in order to persuade the full court that Judge Anderson's opinion accurately reflected Texas constitutional law. In particular, Harlow stressed the ways in which the amendment was intended to eliminate barriers to advancement by women through a constitutional guarantee that all Texans, regardless of sex, be treated according to their abilities, interests, and qualifications rather than according to old but pervasive gender stereotypes. Harlow explained how the sodomy statute was inconsistent with that constitutional guarantee because it "limits women's sex roles to a traditional male/female model." She added that striking down the statute "would allow women to choose female partners without penalty and exercise full individual choice, free from the antiquated idea that they need a man to complete themselves."

In the end, however, legal arguments grounded on the need to promote gender equality apparently proved too much for the full court to handle. In an opinion issued in March 2001, seven of the nine judges rejected all of Harlow's constitutional arguments against the sodomy law. The law did not discriminate on the basis of sex, the court concluded, because it applied equally to men and women. The court also held that it was rational, and therefore constitutional, for the legislature to conclude that same-sex sodomy is more morally problematic than different-sex sodomy. Finally, the majority, in reasoning that closely tracked that of the U.S. Supreme Court in *Bowers v. Hardwick* fifteen years earlier, concluded that the long history of legal, religious, and moral disapproval of homosexuality meant that the Homosexual Conduct Law did not violate privacy guarantees under either the federal or state constitution.[19]

The lone dissenters were the same two judges who initially voted to strike down the law. One of them, Chief Justice Murphy, had announced several weeks earlier that he would soon resign after twenty years on the court. Although he would later deny that his resignation was related to the outcry generated by his willingness to strike down the sodomy law, the timing of the resignation—coming shortly before the full court's decision and while he still had two years remaining in his term—suggested otherwise. In fact, Murphy was so stung by the political outcry that followed the panel's opinion that he at one point stated bluntly that "there are those in the Republican Party who feel that we owe allegiance to the party and whatever the platform might be, regardless of what the law may be."[20]

▲

After the Court of Appeals upheld the constitutionality of the Homosexual Conduct Law, Harlow's next step was to file an appeal with the Texas Court of Criminal Appeals, the highest Texas court that hears criminal cases, which has a reputation for being extremely conservative. Although Harlow suspected that the Court of Criminal Appeals might not have the courage to strike down the sodomy law, she thought that the court would at least entertain the serious constitutional claims raised by two individuals who had been arrested in a home for engaging in consensual sex.

But Harlow was wrong. In what can only be characterized as a judicial passing of the buck, the Texas Criminal Court of Appeals in April 2002 issued a one-sentence statement announcing that it would not hear the appeal. This decision proved bittersweet for Harlow. On the one hand, she had worked hard—along with Goldberg, Katine, and several other lawyers—trying to persuade the Texas courts to strike down the Homosexual Conduct Law, and it was disappointing that that effort had failed. On the other hand, Harlow knew that the U.S. Supreme Court was more likely to reconsider *Hardwick* in a case in which the lower courts had rejected a challenge to a sodomy law involving an actual arrest in the home. In short, the loss before the Texas courts now made a win before the U.S. Supreme Court possible.

▲

Every year, the Supreme Court receives several thousand requests (known as "petitions for certiorari") to hear appeals from lower courts. Of those requests, the Court grants a tiny number, usually less than 1 percent. The fact that a case raises important constitutional issues makes it more likely that the Court will hear the appeal. The Court is also more likely to grant an appeal if lower courts have reached different legal conclusions in similar cases.

Although several state appellate courts during the 1980s and 1990s took different positions on whether sodomy laws were constitutional, those conclusions, at least in cases decided after *Hardwick*, were based solely on the interpretation of *state* constitutions. The lower courts, both state and federal, were required to follow *Hardwick's* holding that sodomy laws did not violate the right of privacy under the federal Constitution. *Hardwick*, however, had not addressed the question of whether a "gay only" sodomy statute (such as that of Texas) violated the federal Equal Protection Clause. Nonetheless, many post-*Hardwick* courts relied on that case to justify their decision not to apply heightened judicial scrutiny to laws and regulations that treated individuals differently depending on their sexual orientation. Not surprisingly, therefore, by the time the *Lawrence* appeal reached the Supreme Court, no post-*Hardwick* appellate court had held that a sodomy statute violated the federal Equal Protection Clause.

The complicated interplay between substantive due process (or right to privacy) and equal protection arguments against sodomy laws played a crucial role in Harlow's reasoning on how to write a petition for certiorari that maximized the chances that the Court would hear her clients' case. Although Harlow, of course, hoped that the litigation would eventually lead to the overruling of *Hardwick*, it was crucial, in order to maximize the chances that the Court would grant the certiorari petition, for the Justices to understand that it was not necessary to overrule *Hardwick* in order to strike down the Texas Homosexual Conduct Law.

Under the doctrine of stare decisis (or "to stand on the decisions"), there is a strong presumption against courts overruling their own precedents. Although parties can sometimes rebut that presumption —by, for example, showing that a court's earlier decision was clearly incorrect under applicable principles of law—judges generally prefer not to disturb their own rulings. A court that changes its mind with some frequency, after all, undermines its own legitimacy.

In order to show that *Lawrence* was not simply *Hardwick* redux, the certiorari petition emphasized the extent to which the Texas law differed from the Georgia sodomy statute upheld by the Court in 1986. The Texas law, unlike the Georgia provision, explicitly singled out lesbians and gay men for punishment. This was the case even though the sexual conduct in question (oral and anal sex) was widely practiced by the population at large. The petition even cited a comprehensive study of Americans' sexual practices which found that three-quarters of the population engages in oral sex and a quarter in anal sex.[21] But the Texas legislature had decided to impose criminal liability on lesbians and gay men only.

As part of a strategy to make it clear that the Court did not have to overrule *Hardwick* in order to side with her clients, Harlow thought it important to first address the equal protection challenge to the Texas law while leaving the due process/right to privacy argument for the end of the petition. If four Justices (the number required for a certiorari petition to be granted) eventually voted to hear the case, Harlow, in consultation with the other attorneys who were helping with the case, could then decide whether it would make more sense to have the defendants' brief lead with the due process argument.[22] But, for now, the goal was to get the case through the Court's door, which Harlow thought was more likely to happen if the Justices looked at the case primarily from an equal protection perspective because that was the best way, as a doctrinal matter, of distinguishing it from *Hardwick*.

To highlight the equal protection aspects of the case meant to emphasize the discriminatory impact that the Texas law had on LGBT people. In particular, the statute stigmatized what Harlow in the petition called the "loving behavior" of same-sex couples by branding them as criminals. In making this argument, the petition emphasized the Court's holding in *Romer v. Evans* that the mere dislike of a group of individuals cannot justify the government's differential treatment of them.

For his part, Assistant District Attorney Delmore in his papers implored the Court not to hear the case, arguing that the question of whether to criminalize sodomy, as the *Hardwick* Court had recognized in 1986, was one for the legislature. But a few months later—much to Harlow's delight—the Justices decided to hear the case. In making the announcement, the Court stated that it would entertain both the equal protection and the due process challenge to the Homosexual Conduct Law. In doing so, the Court noted that it was willing to tackle directly the question of whether *Hardwick* should be overruled. The stage was now set for what would likely be the most important LGBT rights decision in the Court's history.

▲

The next task was to write a brief that would persuade the Court that it was constitutionally necessary to strike down the Homosexual Conduct Law. As Harlow saw it, the legal arguments justifying such an outcome could be boiled down to two easy-to-understand principles: first, that the police do not belong in people's bedrooms; and second, that this is as true for the bedrooms of LGBT people as it is for those of straight ones.

Although the certiorari petition had emphasized the equal protection challenge to Texas's Homosexual Conduct Law by raising that argument first, Harlow believed that the brief should lead off with a long section on why that law violated substantive due process rights. The fact that the Court had granted review not only of the equal protection claim but also of the due process one meant that at least four Justices were open to the idea of overruling *Hardwick*. By beginning the brief with the due process argument, Harlow sought to signal to the Court that the defendants and their lawyers were confident in their view that *Hardwick* had been incorrectly decided.

One of the biggest challenges facing Harlow and the other drafters of the brief was how to talk to the Court about gay sex. The *Hardwick* Court had accepted both the notion that gay sex was morally problematic and that homosexuality and sodomy were indistinguishable. Or bluntly put, the *Hardwick* Court had dismissed LGBT people as immoral sodomites. Given its narrow view of LGBT individuals, it was not surprising that the *Hardwick* Court also concluded that there was no constitutionally relevant connection between gay sex on the one hand and marriage, family, and relationships on the other.

In order to convey to the Court that there was something more momentous at stake in *Lawrence* than the mere right to engage in anal or oral sex, Harlow decided that the brief should use the term "sexual intimacy" rather than "sodomy" or "sex." Using "sexual intimacy," which appeared twenty-three times in the final version, conveyed the idea that same-sex sexual conduct can be accompanied by commitment and love. The *Hardwick* Court had framed the legal issue in the case narrowly by asking whether the Constitution recognized a fundamental right to engage in homosexual sodomy. It was crucial that the *Lawrence* brief persuade the Court to be more expansive in its constitutional analysis by viewing the case as one that implicated not only the right to engage in particular sexual acts, but also the right to make the exceedingly personal and sensitive choice of whom to be sexually intimate with.

For several decades, legal advocates had grounded the due process right at issue in cases such as *Lawrence* in considerations of privacy. Harlow, however, did not want to rely too much on the right to privacy in the brief because she feared that doing so might lead her clients' case to get caught up in the deep disagreements among the Justices about the advisability, and continued viability, of *Roe v. Wade*.

The fundamental right to privacy can be thought of as having two components, one spatial and the other decisional. The former relates to the notion that privacy considerations limit the state's authority to regulate what takes place in certain locations (such as the home). The latter refers to the idea that privacy concerns also limit the state's power to legislate in matters that affect personal and intimate decisions made by individuals (such as whether to procreate). The brief made use of the right to privacy in a spatial sense by emphasizing the need to protect the home from governmental intrusion. Yet, when it came to discussing the need to protect the personal and intimate decisions of individuals, the brief emphasized the concept of "liberty" rather than that of "privacy."

One of the criticisms that conservatives consistently raise against *Roe v. Wade* is that the opinion was grounded in a concept—that of privacy—that is not mentioned in the Constitution. The Fourteenth Amendment does explicitly protect "liberty," thus providing a textual legitimacy to the brief's arguments about personal autonomy that would have been lacking if it had focused more on considerations of decisional privacy.

The question of which personal and intimate decisions are protected by the Constitution is one of the most intractable and difficult in modern American jurisprudence because, not surprisingly, it often arises in the context of controversial issues such as sex, reproduction, and abortion. The main point made by Lambda's brief in *Lawrence* was that wherever the outer boundaries of constitutionally protected liberty might lie, an adult's choice of sexual partners surely fell within them. As the brief put it "the choice of one's partner, and whether and how to connect sexually are profound attributes of personhood where compulsion by the state is anathema to liberty. Thus, the essential associational freedom here is the freedom to structure one's own private sexual intimacy with another adult."

The brief also directly challenged the *Hardwick* Court's assertion that there was no connection between LGBT sexual intimacy and marriage, family, and relationships. Harlow knew that in the years between *Hardwick* and *Lawrence*, the nation had become increasingly aware of the ways in which LGBT people go about forming and maintaining families and relationships. Harlow also knew that the Justices were cognizant of the many family law cases involving LGBT parties, including the challenges to same-sex marriage bans, that had been litigated in the lower courts during those years. These cases undermined the old stereotype of LGBT people as individuals who are uninterested in or incapable of maintaining strong and committed relationships with their partners. To further support this point, the brief cited the findings of the 2000 census that identified more than 600,000 households composed of same-sex partners nationally, 43,000 of which were in Texas alone. The brief also pointed to sources which estimated that a large number of children across the country were being raised by LGBT parents.

While the first part of the brief addressed the substantive due process issues, the second tackled the question of equal protection. The brief did not ask the Court to subject the Homosexual Conduct Law to heightened scrutiny under the Equal Protection Clause. Instead, it contended that the law was unconstitutional even under the highly deferential rational basis standard of review.

To defend that position, the brief noted that when the legislature in the early 1970s decided to repeal the sodomy statute as applied to heterosexuals, it also chose, for the first time, to target LGBT people by explicitly proscribing their sexual intimacy. The result of this un-equal application of the law was that it imposed on LGBT people a "badge of criminality" that made them "unequal in myriad spheres of everyday life." The existence of sodomy laws, the brief pointed out, was frequently used as a reason to deny LGBT individuals the op-portunity to have custody of or visitation with their children, to get jobs in the public sector, and to benefit from the protection afforded by hate-crime legislation.

The only justification that the state was proffering for its sodomy law's differential treatment of LGBT people was that the majority of citizens had a right to have the law reflect their moral views. Lambda's brief raised two objections to this argument: First, the state's justifi-cation was tautological because it amounted to nothing more than a contention that the law was necessary because the citizens of Texas thought that it was necessary. Second, the enforcement of majoritar-ian morality cannot, by itself, serve as a sufficient justification for a law that targets some individuals for criminal prosecution but not others.

Finally, the brief noted that, for several decades now, there had been a steady move across the country to decriminalize sodomy. While in 1960, all fifty states had sodomy statutes on the books, by the time *Lawrence* reached the Court, only thirteen jurisdictions still had them (which was in turn about half the number that had them in 1986 when the Court decided *Hardwick*). Delmore, in the government brief, urged the Court not to focus on this more recent trend but instead to look to the government's long-standing regulation of consensual sex in the United States, one that encompassed not only the criminalization of sodomy but also of adultery and fornication.

Earlier Supreme Court cases had made it clear that in order for a right to be recognized as fundamental, it must be deeply rooted in the nation's history and traditions. The gradual but incomplete decriminalization that had taken place in the last forty years, Delmore argued, was not enough to satisfy this standard. As his brief succinctly put it, "the petitioners mistake new growth for deep roots." Delmore also argued in his brief that the conduct for which the defendants were arrested had nothing to do with what he characterized (in a decidedly nonsecular choice of words) as the "sacred choices" of marriage, conception, and parenthood. Not surprisingly, Delmore on this point relied on what he contended was the ongoing constitutional viability of *Hardwick*. Sixteen years was too short a period for the Court to change its mind about whether there was a fundamental right to engage in homosexual sodomy. As he had done from the beginning of the case, Delmore relied on the need to promote public morality as the sole justification for the enactment of the Homosexual Conduct Law. It is legitimate for the state, Delmore argued, to be concerned with not only the physical well-being of its citizens but also with their moral well-being.

▲

After the briefs were filed, Harlow turned to the question of who should conduct the oral argument. In addition to wanting someone who had extensive experience arguing before the Supreme Court, she also believed it was important that the attorney be a member of the LGBT community and, as such, be personally impacted by the continued existence of sodomy statutes. As Harlow pondered over the list of candidates, she kept returning to Paul Smith, the head of Jenner & Block's Supreme Court practice. Smith, like several other of his firm's lawyers, had volunteered many hours of his time to help with the brief and was intimately familiar with the constitutional issues raised by the case. He was also an experienced oral advocate, having previously argued nine cases before the Court. In addition, he had clerked for Justice Lewis Powell in the early 1980s and was part of the inner circle of highly influential judges and lawyers in Washington, D.C. Finally, Smith had been open about his homosexuality for many years, and

Harlow suspected that most, if not all, of the Justices knew he was gay. For all of these reasons, Harlow chose Smith to argue the case.

On the morning of the oral argument, people flooded the Supreme Court building. All of the seats in the center of the courtroom, which are reserved for members of the Supreme Court bar, were taken by 6:30 a.m., more than four hours before the oral argument was to begin. It seemed that the majority of those present in the courtroom that day were members of the LGBT community. When Smith stood up and walked the handful of steps from the petitioners' table to the podium that faced the nine Justices of the Supreme Court at 11:09 a.m. on March 26, 2003, the air in the room seemed to crackle with excitement and tension.

It is fair to characterize Smith's argument before the Supreme Court in *Lawrence* as largely a one-on-one debate with Justice Antonin Scalia. Smith knew going into the argument that it would be very difficult, if not impossible, to persuade the conservative Justice to strike down Texas's Homosexual Conduct Law. Rightly or wrongly, Scalia through the years had been consistent in his view that the Due Process Clause provides individuals with no substantive (as opposed to procedural) protections. Nonetheless, how Smith responded to the forceful questioning expected from Scalia would likely be crucial in persuading Justices Anthony Kennedy and Sandra Day O'Connor, the two centrists on the Court, to join the four more liberal Justices (Stephen Breyer, Ruth Bader Ginsburg, David Souter, and John Paul Stevens) in striking down the sodomy law.

Of the thirty-five questions that the Justices asked Smith during his thirty-minute argument, twenty-three were posed by Scalia. Early on during their exchange, Scalia revealed just how much of a judicial outlier he was on matters related to substantive due process when he questioned the well-established principle that it is unconstitutional for the state to limit the intimacy choices of married couples. In many ways, Scalia's radical constitutional perspective served Smith's purposes because it allowed him to follow up with the suggestion that perhaps other Justices on the Court might believe that married couples do have constitutionally protected rights to build their relationships around the type of sexual intimacy they deemed best for themselves. Smith added that sexual intimacy can also play an important role in the relationships of unmarried couples, whether they be gay or straight.

The exchange over the extent to which the Constitution provided protection to married couples was followed by another interaction between Scalia and Smith. This time, the Justice took issue with the lawyer's contention that three-quarters of the states had gotten rid of their sodomy statutes because they realized that the laws were inconsistent with "basic American values about the relationship between the individual and the State." Apparently seeking to make the point that such repeals were irrelevant, Justice Scalia asked the lawyer to assume that at one point all of the states had laws prohibiting flagpole sitting, and that eventually the legislatures repealed those laws. Did this mean that flagpole sitting was a fundamental right? No, Smith responded calmly. The Court's past rulings had made it clear that what mattered was not only the history of the regulations in question but also whether the claimed right goes to the core of how people define their lives. The decision to engage in sexual conduct with certain others, unlike the choice to sit on flagpoles, was an exceedingly personal one that implicated some of the most private and intimate considerations faced by individuals.

A few minutes later, in response to Smith's complaint that the Texas law had to be justified in ways other than through the mere disapproval by the majority of a certain minority, Scalia retorted by noting that society frequently makes moral judgments that are then codified into law. Wasn't the prohibition against bigamy, for example, nothing more than a reflection of public morality? Bigamy laws were different, Smith responded, because their purpose was to protect the state-created institution of marriage. In contrast, Texas was not claiming that it was protecting an institution through its sodomy law. Indeed, Smith added, *Lawrence* was quite similar to a case decided by the Court almost forty years earlier in which it struck down a Florida law that prohibited unmarried cohabitation but only when it was engaged in by interracial couples.[23] The Court in the cohabitation case had rejected the government's claim that it was regulating conduct rather than impermissibly imposing a burden on certain groups of individuals. Similarly, Smith argued, the Texas law was not ultimately about the prohibition of certain sexual acts; if it were, then the legislature would prohibit all sodomy regardless of who engages in it. By only proscribing same-sex sexual conduct, the state was targeting individuals rather than conduct.

After Smith finished his argument, Charles Rosenthal, the Harris County district attorney, stood up to represent the government. It was, as the Houston Chronicle put it, "peculiar" that Rosenthal had decided to argue the case himself. Rosenthal's experience as a prosecutor had been limited almost entirely to appearing before trial judges and juries; he had almost no experience arguing before appellate courts. As the newspaper pointed out, many in Houston suspected that Rosenthal chose to argue the case himself—rather than allowing Delmore, a highly experienced appellate advocate who was intimately familiar with the litigation—because he wanted to score political points with Republican activists back home.[24] Regardless of his reasons, Rosenthal's performance before the Supreme Court in Lawrence was not stellar. Linda Greenhouse, the New York Times Supreme Court reporter, wrote the next day that the oral argument "proved to be a mismatch of advocates to a degree rarely seen at the court." USA Today called the arguments "surprisingly lopsided," while the Houston Chronicle characterized Rosenthal's appearance before the Court as "lackluster."[25]

As he had done with Smith, Justice Scalia largely dominated the Court's exchange with Rosenthal. Unlike with Smith, however, the conservative Justice did not seem troubled by the substance of the arguments presented by the people's lawyer. Instead, Scalia appeared exasperated by Rosenthal's inability to present the state's argument in a coherent and persuasive way. For example, at one point early on during Rosenthal's presentation, the prosecutor conceded that the national trend regarding the decriminalization of sodomy was a possible indication that the general public no longer condemned homosexual acts. But Justice Scalia had no interest in accepting such a concession. Didn't the fact that Congress had on several occasions refused to enact a law prohibiting discrimination on the basis of "sexual preference" show that the public did not approve of "homosexual acts"? Rosenthal sheepishly agreed that it did.

As the argument proceeded, Justice Stephen Breyer, along with Justice David Souter, tried repeatedly to pin Rosenthal down on what harm sodomy laws were meant to prevent. The two Justices noted that laws against adultery protected the institution of marriage while those against drug use protected individuals from bodily harm. But what was the harm to others inflicted by consensual sodomy? In the end, Rosenthal could not respond, except to repeat, yet again, that the state had the right "to prohibit certain immoral conduct." This type of reasoning was probably enough to satisfy Justice Scalia, as well as Chief Justice William Rehnquist and Justice Clarence Thomas, the other two conservatives on the Court, but it was unlikely to carry much weight with the four liberals. The case would therefore likely come down to the votes of the two Justices (Kennedy and O'Connor) who constituted the court's ideological center and who remained largely silent during the oral argument.

After the oral argument, Rosenthal returned to Texas and did not speak much about the case or his performance. Several years later, however, Rosenthal's involvement in *Lawrence* took a rather ironic twist. In 2008, the media revealed that Rosenthal, who was married, had used his office computer to send amorous e-mails to his secretary, with whom he had had an affair. The press also reported that Rosenthal used his work e-mail to send messages containing sexual and racial jokes, as well as pornographic images. When this information became public, Rosenthal—the same career prosecutor who had tried to persuade the U.S. Supreme Court not to recognize a right to privacy in the sodomy litigation—argued before a trial judge that his right to privacy under *Lawrence* allowed him to keep his e-mails private. The judge rejected Rosenthal's legal position and ordered that all of the district attorney's work e-mail be made public. Shortly thereafter, the Harris County Republican Party announced that it would no longer support Rosenthal's reelection for a third term. A few weeks later, Rosenthal, a seemingly broken man, resigned only hours after the state attorney general filed a suit seeking his removal.[26] It is an interesting historical footnote that the careers of the two lawyers (Michael Bowers and Charles Rosenthal) whose offices defended the Georgia and Texas sodomy statutes before the Supreme Court eventually ended their public careers in disgrace related to sexual matters.

▲

The Supreme Court frequently waits until the end of its term in late June to release its hardest-fought and most controversial decisions. In June 2003, with four days remaining in the term, Harlow traveled from New York to Washington, D.C. It was her intention to sit in the courtroom during those days until the Justices released their ruling in *Lawrence*. Three of the days went by without the issuance of the opinion, meaning that the Court would rule on the case on the term's very last day.

Given how the oral argument went, Harlow was guardedly optimistic that her clients would prevail on their equal protection claim, but she feared that there might not be the necessary five votes to overrule *Hardwick* by holding that the Constitution protects the ability of LGBT people to engage in sexual intimacy. She was thrilled, therefore, when Justice Kennedy, in reading the Court's opinion from the bench, started by discussing the ways in which the Constitution protects the rights of liberty and autonomy of individuals to make important decisions about their lives. A few minutes later, as Kennedy explained how the Court had made a terrible mistake in *Hardwick* and how that case had to be overruled, tears welled up in Harlow's eyes. And she was not alone. There were others in the packed courtroom quietly sobbing as Justice Kennedy spoke. The same Court that in *Hardwick* had dismissed the notion that the Constitution provided protection in matters of sexual intimacy to LGBT people as "facetious" was at that very moment issuing an opinion in which it recognized the basic human dignity of LGBT individuals. The contrast between what had happened seventeen years earlier and what was taking place on that June day in 2003 could not have been starker.

The Court in *Hardwick*, Kennedy explained, failed to understand the extent of the liberty interest at issue in that case. The litigation over the Georgia statute had not been, as the Court had concluded in 1986, about the right to engage in sodomy. To think of the claim in that narrow way was demeaning to Mr. Hardwick in the same way that it would be demeaning to a married couple to suggest that their marriage was only about sexual intercourse. Sodomy laws, in addition to proscribing particular sexual acts, Kennedy explained, also seek to control personal relationships. Kennedy added that the Constitution requires that individuals, in the absence of demonstrated harm to self or others, be allowed to participate in intimate relationships of their choice, especially within the confines of their homes. Kennedy made clear that this constitutional right applied to everyone, including LGBT people.

Most of Kennedy's opinion involved a detailed critique of *Hardwick*. Not only did the Court in that case frame the issue too narrowly, it also simplified the historical record. There is no long-standing tradition in this country of laws aimed exclusively at same-sex sexual conduct. While it was true that American sodomy laws could be traced back to the English Reformation Parliament of 1533, it was not until the 1970s that a handful of states explicitly criminalized same-sex sexual relations. Prior to that point, Kennedy explained, sodomy laws were aimed at condemning nonprocreative sex in general rather than gay sex in particular.

Kennedy also noted how the *Hardwick* opinion was inconsistent with what he called an "emerging awareness" that adults have important liberty interests in making decisions about their sexual lives. This recognition was reflected in the clear trend among states, starting in the 1960s, to decriminalize sodomy. Furthermore, although the Court in *Hardwick* had relied on what it took to be Western civilization's clear condemnation of homosexuality, Kennedy noted that the European Court of Human Rights had several years before that case held that the criminalizing of consensual same-sex sexual conduct violated the European Convention on Human Rights.[27]

Finally, Kennedy explained that the Court's substantive due process precedents did not allow the state to criminalize conduct based solely on moral judgments. This was particularly true when the conduct in question implicated the liberty interests of individuals to make decisions about their sexual practices. Those who engage in same-sex sexual conduct, Kennedy wrote, "are entitled to respect for their private lives. The State cannot demean their existence or control their destiny by making their private sexual conduct a crime."

The four liberal Justices on the Court (Breyer, Ginsburg, Souter, and Stevens) joined Kennedy's opinion. Justice O'Connor also voted to strike down Texas's Homosexual Conduct Law but unlike the majority, she did so on equal protection grounds. O'Connor was one of only two sitting Justices (the other was Rehnquist) who had voted with the majority in *Hardwick*. Rather than agreeing to overrule *Hardwick*, O'Connor concluded that the sodomy statute was unconstitutional because it represented nothing more than an effort to harm and stigmatize a politically unpopular group.

Although Kennedy in his opinion had also noted the sodomy law's stigmatizing impact on LGBT people, he reasoned that it was necessary to strike that law down on substantive due process grounds because otherwise it might be claimed that a sodomy statute that applied both to same-sex and to different-sex couples would pass constitutional muster. In her concurrence, O'Connor explained that an effort to apply equally a sodomy law against gays and straights "would not long stand in our democratic society." O'Connor, in other words, was optimistic about the ability of the political process to dispense with laws that prohibited everyone from engaging in sodomy. In her estimation, it was enough for the Court to hold that lesbians and gay men could not be singled out for differential treatment by criminalizing their (and only their) consensual sexual conduct. Interestingly, while Justice O'Connor was willing to leave undisturbed *Hardwick's* holding that moral considerations were enough to insulate a law from a due process challenge, those same considerations, in her view, were not enough to withstand an equal protection challenge. When it came to the differential treatment of otherwise similarly situated individuals, O'Connor explained, the state must provide a rationale that goes beyond mere disapproval of those individuals.

The dissenters were Chief Justice Rehnquist, Justice Thomas, and Justice Scalia. Unsurprisingly, it was Scalia who wrote the opinion explaining the views of all three men. He began by taking the majority to task for so willingly overruling *Hardwick* while refusing, in earlier cases, to overrule *Roe v. Wade.* The overruling of *Hardwick,* Scalia predicted, will lead to "a massive disruption of the current social order" because it would likely render unconstitutional laws grounded on notions of morality that prohibited "bigamy, same-sex marriage, adult incest, prostitution, masturbation, adultery, fornication, bestiality, and obscenity." In contrast, the overruling of *Roe* would only return the nation to the abortion regime that existed for decades prior to 1973, one in which states were allowed to decide whether and how to restrict access to abortions.

For Scalia, it did not matter whether sodomy laws prior to the 1970s targeted sodomy in general or same-sex sodomy in particular. What was important was that homosexual sodomy had been against the law in most states for most of the nation's history, which meant that the Constitution did not recognize a fundamental right to engage in that conduct. The decriminalization that began in the 1960s was irrelevant because it was too recent. The fundamental right in question, Scalia noted, must be deeply rooted in the nation's history and tradition. By definition, the majority's discussion of an "emerging awareness" about the importance of freedom in matters of consensual sexual conduct could not be "deeply rooted" in the nation's past.

Finally, as he had done in *Romer v. Evans,* Scalia dismissed the majority's opinion as "the product of a Court, which is the product of a law-profession culture, that has largely signed on to the so-called homosexual agenda." The Court, in other words, was once again doing nothing more than taking sides in the culture wars, rather than acting as a neutral arbiter making sure "that the democratic rules of engagement are observed." According to Scalia, what the people in Texas had done through their legislators in enacting the Homosexual Conduct Law was "well within the range of traditional democratic action." He warned that the Court was making it possible for future courts to deprive the people of the opportunity to use the democratic process to express their disapproval of same-sex marriages.

▲

The LGBT community across the country held rallies to celebrate the Court's ruling in *Lawrence*. In Houston, several hundred people gathered in front of City Hall for a celebration that included an appearance by Lawrence and Garner. Celebratory rallies were also held in Boston, Chicago, Detroit, Los Angeles, New York, and several other cities. There was much for LGBT people to be happy about: The Supreme Court had lifted from their collective backs the heavy stigma that came with the fact that, until a few hours earlier, their intimate sexual conduct could be deemed criminal by the state. And, just as important, the Court had done so in a way that acknowledged their basic human dignity while recognizing that their sexual lives and relationships, like those of heterosexuals, were entitled to constitutional respect.

## The Impact

In the late 1970s, Gallup began polling Americans on the question of whether it was appropriate for gay sex to be criminalized. In those early polls, respondents were equally divided, with about 45 percent agreeing that "homosexual relations between consenting adults should be legal" and roughly 45 percent disagreeing (with the rest unable or unwilling to provide an answer). During the decades that followed, the percentage of respondents who agreed that "homosexual relations" should be legal increased gradually to the point that by May 2003, the month before the Supreme Court issued its opinion in *Lawrence*, 60 percent of respondents stated that homosexual relations should be legal.[28]

Interestingly, that number dropped to 50 percent in the weeks following *Lawrence* and remained at that level for two years (before going back up to 56 percent in 2006 and remaining steady since). It can be argued, therefore, that the immediate impact of *Lawrence* was to increase the public's support for laws criminalizing consensual gay sex, but it is not that simple. In the aftermath to *Lawrence*, there was little criticism of the opinion for having struck down a sodomy law as such. Instead, conservative activists, commentators, and politicians attacked the Court's ruling because they viewed it as paving the way for the recognition of same-sex marriages. The *Lawrence* Court's holding that majoritarian morality was not enough to justify sodomy laws suggested that morality would also not be enough to defend same-sex marriage bans.

In the months that followed *Lawrence*, social conservatives expressed a growing sense of anxiety about what that opinion might bring. This led right-wing groups to announce, in September 2003, that they were "redirecting resources from the antiabortion movement and the school voucher fight to a new effort to stop the expansion of gay rights." Much of this effort focused on the issue of same-sex marriage, with the president of the Family Research Council, for example, warning that "unless the American people rise up to defend this indispensable institution, we could lose marriage in a very short time." For his part, James Dobson, the leader of Focus on the Family, told his supporters in a letter that "the homosexual activist movement . . . is poised to administer a devastating and potentially fatal blow to the traditional family."[29] Also, following *Lawrence*, the Southern Baptist Convention approved a resolution condemning same-sex unions, while the U.S. Conference of Catholic Bishops endorsed a federal constitutional amendment to ban same-sex marriages.

Social conservatives' worst fears about the impact of *Lawrence* seemed to be realized only five months later when the Massachusetts Supreme Judicial Court, in *Goodridge v. Department of Public Health*, became the first appellate court in the country to call for the recognition of same-sex marriages.[30] It would be incorrect to contend that *Lawrence* compelled *Goodridge*. The former case was decided on federal constitutional grounds while the plaintiffs in *Goodridge* relied

exclusively on state constitutional arguments to challenge Massachusetts's same-sex marriage prohibition. In addition, the sodomy case
was about the explicit use of the state's coercive powers (through the
application of a criminal law) while the marriage case was about access to rights and benefits that the government distributes through
the institution of marriage.

Despite these differences, it is unlikely that the Massachusetts court
would have had the legal fortitude to call for the recognition of same-
sex marriages if the Supreme Court in *Lawrence* had not used highly
inclusive language to conclude that the choice of sexual partners by
lesbians and gay men is as important, and as worthy of constitutional
respect, as is that of heterosexuals. It seems that the Supreme Court's
embrace of the idea that LGBT people share a basic human dignity
arising from their sexuality encouraged the Massachusetts court to
also rely on that commonality in reaching its holding.

The Massachusetts court left no doubt that it had been deeply influenced by *Lawrence* when it noted that the Supreme Court's sodomy decision had affirmed the principle that the federal Constitution
protects "the core concept of common human dignity" and that, as
such, it limits the power of the government to intrude "into the deeply
personal realms of consensual adult expressions of intimacy and one's
choice of intimate partner." The state court also explained that the
Massachusetts constitution frequently provides more protection to
individuals than does the federal Constitution, even in instances
when both documents contain essentially the same language. In doing
so, the state constitution protects both "'freedom from' unwarranted
government intrusion into protected spheres of life and 'freedom to'
partake in benefits created by the State for the common good." And
there can be no more basic liberty and due process right, the court
concluded, than the freedom to decide "whether and whom to marry,
how to express sexual intimacy, and whether and how to establish a
family."

If *Lawrence* made social conservatives nervous, *Goodridge* made
them angry. In the twelve months following the Massachusetts court's
same-sex marriage ruling, right-wing political groups succeeded in

persuading voters in thirteen states to amend their constitutions to prohibit same-sex marriages. Voters in an additional ten states did the same in 2005 and 2006.

This fevered rush to amend state constitutions in order to limit the rights of individuals seemed driven less by a realistic fear that judges would strike down bans on same-sex marriage—many of the constitutional amendments, after all, were approved in states (like Alabama and Mississippi) with highly conservative judiciaries—than by the urgency felt by many social conservatives to send an unequivocal message of disapproval of same-sex marriage. In fact, it would take another five years after *Goodridge* before a second state supreme court (that of California) held that its state constitution required the recognition of same-sex marriages.[31]

During that intervening period, appellate courts in Arizona, Maryland, New York, and Washington rejected the claim by LGBT plaintiffs that the state had a constitutional obligation to recognize same-sex marriages despite the absence, in the respective state constitutions, of provisions explicitly banning same-sex marriages.[32] The New York Court of Appeals in particular disagreed with the notion that *Lawrence* was relevant to the issue of same-sex marriage by pointing out that the litigants in the Texas sodomy case had asked for protection against governmental interference with intimate sexual conduct. In contrast, the LGBT plaintiffs in marriage cases were seeking access to "a state-conferred benefit." While the government, after *Lawrence*, clearly lacked the authority to prohibit adults from engaging in consensual sexual relationships in private, that did not mean that it was constitutionally required to legally recognize those relationships. Unlike the Massachusetts court, the New York court concluded that substantive due process principles imposed negative obligations on the state not to interfere with same-sex relationships but did not mandate an affirmative obligation to recognize them as marital.[33]

The majority in *Lawrence* tried to steer clear of the marriage issue by emphasizing that the case did not involve the question of legal recognition of relationships. Nonetheless, in explaining why the sodomy statute was unconstitutional, the opinion paid considerable attention to the implications of the Texas law for those in sexual relationships. For the Court, the case was not just about the liberty implications of restricting sexual *conduct* as such; it was also about the impact of those restrictions on intimate *relationships*. In fact, for the Court, it made no sense to discuss the freedom to engage in sexual conduct without also discussing the ability of individuals to form and maintain personal relationships. As Justice Kennedy explained, in one of the majority opinion's most notable sentences, "when sexuality finds overt expression in intimate conduct with another person, the conduct can be but one element in a personal bond that is more enduring."

The *Lawrence* Court understood that relationships are central to the dignity and autonomy of all individuals, including those who are gay or lesbian. As the Court saw it, what was ultimately at issue in the case was the ability of individuals to "retain their dignity as free persons" in the face of regulations such as Texas's sodomy statute that "seek to control . . . personal relationship[s]." Once the understanding of the liberty interests protected by the Due Process Clause in matters of sexuality is expanded, as it was in *Lawrence*, to include not only sexual conduct but sexual relationships as well, then the state's burdening of same-sex relationships through its refusal to recognize them becomes constitutionally suspect. Whether courts, going forward, accept that argument remains to be seen. What is clear is that *Lawrence* helps to lay the foundation for the claim that the government's failure to recognize same-sex marriages has important implications for personal liberty and autonomy because it burdens relationships that are otherwise constitutionally protected.

▲

Another issue that has arisen in the aftermath of *Lawrence* is the extent to which the opinion held that the Constitution recognizes a *fundamental right* to engage in consensual sexual activity. Although the Court had previously concluded that individuals have a fundamental right to use contraceptives, and that women have such a right to decide whether to carry a fetus to term, it had never, prior to *Lawrence*, held that there was a fundamental right to engage in sexual activity independent of the child-creating and childbearing implications of the earlier cases. There is much to *Lawrence* which suggests that the ruling is a fundamental rights one, including the Court's extended discussion of the importance of personal autonomy and dignity as related to the ability of individuals to choose sexual partners, as well as its repeated reference to the earlier fundamental rights cases involving contraception and abortion. The Court, however, did not state explicitly that a fundamental right was implicated in the case. Further complicating matters, the Court, in the end, struck down the statute because it did not further "a legitimate state interest," which is the standard that is usually applied in rational basis cases.

As a matter of judicial review, it makes all the difference whether *Lawrence* is a fundamental rights case. If adults have a fundamental right to engage in consensual sexual conduct, then government regulations and policies that interfere with that right are presumed unconstitutional, a presumption that can be overcome only if the state establishes the existence of a compelling interest. On the other hand, if *Lawrence* is not a fundamental rights case, then those same regulations and policies will be upheld by courts as long as there is any rational justification for their adoption.

At the time the Supreme Court issued its opinion in *Lawrence*, the ACLU was in the process of challenging a Florida law that prohibits lesbians and gay men from adopting. After *Lawrence*, the ACLU filed a supplemental brief before the U.S. Court of Appeals for the Eleventh Circuit arguing that Florida's adoption ban was unconstitutional because it impermissibly burdened the fundamental right of individuals to engage in private sexual intimacy as recognized by the Supreme Court in the Texas sodomy case. More specifically, the ACLU took the position that Florida was violating the fundamental right of LGBT people to choose their sexual partners by denying them the opportunity to adopt solely because of whom they chose to be sexually intimate with. But the Court of Appeals rejected that argument, noting that the *Lawrence* Court did not explicitly hold that the case implicated a fundamental right; nor did it apply heightened scrutiny to strike down the Texas statute. Furthermore, the federal court, like the New York Court of Appeals in the same-sex marriage case, distinguished between the negative right to be free from governmental regulation (implicated by a sodomy law) and the positive right to enjoy certain state-provided benefits (such as the opportunity to adopt children).[34]

Other courts have disagreed with the Eleventh Circuit's conclusion that *Lawrence* calls only for the application of rational basis review. For example, the U.S. Court of Appeals for the Ninth Circuit, relying on *Lawrence,* has called for the application of heightened scrutiny in determining whether the military's exclusion of openly gay service members violates their substantive due process rights. The Ninth Circuit has reasoned that the higher level of scrutiny is appropriate not only because the *Lawrence* Court relied extensively on fundamental rights cases in striking down the sodomy law but also because it overruled *Hardwick* on the ground that that case was insufficiently sensitive to the liberty implications at stake when the government proscribes consensual sodomy. The Court of Appeals interpreted this to mean that the *Lawrence* Court wanted courts in future cases to focus on the challenged regulation's impact on sexual liberty and privacy rather than on whether there is a rational basis for its implementation.[35]

The Ninth Circuit did not strike down the military's "Don't Ask, Don't Tell" policy; instead, it remanded the case to the lower court for further proceedings. In doing so, however, the court held that when the government "attempts to intrude upon the personal and private lives of homosexuals, in a manner that implicates the rights identified in *Lawrence,* [it] must advance an important governmental interest, the intrusion must significantly further that interest, and the intrusion must be necessary to further that interest."

Much of the government-sponsored discrimination faced by LGBT people is the result of regulations and policies that seek to discourage homosexuality based on outdated notions about the negative impact, both on society and on the individuals in question, of same-sex sexual intimacy. It is unlikely that such regulations and policies, including perhaps the military's "Don't Ask, Don't Tell" policy, can withstand the kind of heightened scrutiny that the Ninth Circuit, in the aftermath of *Lawrence*, believes is appropriate in these types of cases.

As with its impact on the issue of same-sex marriage, the question of whether *Lawrence* is a fundamental rights case is one that is still being played out in the courts. It may be that the Supreme Court will eventually clarify this matter by holding explicitly that adults have a fundamental right to engage in consensual and private sexual conduct. In the meantime, the Ninth Circuit's ruling bodes well for future efforts to do away with regulations and policies that place burdens on LGBT people solely because of their choice of sexual partners.

▲

One area where *Lawrence* should have a positive impact is that of family law. Prior to *Lawrence*, courts frequently relied on the existence of sodomy statutes to deny LGBT people custody of their children when a heterosexual, whether a former spouse or a family member, also sought custody. For these courts, the fact that the state criminalized consensual same-sex sexual conduct meant that all sexually active LGBT people were either actual or potential criminals. In choosing between a criminal (i.e., an LGBT parent) and a noncriminal (i.e., a straight parent or guardian), these courts chose the latter.[36]

Now that the state, after *Lawrence*, lacks the constitutional authority to enforce sodomy statutes, it is no longer possible to equate homosexuality with criminality. It would seem clear, therefore, that the mere fact that some parents engage in consensual same-sex sexual conduct cannot be used to deny them custody of their children.

Starting approximately a decade before *Lawrence*, some state appellate courts began rejecting the application of a categorical or per se rule that deemed LGBT parents incapable of promoting the best interests of their children. These courts called for a more nuanced determination that looked for a nexus between the same-sex sexual orientation of parents and the likelihood of harm to their children.[37] Even when applying the so-called "nexus test," however, some courts seemed to require LGBT parents to either hide or minimize their relationships with their partners in order to receive or maintain custody of their children while not asking the same of heterosexual parents. For example, in the years leading up to *Lawrence*, the Alabama Supreme Court denied custody to a lesbian mother because she was open with her children about her relationship with another woman, while the North Carolina Supreme Court took custody away from a gay dad because his partner moved in with him.[38] In a similar vein, some courts have permitted LGBT parents to visit with their children only so long as their partners are not also present.[39]

These types of judicial decisions require parents to make the extremely difficult and painful choice between having custody of or visitation with their children, and maintaining their relationships with their partners. In doing so, it would seem clear that they violate the right of all individuals, recognized in *Lawrence*, to make choices about sexual partners without state interference. Indeed, short of incarcerating LGBT people for engaging in consensual sex, it is difficult to imagine what could be more coercive than to deny them custody of or visitation with their children on the basis of their participation in an intimate relationship with another adult of the same sex. For this reason, one would expect that *Lawrence* will lead future courts to stop forcing LGBT parents to choose between their children and their partners.

▲

One of the most important effects of *Lawrence* is that, by overruling *Hardwick*, it took away from gay rights opponents the ability to defend discriminatory policies against LGBT people on the ground that the Supreme Court of the United States had given its constitutional stamp of approval to the use of the criminal law as a means to discourage homosexuality. *Lawrence's* importance, however, lies not only in its overruling of *Hardwick* but also in the way in which it did so. While the *Hardwick* Court summarily dismissed the notion that there was any connection between homosexuality and the types of relationships and families valued by heterosexuals, the *Lawrence* Court spoke of a common human dignity that is implicated whenever individuals make decisions related to sexual intimacy and relationships.

What this means in practice is perhaps best reflected in an immigration case decided two years after *Lawrence*. In 1998, Nasser Karouni, a gay immigrant from Lebanon, applied for asylum. Karouni, who came to the United States in the late 1980s on a tourist visa and then failed to return home upon its expiration, argued in his asylum petition that he feared persecution if he returned to Lebanon. In support of his petition, Karouni introduced evidence that Lebanese government officials, as well as Hezbollah militiamen, had harassed and victimized him because of his sexual orientation. In particular, he related how armed militiamen one night stormed into his apartment threatening to kill him because he was in a sexual relationship with another man. Although the militiamen did not kill him that night, they did, several weeks later, kill his gay cousin.

In arguing that Karouni was not entitled to remain in the United States as a refugee, the government contended in court that he faced persecution if he returned to Lebanon not because of his *status* as a gay man but because he might engage in homosexual *acts*. As long as Karouni refrained from engaging in those acts, the government argued, he had no reason to fear persecution. This type of legal argument would have likely succeeded prior to *Lawrence*. After all, same-sex sexual acts, following *Hardwick*, were not subject to constitutional protection.

Not so after *Lawrence*. In Mr. Karouni's case, the U.S. Court of Appeals for the Ninth Circuit rejected the government's effort to force him to make, what the court described as, "the Hobson's choice of returning to Lebanon and either (1) facing persecution for engaging in future homosexual acts or (2) living a life of celibacy." Forcing Karouni to make such a choice, the court ruled, was inconsistent with the *Lawrence* Court's recognition of the link between sexuality on the one hand and personal bonds and relationships on the other. As the Court of Appeals put it, by arguing that Karouni could avoid persecution by abstaining from future homosexual acts, the [government] is essentially arguing that the [Immigration and Naturalization Act] requires Karouni to change a fundamental aspect of his human identity, and forsake the intimate contact and enduring personal bond that the Due Process Clause of the Fourteenth Amendment protects from impingement in this country [as recognized in *Lawrence*].[40]

In the end, the court rejected the government's contention that the immigration law required Karouni to change such an important part of who he was or to relinquish, as the *Lawrence* Court put it, such an "integral part of [his] human freedom."

The government's position in the *Karouni* case is particularly interesting because it was LGBT rights proponents who, prior to *Lawrence*, frequently attempted to distinguish between conduct and status. Even if the government, in other words, could proscribe gay sex after *Hardwick*, the reasoning went, that did not mean it could treat gay individuals differently simply because of their status as homosexuals. This type of argument was particularly common in cases challenging the military's ban on gay service members. In several of those cases, LGBT rights lawyers chose to proceed with plaintiffs for whom the military lacked evidence of participation in homosexual acts and who thus could be thought of as being celibate.[41] Although relying on this category of plaintiffs to challenge the military's exclusionary policy made a certain amount of strategic sense while operating under the *Hardwick* constitutional regime, it was also problematic to the extent that it suggested that LGBT people were entitled to constitutional protection only if they refrained from engaging in any same-sex sexual conduct.

As *Karouni* shows, after *Lawrence*, it is the government that has sometimes attempted to disaggregate the status of being gay from gay sexual acts. As the Ninth Circuit noted, however, such a disaggregation is ultimately dehumanizing because it assumes that it is possible for individuals to lead full human lives without having the option of being sexually intimate with others of their choice. It was precisely that assumption which became untenable after *Lawrence,* and the *Karouni* case is but one illustration of how the Constitution, properly interpreted, does not allow the government to use it as a justification for regulations and policies that place special burdens on LGBT people because of their relationship choices.

# Conclusion

ALTHOUGH THIS BOOK has focused on the LGBT rights movement's judicial strategy, that strategy has been only one part of its larger political and social struggle on behalf of sexual minorities. The movement has sought to advance the interests of LGBT people in many ways other than through the courts, including by lobbying legislatures at the local, state, and federal levels to enact antidiscrimination and hate crime laws; by persuading private and public employers to provide domestic partnership benefits; and by encouraging entertainment and media outlets to accurately portray the lives of LGBT people.

None of the tactics pursued by the LGBT rights movement, however, has proved to be as controversial as its legal strategy. This is primarily because social conservatives have loudly and repeatedly—often to great political effect—questioned the legitimacy of relying on judicial rulings to advance LGBT rights positions. I end this book by noting some themes that run across the five cases profiled here which I believe help to legitimize the LGBT rights movement's judicial strategy. While defending the legitimacy of that strategy, I also explain why it is likely, going forward, that the movement will rely less on the courts to achieve its goals in the next two decades than it has during the last two.

▲

The five lawsuits profiled in this book share several similarities. All five cases involved LGBT litigants who used the courts, with the assistance of LGBT rights lawyers, to protect not only their interests as individuals but also those of the broader LGBT community. There are other, perhaps less evident, themes common to the five lawsuits that reveal vital aspects of the LGBT rights movement's judicial strategy and help defend its legitimacy and appropriateness.

GRADUALISM   No social movement that adopts a judicial strategy can expect to achieve all, or even most, of its goals through one lawsuit. Not even *Brown v. Board of Education,* the most important civil rights case in the nation's history, achieved such a result. In fact, it bears remembering that the civil rights movement began pursuing a judicial strategy several decades before *Brown.* In those earlier cases, the NAACP Legal Defense Fund successfully challenged racially discriminatory policies in areas ranging from access to voting to segregation in higher education. It was only after those undoubtedly significant, but nonetheless limited, victories were firmly in place that civil rights lawyers asked the Supreme Court, in *Brown,* to render unconstitutional the "separate but equal" principle that had served as the foundation of legal segregation since Reconstruction.

It is also important to keep in mind that *Brown* was not the end of the road for the legal component of the civil rights struggle. It took additional decisions by the Supreme Court, as well as resolute actions by the legislative and executive branches of the federal government, to sweep away the resilient vestiges of the Jim Crow regime.

The LGBT rights movement, like the civil rights movement before it, has pursued a gradualist legal strategy. In doing so, the movement has focused on challenging particular manifestations of homophobia and anti-LGBT discrimination through relatively narrow cases rather than on attempting to put an end to all such manifestations in one or two fell swoops.

Of the five cases profiled in this book, none reflects the movement's gradualist approach better than *Braschi*. Rather than seeking to have same-sex relationships recognized simultaneously in many different contexts, the *Braschi* litigation sought to persuade New York courts to hold that a committed same-sex relationship could constitute a family within the meaning of the Rent Control Law. It was only after that victory was firmly in hand that the movement then used the reasoning of the New York Court of Appeals, as well as the political momentum that the judicial victory created, to try to persuade government officials to recognize that same-sex couples were entitled to some of the other benefits that accompany the legal recognition of heterosexual relationships.

Similarly, the *Nabozny* litigation sought to make the essential but circumscribed point that the Constitution is violated when school officials fail to protect students from repeated antigay harassment perpetrated by other students. As a policy matter, there are many ways in which school officials can help to maximize the educational experience of LGBT students other than by protecting students from peer-on-peer harassment. For example, officials can offer a curriculum that includes issues of concern and interest to LGBT students, and they can help to create an institutional atmosphere that is tolerant of difference and diversity. The judicial victory in *Nabozny* did lead some school districts to institute these kinds of policies, but that was not the focus of the case; instead, the litigation's primary objective was to prevent LGBT students from being physically and verbally accosted in school hallways and bathrooms. Once that objective was accomplished, activists were able to turn their attention to the additional ways in which officials can make it possible for LGBT students to participate equally in the offerings and lives of their schools.

It may at first blush seem that the *Romer* and *Lawrence* lawsuits constituted less gradualist forms of litigation than either *Braschi* or *Nabozny*. The two former cases, after all, resulted in U.S. Supreme Court opinions that struck down as unconstitutional entire classes of law—restrictions on the scope of antidiscrimination provisions in *Romer* and sodomy laws in *Lawrence*. When we place the cases in their proper context, however, it becomes clear that they also reflect the LGBT rights movement's gradualist legal strategy.

In *Romer*, the LGBT rights lawyers did not attempt, once the trial ended, to use the litigation to get a broad ruling that sexual orientation constituted a suspect classification, one that would prospectively require courts to apply heightened judicial scrutiny whenever the government attempts to make distinctions among individuals based on their sexual orientation. Instead, when the case was appealed to the Colorado Supreme Court, and later to the U.S. Supreme Court, the LGBT rights lawyers challenged Amendment 2 on more circumscribed grounds based on the rights of individuals to participate equally in the political process and on the constitutional illegitimacy of Colorado's targeting of one highly stigmatized group in order to deny its members (and no others) antidiscrimination protection under the law.

The gradualist strategy pursued by the LGBT rights movement in *Romer* is also reflected in the fact that after the initial victory in the Colorado courts, the LGBT rights lawyers sought to prevent Supreme Court review. The goal of the litigation was to have the courts strike down Amendment 2, rather than to have the U.S. Supreme Court issue a broad opinion about the equality rights of LGBT people. The fact that the Court did, in the end, speak in highly inclusive language in rendering unconstitutional Colorado's effort to relegate lesbians and gay men to the status of second-class citizens, while obviously welcomed by the movement, was not the litigation's main purpose.

Similarly, *Lawrence* was the culmination of the movement's long and methodical effort to challenge sodomy laws, which during the 1970s focused primarily on the federal courts and then, in the late 1980s after *Bowers v. Hardwick*, shifted to the state courts. In the end, the movement spent more than a generation chipping away at sodomy laws, a process that paved the way for the Court's ruling in *Lawrence* that those laws, by the beginning of the twenty-first century, had become constitutional outliers because they had fallen outside of mainstream understandings of the type of personal liberty and autonomy that the government must respect.

It seems clear, in hindsight, that the background conditions that might have led the Supreme Court to strike down sodomy laws in 1986, when it decided *Hardwick*, were not then in place. At the time, only a handful of lower courts had held that sodomy laws were unconstitutional, leaving such laws firmly in place in half of the states. In contrast, by the time the Court agreed to hear the appeal in *Lawrence* almost twenty years later, several state courts had held that sodomy laws violated basic principles of privacy and equality under their respective state constitutions. In addition, during that period, courts heard dozens of family law cases, including several involving same-sex marriage, that highlighted the relationships of love and care that LGBT people have with their partners and, for those who have them, with their children. By 2003, therefore, it was much more difficult for the Court, as it had done in 1986, to dismiss out of hand the idea that the Constitution afforded protection to the intimacy choices of LGBT people.

At the core of a gradualist legal strategy is the recognition that judges do not decide cases in a vacuum, disconnected from social and cultural understandings that they share with other members of society. A gradualist legal strategy is driven by realist considerations of what is achievable through the courts given not only the state of the law at the time of the litigation, but also the degree of familiarity that judges can be expected to have with the lives, interests, and aspirations of the individuals involved. By the time *Lawrence* was decided, a growing number of judges, including a few who sit on the Supreme Court, had come to view LGBT people as full members of society with constitutional rights like everybody else.

The one case chronicled in this book that seems to depart from the movement's gradualist legal strategy is *Baehr*. In many ways, *Baehr* is different from the other cases explored here because it was not, at the beginning, a "movement case." When the *Baehr* litigation started, most LGBT rights lawyers and activists, hewing to a gradualist legal strategy, believed that more limited steps toward the legal recognition of same-sex relationships had to be taken before the movement asked courts to render unconstitutional prohibitions against same-sex marriage. Many members of the LGBT community, however, saw the issue differently; while movement leaders, with the notable exception of Evan Wolfson and a few others, believed that seeking marriage rights through the courts was a risky (and possibly reckless) proposition, many members of the LGBT community saw the pursuit of marriage as a natural next step in the fight for equality.

Starting in the mid-1980s, same-sex couples by the thousands began participating in commitment ceremonies, which, while not legally valid, captured the symbolism (and joy) of marital ceremonies. At around the same time, the advent of the AIDS epidemic made LGBT people feel especially vulnerable—as they faced the possible loss of employment, housing, and health insurance—by the lack of legal recognition of and protection for their relationships. The 1980s also saw a large increase in the number of LGBT people who were raising children. For many members of the community, therefore, the seeking of marriage seemed, by the early 1990s, like a reasonable next step to take in the struggle for equal rights.

A social movement's gradualist approach to using the courts as a way of advancing the interests of its members can serve to legitimize that use. There will always be those who will argue that the pursuit of LGBT rights through the courts is per se illegitimate because it bypasses democratic processes and instead relies on the actions of (largely) unelected judges. But under our system of government, courts have the responsibility of enforcing constitutional provisions, even when it means striking down laws or policies that have majoritarian support. (This is a point that many conservative opponents of LGBT rights conveniently forget in other contexts when they turn to the judiciary, for example, to protect religious rights, property rights, and even, as happened during the contested 2000 election, to stop the counting of votes.)[1]

If we begin with the assumption, as our historical tradition and constitutional structure require us to do, that it is sometimes necessary for courts to come to the aid of minorities against the expressed wishes of the majority, then the fact that the LGBT rights movement's judicial strategy has been gradualist in nature serves to legitimize that strategy by belying the accusation, often made by opponents, that the movement is radical and reckless in its push for change. The movement's gradualist approach, as reflected in the cases profiled in this book, shows that LGBT rights lawyers and activists have taken prudent, measured, and incremental steps in legally challenging policies and regulations that discriminate against LGBT people.

REALISM  All of the cases profiled in this book arose from real circumstances and events—the five lawsuits, rather than constituting controversies engineered by lawyers in the pursuit of test cases, instead arose organically, that is, in response to actual instances of discrimination faced by real LGBT people leading real lives. Miguel Braschi, for instance, turned to the courts when he was in danger of losing his home after the death of his same-sex partner. Jamie Nabozny did the same after years of suffering severe antigay harassment perpetrated by fellow students, a pattern of abuse ignored by school officials. The *Romer* plaintiffs sued only after Colorado voters denied lesbians and gay men the opportunity to seek antidiscrimination protection under the law based on their sexual orientation. Genora Dancel and Ninia Baehr turned to the courts after they were unable to name each other as beneficiaries of their health and life insurance policies, an opportunity that is offered to legal spouses as a matter of course. And, despite accusations to the contrary by some conservatives at the time, John Lawrence and Tyron Garner did not participate in an organized effort by LGBT rights activists to challenge Texas's sodomy law; instead, the two men found themselves, entirely unexpectedly, under arrest and charged with a crime for having done nothing more than engage in consensual sex in the home.[2]

The fact that the LGBT rights movement's judicial strategy has consistently focused on the challenges and burdens confronted by real people facing real discrimination also serves to legitimize that strategy by showing that it is not grounded in artificial or politically motivated disputes. Rather, the legal controversies that have been part of the movement's judicial strategy have been driven by the need to protect identifiable individuals from discriminatory regulations and policies that harm them in tangible ways.

LOCALISM Another similarity among the cases chronicled in this book is that all of them, with the exception of *Nabozny*, were initially brought in state courts. There are many factors that go into the decision of whether to bring a civil rights case in state or federal court, including the extent to which the claim is based on principles of state or federal law (or a combination of the two). In addition, there is the strategic question of which type of court is more likely to be receptive to the arguments that are part of the civil rights claim in question.

The civil rights movement of the 1940s and 1950s relied almost exclusively on the federal courts in pursuing its judicial strategy. One reason for this is that state judges, in particular those in the South, had a reputation (in many cases deserved) as implacable foes of racial equality. This state of affairs left the civil rights movement with little choice but to turn to a federal judiciary that was generally willing to enforce the Constitution to protect the rights of African Americans despite considerable public opposition.

During the 1950s and 1960s, the Supreme Court, under the leadership of Chief Justice Earl Warren, did not shy away from protecting Americans' civil rights and civil liberties. This was the case not only in the area of race discrimination but in many others as well, including that of free speech, participation in the political process, and the enforcement of criminal laws. Starting in the early 1970s, the Court began to change course, initially by refusing in some instances to expand the scope of civil rights and civil liberties protections, and then more aggressively by cutting back on those protections. The Court's growing conservatism, in turn, increasingly led civil rights lawyers to look to state constitutions and state courts to protect their clients from discrimination.

*Baehr* and *Lawrence* are but two examples of this phenomenon. In the former case, the LGBT litigants relied exclusively on state constitutional arguments, including one based on the Hawaii Constitution's explicit protection of the right to privacy, to challenge the state's refusal to permit same-sex couples to marry. In the latter case, the LGBT rights lawyers asked state judges to rule that the state constitution rendered Texas's sodomy statute invalid even though the U.S. Supreme Court had earlier held in *Hardwick* that states could, without violating the federal Due Process Clause, criminalize consensual same-sex sodomy. Although the effort to void the Texas sodomy law on state constitutional grounds eventually failed in *Lawrence*, similar efforts in other jurisdictions succeeded in the years leading up to that case.[3]

*Romer* also illustrates the extent to which LGBT rights lawyers have turned to state courts. Even though the constitutional challenge to Amendment 2 was initially grounded in both the state and federal constitutions, it was not part of the LGBT rights lawyers' strategy in that case—as it was in *Baehr* and *Lawrence*—to try to persuade the state courts that the state constitution provided the plaintiffs with more protection than the federal one. *Romer* was, from the beginning, essentially a federal constitutional case, and was treated as such by the lawyers and the Colorado courts. This means that the LGBT rights lawyers could have brought the case in federal court, and limited their arguments to ones grounded in the federal Constitution, without much difficulty. The fact that the lawyers instead chose to pursue their federal constitutional claims in state court is illustrative of the extent to which the LGBT rights movement has turned to state courts in the effort to advance the interests of LGBT people through the judicial process.

For opponents who believe that it is illegitimate to try to advance LGBT rights causes through the courts, it does not matter whether the litigation is brought in federal or state court. But, in my estimation, the fact that the LGBT rights movement has relied extensively on state courts serves to legitimize its judicial strategy because it shows a willingness to trust local judges to make (what the movement deems to be) the right decisions in cases involving sexual minorities. This is not to deny that the federal courts, as the primary enforcers of federal constitutional law, have a vital (and entirely legitimate) role in protecting the rights of minorities in this country. But the extent to which the LGBT rights movement has looked to state judges for protection helps to legitimize its judicial strategy by showing that it does not have to rely exclusively on federal judges, who are, as a general matter, not as closely linked to the communities and regions where the cases arise as are state judges.

The fact that in *Romer*, for example, state judges had earlier raised troubling questions about the fundamental fairness, and constitutional appropriateness, of Amendment 2, went a long way in legitimizing the U.S. Supreme Court's later decision to strike down the Amendment. This was not, after all, an instance of a faraway federal court voiding a law, approved by state voters, that had passed constitutional muster in the state courts. Instead, this was an instance in which state judges, all of whom were Coloradans with presumed deep roots in that state, had already concluded that Amendment 2 violated basic constitutional principles of equality.

▲

This book has been retrospective in nature as I have explored the factual and legal backgrounds, as well as the impact, of five important LGBT rights lawsuits. If we shift the focus to a prospective one, it would seem that the movement is poised to begin relying less on the courts going forward than it has in the past.

One reason for this, quite simply, is that the movement's legal successes have lessened the need for further litigation. For example, after *Lawrence*, the criminal regulation of private and consensual same-sex sodomy, the proscription of which was part of the law of every state in the union as recently as 1960, is no longer an issue that the movement needs to address. Similarly, *Romer* ended efforts by social conservatives to deny LGBT people the opportunity to seek the protection of antidiscrimination laws, a tactic that gay rights opponents pursued regularly during the preceding twenty years. This has permitted the movement to concentrate its resources on expanding the number of

states and municipalities that protect LGBT people from discrimination. In the particular context of employment, twelve states have
enacted gay rights laws since *Romer* was decided (bringing the total
to twenty-one), while dozens of municipalities have done the same.
The movement has also, since *Romer*, focused more intently on having Congress enact the Employment Non-Discrimination Act, a law
that would prohibit employment discrimination on the basis of sexual
orientation—and hopefully gender identity as well—at the federal
level. There is a good chance that Congress will approve such a law in
the next few years.

The LGBT rights movement has also begun to pay greater attention to the legislative arena when it comes to the legal recognition
of same-sex relationships, an effort that is bearing fruit. In fact, between 2007 and 2009 alone, the legislatures of Nevada, Oregon, and
Washington enacted comprehensive domestic partnership laws, while
those of Maine, New Hampshire, and Vermont approved same-sex
marriage laws. (The Maine law was later voided by voters.) Although
it is unlikely that any of these laws would have passed but for the
ability of the same-sex marriage litigation strategy to raise the nation's
consciousness regarding the lack of legal recognition and protection
afforded to same-sex couples, it is nonetheless the case that all five
legislatures acted because they chose to do so, not because they were
required by courts.

This is not to suggest that there will no longer be litigation involving the question of same-sex marriage. We are likely, for example, to
see more federal constitutional challenges to the Defense of Marriage
Act and to the state constitutional provisions prohibiting the recognition of same-sex marriages. But as a general matter, there appears to
be a growing recognition by many in the LGBT rights movement that
the time has come to rely somewhat less on the courts and more on
political organizing and grass-roots mobilizing aimed at persuading
government officials and the public of the need to provide same-sex
relationships with at least some of the legal protections available to
married heterosexual couples.

Fifteen years ago, the decision of whether to seek same-sex marriage through the courts or through the political process was an easy one because although the odds were not great either way, they were particularly poor in the political arena. The choice of courts versus political process is more complicated these days, primarily because the ongoing national conversation about same-sex relationships engendered by the marriage lawsuits has made political victories in a growing number of states possible.

It is likely that the future will bring a reduced judicial role in other LGBT rights matters as well. One of these is the question of gays in the military. In contrast to the issues of sodomy and the availability of antidiscrimination protection (for civilians) under the law, the reason for a reduced judicial role in this area has less to do with the movement's judicial successes and more to do with its failures. Most constitutional challenges to the military's "Don't Ask, Don't Tell" policy have failed. In contrast, there is a growing recognition outside of the courts that the policy undermines rather than promotes military preparedness because it results in the dismissal of highly qualified service members. In fact, some influential (retired) military officials who supported the policy when it was first proposed now contend that it is unnecessary and counterproductive. These growing calls for reform have resulted in the introduction of bills in Congress that would require the military to permit openly gay service members to serve their country. All of this suggests that if discrimination against LGBT people in the military is to cease, it will be as a result of legislative changes rather than of judicial edicts.

For different reasons, then, it seems likely that the LGBT rights movement will lessen its reliance on a judicial strategy in the decades to come. Such a development would be consistent with the trajectory of other social movements that have turned to the courts to advance their causes. The civil rights movement during the 1940s and 1950s and the women's rights movement during the 1970s relied heavily on the courts to challenge a long list of regulations and policies that treated racial minorities and women as second-class citizens. There came a time, however, when both movements shifted their approach from one that focused heavily on the courts to one that also sought to engage legislative and political processes.

When the experience of the LGBT rights movement is added to that of the civil rights and women's movements, it seems clear that civil rights struggles in the United States, at least since World War II, have largely occurred in stages. The pursuit of a judicial strategy has been especially important when the group in question is so stigmatized and politically impotent that the judiciary is, as a practical matter, the only governmental institution willing to entertain its claims for equal citizenship. As the movements begin to achieve important judicial victories, the broader society is required to take more seriously the interests and needs of these groups. This, in turn, makes legislative and political victories more likely.

At the same time, however, the experiences of the civil rights and women's movements suggest that struggles against long-standing and deeply entrenched discrimination are neither completely linear nor bounded by finite end points. Those experiences show that the struggles include many disappointments, defeats, and setbacks along the way, ones that make the attainment of equality by stigmatized groups less of an end result than a process. From this perspective, the most important accomplishment of the LGBT rights movement's judicial strategy, as illustrated by the five cases profiled in this book, is that it has gotten that process started for LGBT people. Ultimately, however, it will be up to society at large, and not just the courts, to determine whether sexual minorities are to be viewed and treated as true equals in our democracy.

# Where Are They Now?

*Bill Rubenstein* (Chapter 1): Professor of Law, Harvard University.

*Patricia Logue* (Chapter 2): Associate Circuit Judge, Cook County, Illinois.

*Matthew Coles* (Chapter 3): Director, Lesbian Gay Bisexual Transgender Project, American Civil Liberties Union.

*Suzanne Goldberg* (Chapter 3): Professor of Law, Columbia University.

*Evan Wolfson* (Chapter 4): Executive Director, Freedom to Marry.

*Daniel Foley* (Chapter 4): Associate Judge, Court of Appeals of Hawaii.

*Ruth Harlow* (Chapter 5): Counsel, Linklaters, LLP.

# Acknowledgments

THIS BOOK COULD NOT have been written without the assistance of Matthew Coles, Daniel Foley, Suzanne Goldberg, Ruth Harlow, Patricia Logue, Bill Rubenstein, and Evan Wolfson. These seven lawyers spent many hours speaking to me about their lives, careers, and, most important, their recollections of the lawsuits chronicled in this book. I hope that I have been able to do justice to their remarkable work on behalf of the LGBT community.

I have been lucky through the years to have received encouragement for my work by colleagues in the legal academy, many of whom have become friends. I would like in particular to thank Michelle Anderson, Beth Hillman, Kit Kinports, Andy Leipold, Phil McConnaughay, Nancy Polikoff, Laurie Reynolds, Steve Ross, and Ed Stein.

I am also appreciative of the research assistance provided by Kris Harrison, Cynthia Helzner, and Giancarlo Urey. And I would like to thank Beacon Press's Michael Bronski, Joanna Green, and Gayatri Patnaik. It has been a true pleasure working with them on this project.

Finally, I would like to thank Tony and Katia Prado, for teaching me that it is possible to live one's values every day; my partner, Richard Storrow, for his generous spirit, his loving care, and his beautiful smile; and our sons, Emmanuel and Sebastian, for allowing me to love in ways that I never imagined possible.

# Notes

INTRODUCTION

1. Opinion and Order, Texas v. Driskill Bar and Grill, No. 739, 130–31, Municipal Court, City of Austin, Travis County, April 16, 1980, 10.

2. Guillermo Garcia, "Gays Win Suit against Driskill Disco," *Austin American-Statesman*, June 11, 1979, 1.

3. Interview with Matthew Coles, New York City, September 2006.

4. Guillermo Garcia, "Gay Rights Recognized Lawyer Says," *Austin American-Statesman*, July 15, 1979, B3.

5. In re Thom, 337 N.Y.S.2d 588 (App. Div. 1972), reversed by 301 N.E.2d 542 (N.Y. 1973).

6. Vern L. Bullough, "Lesbianism, Homosexuality, and the American Civil Liberties Union," *Journal of Homosexuality* 13 (1986): 23–32; William N. Eskridge Jr., *Dishonorable Passions: Sodomy Laws in America 1861–2003* (New York: Viking, 2008), 152 (quoting ACLU policy statement on homosexuality, January 7, 1957).

7. Boutilier v. Immigration and Naturalization Service, 387 U.S. 118 (1967).

8. Bowers v. Hardwick, 478 U.S. 186 (1986).

9. It is also important to note that many lawyers contributed to the five lawsuits chronicled in this book. The fact that those suits are explored here largely through the eyes of the lead LGBT rights attorneys in the respective cases is not meant to suggest that they were solely responsible for the judicial victories that ensued.

10. See, e.g., Michael J. Klarman, *From Jim Crow to Civil Rights: The Supreme Court and the Struggle for Racial Equality* (New York: Oxford University Press, 2004); Gerald N. Rosenberg, *The Hollow Hope: Can Courts Bring About Social Change?* (Chicago: University of Chicago Press, 1991).

CHAPTER I—FAMILY

1. Centers for Disease Control and Prevention, "Pneumocystis Pneumonia—Los Angeles," *Morbidity & Mortality Weekly Report* 30, no. 21 (June 1981): 1–3; Lawrence Altman, "Rare Cancer Seen in 41 Homosexuals," *New York Times*, July 3, 1981, A20.

2. Michael Weber, "Yellow Iris Farm: The Northern New Jersey Retreat of Leslie Blanchard," *Architectural Digest*, June 1986, 100.

3. Chris Smith, "Crazy As He Wants To Be," *New York Magazine*, August 2, 1999.

4. Telephone interview with Laura Hudson, November 2006.

5. John-Manuel Andriote, *Victory Deferred: How AIDS Changed Gay Life in America* (Chicago: University of Chicago Press, 1999), 344.

6. Once the hospital changed its policies, the court dismissed the case as moot. Dallas Gay Alliance, Inc. v. Dallas County Hospital District, 719 F.Supp. 1380 (N.D. Texas 1989).

7. Gelman v. Castaneda, *New York Law Journal*, October 22, 1986, 13 (Civ. Ct.); Two Associates v. Brown, 502 N.Y.S.2d 604 (Sup. Ct. 1986); Yorkshire Towers v. Harpster, 510 N.Y.S.2d 976 (Civ. Ct. 1986).

8. Braschi v. Stahl Associates, 531 N.Y.S.2d 562 (App. Div. 1988).

9. Matter of Adoption of Robert Paul P., 471 N.E.2d 424 (N.Y. 1984).

10. McMinn v. Town of Oyster Bay, 488 N.E.2d 1240 (N.Y. 1985); Group House of Port Washington v. Board of Zoning and Appeals, Town of Hempstead, 380 N.E.2d 207 (N.Y. 1978).

11. Baer v. Brookhaven, 537 N.Y.2d 619 (N.Y. 1989).

12. Braschi v. Stahl Associates Co., 543 N.E.2d 49 (N.Y. 1989).

13. Arnie Realty Corp. v. Torres, 742 N.Y.S.2d 240 (App. Div. 2002); St. Mark's Assets, Inc. v. Hertzog, 760 N.Y.S.2d 608 (App. Term 2003).

14. Picon v. O.D.C. Associates, No. 86–22894 (Sup. Ct. N.Y. Co., January 28, 1991); Arnie Realty v. Torres, *New York Law Journal*, June 3, 1999, 27 (App. Term).

15. Colon v. Frias, 615 N.Y.S.2d 618 (Civ. Ct.1994).

16. In re Guardianship of Kowalski, 478 N.W.2d 790 (Minn. Ct. App. 1991); Stewart v. Schwartz Brothers-Jeffer Memorial Chapel, 606 N.Y.S.2d 965 (Sup. Ct. 1993).

17. Estate of Cooper, 592 N.Y.S.2d 797 (App. Div. 1993); Raum v. Restaurant Associates, 675 N.Y.S.2d 343 (App. Div. 1998).

18. Alison D. v. Virginia M., 572 N.E.2d 27 (N.Y. 1991).

19. Matter of Jacob, 660 N.E.2d 397 (N.Y. 1995).

20. Hernandez v. Robles, 855 N.E.2d 1 (N.Y. 2006).

## CHAPTER 2 — HARASSMENT

1. During Lambda's third decade (1993–2003), the organization handled twelve LGBT youth cases, including lawsuits (such as Jamie's) that addressed antigay harassment in the schools. Ellen Ann Andersen, *Out of the Closets & Into the Courts: Legal Opportunity Structure and Gay Rights Litigation* (Ann Arbor: University of Michigan Press, 2004), 48–49.

2. Paul Gibson, "Gay Male and Lesbian Youth Suicide," in *Report of the Secretary's Task Force on Youth Suicide*, vol. 3 (Washington, D.C.: U.S. Department of Health & Human Services, 1989); Joyce Hunter, "Violence Against Lesbian and Gay Male Youths," *Journal of Interpersonal Violence* 5, no. 3 (1990): 295–300.

3. Equality Foundation of Greater Cincinnati v. Cincinnati, 838 F.Supp. 1235 (S.D. Ohio 1993). Logue continued to work on the constitutional challenge to the Cincinnati ballot measure for many years. Although the U.S. Court of Appeals for the Sixth Circuit ultimately upheld the constitutionality of the provision, see 128 F.3d 289 (6th Cir. 1997), Cincinnati voters in 2004 changed their minds and repealed the ban on gay rights laws.

4. Nabozny v. Podlesny, 92 F.3d 446 (7th Cir. 1996).

5. "Gay Ashland Student Awarded Nearly $1 Million," *Capital Times* (Madison, WI), Nov. 21, 1996, 7A.

6. "They Don't Even Know Me: Understanding Anti-Gay Harassment and Violence in Schools," Safe Schools Coalition of Washington State (1999), www.safeschoolscoalition.org/theydontevenknowme.pdf.

7. Montgomery v. Independent School District No. 709, 109 F.Supp.2d 1081 (D. Minn. 2000).

8. Flores v. Morgan Hill Unified School District, 324 F.3d 1130 (9th Cir. 2003); Stacy Finz, "Emerging from a Secret: Taunts and Internal Conflict Pushed Student to the Brink," *San Francisco Chronicle*, June 12, 2000, A1.

9. Joseph G. Kosciw and Elizabeth M. Diaz, "The 2005 National School Climate Survey: The Experiences of Lesbian, Gay, Bisexual and Transgender Youth in Our Nation's Schools" (New York: GLSEN, 2006).

## CHAPTER 3 — DISCRIMINATION

1. Amendment 2 did not address gender identity. At the time, discrimination on the basis of gender identity was not prohibited by any state or local law in Colorado.

2. Bay Area Peace Navy v. United States, 914 F.2d 1224 (9th Cir. 1990).

3. Bay Area Network of Gay & Lesbian Educators v. City of Concord, No. C91-05417 (Cal. Super. Ct. 1992).

4. Citizens for Responsible Behavior v. City of Riverside, 1 Cal.App.4th 1013 (Cal. Ct. App. 1991).

5. See, e.g., NAACP v. Button, 371 U.S. 415 (1963); NAACP v. Alabama, 357 U.S. 449 (1958).

6. Palmore v. Sidoti, 466 U.S. 429 (1984); Evans v. Romer, 1993 WL 19678 (Colo. Dist. Ct.).

7. Harper v. Virginia State Board of Elections, 383 U.S. 663 (1966); Kramer v. Union Free School District, 395 U.S. 621 (1969).

8. Reynolds v. Sims, 377 U.S. 533 (1964).

9. Reitman v. Mulkey, 387 U.S. 369 (1967).

10. Hunter v. Erickson 393 U.S. 385, 393 (1969) (Harlan, J., concurring).

11. Evans v. Romer, 854 P.2d 1270 (Co. 1993) (Evans I).

12. The state appealed the Colorado court's ruling to the Supreme Court. The latter, however, refused to hear the case. 510 U.S. 959 (1993).

13. See, e.g., High Tech Gays v. Defense Industrial Security Clearance Office, 895 F.2d 563 (9th Cir. 1990).

14. Robert P. George, *Making Men Moral: Civil Liberties and Public Morality* (New York: Oxford University Press, 1993).

15. Dean H. Hamer et al., "A Linkage Between DNA Markers on the X Chromosome and Male Sexual Orientation," *Science* 261 (1993): 320-27

16. Evans v. Romer, 1993 WL 518586 (Col. Dist. Ct., December 14, 1993).

17. Evans v. Romer, 882 P.2d 1335 (Co. 1994) (Evans II).

18. James v. Valtierra, 402 U.S. 137 (1971).

19. Romer v. Evans, 517 U.S. 620, 623 (1996).

20. Matthew Coles, "The Meaning of *Romer v. Evans*," *Hastings Law Journal* 48 (1997): 1343, 1361.

21. See, e.g., High Tech Gays v. Defense Industrial Security Clearance Office, 895 F.2d 563 (9th Cir. 1990); Woodward v. United States, 871 F.2d 1068 (Fed. Cir. 1989); Padula v. Webster, 822 F.2d 97 (D.C. Cir. 1987).

22. See, e.g., High Tech Gays v. Defense Industrial Security Clearance, 668 F.Supp. 1361 (N.D. Cal. 1987), reversed by 895 F.2d 563 (9th Cir. 1990); Jantz v. Muci, 759 F.Supp. 1543 (D. Kan. 1991), reversed by 976 F.2d 623 (10th Cir. 1992).

23. Nabozny v. Podlesny, 92 F.3d 446, 458 n. 12 (7th Cir. 1996).

24. Stemler v. City of Florence, 126 F.3d 856, 873 (6th Cir. 1997).

25. Finstuen v. Edmondson, 497 F.Supp.2d 1295 (W.D. Okla. 2006), affirmed on other grounds, 496 F.3d 1139 (10th Cir. 2007).

26. Kansas v. Limon, 122 P.3d 22 (Ka. 2005).

27. Weaver v. Nebo School District, 29 F.Supp.2d 1279 (D. Utah 1998).

28. Quinn v. Nassau County Police Department, 53 F.Supp.2d 347 (E.D.N.Y. 1999).

29. Lofton v. Secretary of Department of Children and Family Services, 358 F.3d 804 (11th Cir. 2004).

30. Lofton v. Secretary of Department of Children and Family Services, 377 F.3d 1275, 1303 (11th Cir. 2004) (Barkett, J., dissenting from denial of en banc review).

31. Equality Foundation of Greater Cincinnati v. Cincinnati, 128 F.3d 289 (6th Cir. 1997).

32. The twelve states are: Colorado (2007), Delaware (2009), Illinois (2006), Iowa (2007), Maine (2005), Maryland (2001), Nevada (1999), New Hampshire (1998), New Mexico (2003), New York (2003), Oregon (2008), and Washington (2006). As of 2009, laws in twenty-one states prohibit discrimination on the basis of sexual orientation in the workplace. Twelve of those states, including Colorado, also prohibit discrimination on the basis of gender identity.

CHAPTER 4 — MARRIAGE

1. Ninia Baehr, *Abortion without Apology: A Radical History for the 1990s* (Boston: South End Press, 1990).

2. The other two same-sex couples who sought marriage licenses on that day were Joseph Melilio and Patrick Lagon, who had been together for thirteen years, and Tammy Rodrigues and Antoinette Pregil, who had been a couple for nine years and who were jointly raising the latter's biological daughter.

3. One of Wolfson's conservative debating opponents was Richard Brookheiser, who eventually became a senior editor at the *National Review*. Another was Lee Lieberman, a future cofounder of the Federalist Society and clerk to Justice Antonin Scalia of the U.S. Supreme Court, who became responsible for vetting candidates for the federal bench on behalf of the first Bush administration.

4. Singer v. Hara, 522 P.2d 1187, 1192 (Wa. Ct. App. 1974); Jones v. Hallahan, 501 S.W.2d 588, 589 (Ky. Ct. App. 1973).

5. DeSanto v. Barnsley, 476 A.2d 952, 956 (Pa. Super. Ct. 1984); Adams v. Howerton, 486 F.Supp. 1119, 1123 (C.D. Cal. 1980), affirmed by 673 F.2d 1036 (9th Cir. 1982).

6. Order Granting Defendant's Motion for Judgment on the Pleadings, Baehr v. Lewin, Hawaii Circuit Court, No. 91-1394-05, October 1, 1991.

7. Standing Committee Report No. 69, Committee on the Bill of Rights, Suffrage and Elections, *Proceedings of the Constitutional Convention of Hawaii of 1978* 1 (1978): 671, 675.

8. State v. Kam, 748 P.2d 372 (Haw. 1988).

9. State v. Mueller, 671 P.2d 1351 (Haw. 1983).

10. The discarded language, which was removed because the legislature concluded in 1984 that it discriminated against the elderly and individuals with dis-

abilities, required that the marriage applicants "show that they are not impotent or that they are not physically incapable of entering into a marriage." 1994 Hawaii Session Laws, Act 217, section 1.

11. Baehr v. Lewin, 852 P.2d 44 (Haw. 1993).

12. See, e.g., Turner v. Safley, 482 U.S. 78 (1987); Zablocki v. Redhail, 434 U.S. 374 (1978).

13. Loving v. Virginia, 388 U.S. 1 (1967).

14. John Gallagher, "Till Death Do Us Part: A Hawaii Court Upholds a Challenge to the Denial of Same-Sex Marriages," *Advocate*, June 15, 1993, 24, 26; Richard Borreca, "Waihee Opposed Same-Sex Marriage," *Honolulu Star-Bulletin*, May 11, 1993.

15. John Gallagher, "The Great Gay Marriage Debate," *Advocate*, February 20, 1996, 35.

16. Charles Krauthammer, "Election Year Diversion," *Washington Post*, May 31, 1996, A23; Don Feder, "Rule by Judges' Whim is not Democracy," *Boston Herald*, December 11, 1996, 35.

17. Baker v. Vermont, 744 A.2d 864 (Vt. 1999).

18. Goodridge v. Department of Public Health, 798 N.E.2d 941 (Mass. 2003); In re Marriage Cases, 183 P.3d 384 (Ca. 2008); Kerrigan v. Commissioner of Public Health, 957 A.2d 407 (Conn. 2008); Varnum v. Brien, 763 N.W.2d 862 (Iowa 2009).

19. Perez v. Sharp, 198 P.2d 17 (Ca. 1948).

CHAPTER 5 — SEX

1. Douglas Martin, "Tyron Garner, 39, Plaintiff in Pivotal Sodomy Case, Dies," *New York Times*, September 14, 2006, D8.

2. Dale Carpenter, "The Unknown Past of *Lawrence v. Texas*," *Michigan Law Review* 102 (2004): 1464, 1482, 1488.

3. William N. Eskridge Jr., *Dishonorable Passions: Sodomy Laws in America 1861–2003* (New York: Viking, 2008), 300.

4. Carpenter, "The Unknown Past of *Lawrence v. Texas*," 1483.

5. Ruth Harlow, "Gay Youth and the Right to Education" (with Donna Dennis), *Yale Law and Policy Review* 4 (1986): 446–78.

6. Gay Men's Health Crisis v. Sullivan, 792 F.Supp. 278 (S.D. N.Y. 1992).

7. Howe v. Hull, 873 F.Supp. 72 (N.D. Ohio 1994).

8. Frank Prial, "Two Homosexuals Say U.S. Agents Assaulted Them," *New York Times*, November 1, 1990, P3.

9. Shahar v. Bowers, 836 F.Supp. 859 (N.D. Ga. 1993), reversed by 70 F.3d 1218 (11th cir. 1995), vacated by 114 F.3d 1097 (11th Cir. 1997) (en banc).

10. Kevin Sack, "Georgia Candidate Admits Adultery and Resigns Commission in Guard," *New York Times*, June 6, 1997, A29.

11. Wainwright v. Stone, 414 U.S. 21, 22–23 (1973).

12. Griswold v. Connecticut, 381 U.S. 479 (1965); Eisenstadt v. Baird, 405 U.S. 438 (1972); Roe v. Wade, 410 U.S. 113 (1973).

13. For cases that failed, see, e.g., Doe v. Commonwealth's Attorney, 403 F.Supp. 1199 (D. Va. 1975), affirmed by 425 U.S. 901 (1976); Baker v. Wade, 769 F.2d 289 (5th Cir. 1985) (en banc). For cases that succeeded, see, e.g., New York v. Onofre, 415 N.E.2d 936 (N.Y. 1980); Commonwealth v. Bonadio, 415 A.2d 47 (Pa. 1980).

14. Bowers v. Hardwick, 478 U.S. 186 (1986).

15. Commonwealth v. Wasson, 842 S.W.2d 487 (Ky. 1992).

16. Jegley v. Picado, 80 S.W.3d 332 (Ark. 2002); Powell v. State, 510 S.E.2d 18 (Ga. 1998); Gryczan v. State, 942 P.2d 112 (Mont. 1997); Campbell v. Sundquist, 926 S.W.2d 250 (Tenn. Ct. App. 1996).

17. Lawrence v. Texas, Texas Court of Appeals, Nos. 98-48530, 98-48531, June 8, 2000, 8.

18. Alan Bernstein, "Texas Republican Convention," *Houston Chronicle*, June 17, 2000, A1; Alan Bernstein, "Republicans Target One of their Own," *Houston Chronicle*, July 4, 2000, A1; Alan Bernstein, "Justice Says Retirement Not Spurred by Ridicule," *Houston Chronicle*, February 3, 2001, A27; Julie Mason, "G.O.P. Chairman Raises Eyebrows with Letter to Appeals Judge," *Houston Chronicle*, July 9, 2000, A34. When first elected in 1980, Murphy was only the second Republican to be elected to the Texas Court of Appeals in the twentieth century.

19. Lawrence v. Texas, 41 S.W.3d 349 (Tex. Ct. App. 2001).

20. Bill Murphy, "Not Leaving the Bench Yet," *Houston Chronicle*, March 31, 2001, A39.

21. Edward Laumann et al., *The Social Organization of Sexuality* (Chicago: University of Chicago Press, 1994), 98–99.

22. There were, in addition to Harlow, several other lawyers who worked on the case once it reached the Supreme Court. William Hohengarten, a litigation partner at Jenner & Block, played an instrumental role in helping to draft the certiorari petition and the brief. In addition, Lambda's Susan Sommer coordinated the writing of amicus briefs.

23. McLaughlin v. Florida, 379 U.S. 184 (1964).

24. John Williams and Patty Reinert, "Rosenthal Testimony [*sic*] Lackluster in Capital," *Houston Chronicle*, March 30, 2003, A33.

25. Linda Greenhouse, "Court Appears Ready to Reverse a Sodomy Law," *New York Times*, March 27, 2003, A18; Joan Biskupic, "Justices Hear Anti-Sodomy Case," *USA Today*, March 27, 2003, 13A; Williams and Reinert, "Rosenthal Testimony [*sic*] Lackluster in Capital."

26. Alan Bernstein, "Rosenthal Critics Turn Up Heat," *Houston Chronicle*, January 1, 2008, B1; Brian Rogers, "More E-Mails Emerge in DA Scandal," *Houston Chronicle*, January 9, 2008, A1; Ralph Blumenthal, "Under Pressure, Prosecutor in Texas Won't Run Again," *New York Times*, January 3, 2008, A21.

27. Lawrence v. Texas, 539 U.S. 558 (2003); Dudgeon v. United Kingdom, Series A, No. 45, European Court of Human Rights (October 22, 1981).

28. "Americans Evenly Divided on Morality of Homosexuality," June 18, 2008, Gallup 2008 Values and Beliefs poll, www.gallup.com/poll/108115/americans-evenly-divided-morality-homosexuality.aspx.

29. Mary Leonard, "Gay Marriage Stirs Conservatives Again," *Boston Globe*, September 28, 2003, A1.

30. Goodridge v. Department of Public Health, 798 N.E.2d 941 (Mass. 2003).

31. In re Marriage Cases, 183 P.3d 384 (Ca. 2008).

32. Standhart v. Superior Court, 77 P.3d 451 (Ariz. Ct. App. 2003); Conaway v. Deane, 932 A.2d 571 (Md. 2007); Andersen v. King County, 138 P.3d 963 (Wash. 2006).

33. Hernandez v. Robles, 855 N.E.2d 1 (N.Y. 2006).

34. Lofton v. Secretary of Department of Children and Family Services, 358 F.3d 804 (11th Cir. 2004).

35. Witt v. Department of the Air Force, 527 F.3d 806 (9th Cir. 2008).

36. See, e.g., Ex parte J.M.F., 730 So.2d 1190 (Ala. 1998); Bottoms v. Bottoms, 457 S.E.2d 102 (Va. 1995).

37. For examples of courts that have applied the nexus test in an appropriate way, see, e.g., Jacoby v. Jacoby, 763 So.2d 410 (Fla. Ct. App. 2000); Inscoe v. Inscoe, 700 N.E.2d 70 (Oh. Ct. App. 1997).

38. Ex parte J.M.F., 730 So.2d 1190 (Ala. 1998); Pulliam v. Smith, 501 S.E.2d 898 (N.C. 1998).

39. See, e.g., Ex parte D.W.W., 717 So.2d 793 (Ala. 1998); In re Marriage of Diehl, 582 N.E.2d 281 (Ill. Ct. App. 1991).

40. Karouni v. Gonzales, 399 F.3d 1163, 1173 (9th Cir. 2005).

41. See, e.g., Thomasson v. Perry, 80 F.3d 915 (4th Cir. 1995) (en banc); Steffan v. Perry, 41 F.3d 677 (D.C. Cir. 1994) (en banc).

CONCLUSION

1. Bush v. Gore, 531 U.S. 98 (2000).

2. Shortly after the arrests of Lawrence and Garner, the Harris County Republican chairman told the press that he "wonder[ed] if this case was ... set up as a challenge. The facts themselves sound suspicious." Steve Brewer, "Stage

Set for Showdown over State's Sodomy Law," *Houston Chronicle*, November 21, 1998, A1.

3. Jegley v. Picado, 80 S.W.3d 332 (Ark. 2002); Powell v. State, 510 S.E.2d 18 (Ga. 1998); Gryczan v. State, 942 P.2d 112 (Mont. 1997); Campbell v. Sundquist, 926 S.W.2d 250 (Tenn. Ct. App. 1996); Commonwealth v. Wasson, 842 S.W.2d 487 (Ky. 1992).

# Index